Early Childhood Classroom Processes

Language and Social Processes
Judith Green, editor

Early Childhood Classroom Processes

edited by

Rebecca Kantor
David Fernie
The Ohio State University

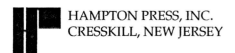

HAMPTON PRESS, INC.
CRESSKILL, NEW JERSEY

Printed in the United States of America

Library of Congress Cataloging-in-Publication Data

Early childhood classroom processes / edited by Rebecca Kantor, David Fernie.
     p. cm. -- (Language and social processes)
    Includes bibliographical references and index.
    ISBN 1-57273-461-2 (cloth) -- ISBN 1-57273-462-0 (pbk.)
     1. Early childhood education. 2. Education, preschool. I. Kantor, Rebecca.
Fernie, David. III. Language & social processes.

    LB1139.23.E25 2003
    372.5--dc21

                          2003042348

Hampton Press, Inc.
23 Broadway
Cresskill, NJ 07626

Contents

Preface

This volume is the culminating project of 10 years of collaborative study in a preschool classroom, where each year, 3- and 4-year-olds and their teachers meet daily to construct a life together in an early childhood program. Over these years of observation and participation in the A. Sophie Rogers Lab School at the Ohio State University, we have come to interpret what we see there in particular ways. In this volume, we share what we have learned from this collective research experience.

In this research, faculty, graduate students, and classroom teachers worked together to take on a new perspective and method, to reduce traditional role hierarchies, and to support an essential commitment to open dialogue and critique, as we sought to interpret the complexity of classroom life in a first school experience. The process of doing this work was exciting and gratifying—a good reason to be an academic and to be doing research.

Given this collaborative process, the traditional parsing of a volume into discrete chapters with single authors is less than satisfying. It does not convey the group spirit felt in this work (as faculty and students typically worked together), nor the many ways that each detail of life is knitted together to form not pieces, but a whole fabric of daily classroom life. Nonetheless, each author took the lead in conceptualizing, carrying out, and writing up an important aspect of the research project in a master's thesis or a dissertation, and wrote the chapter that appears in this volume. We extend our first sincere thanks to chapter authors and colleagues, Peg Elgas, Paula McMurray, Sandy Miller, James Scott, Cheri Williams, and Donna Williams for their work here, and their work with us and with each other.

Our continuing professional collaboration with each other is strongly rooted in this work. In this volume, our chapters are like bookends that provide context, interpretation, summary, and theory development across the overall project. We created each of these chapters at the word processor, discussing, debating, and "wordsmithing" in a comfortable style that evolved during our project.

Feeling a co-equal commitment and involvement in the project, we struggled with the book authorship order inherent in a language with a linear presentation format, and ultimately decided our order as "first" and "second" authors of the book with the time-honored procedure of a coin toss—this work is clearly and entirely a shared endeavor.

At the same time, there are many others who do not appear as authors here and who contributed to the ideas represented in the book. We would like to thank the following contributors to our project who either conducted analyses that informed our collective interpretations, presented papers at conferences with us, or wrote articles and book chapters that appear elsewhere: Bronwyn Davies, Judith Green, John Kesner, Elisa Klein, Carol Meyer, Kim Whaley, and Kate Zutell.

We have had great support at Ohio State University. The late Dean Bailey provided professional and personal support and encouragement to Rebecca that is still a part of her energy. Our respective Department Chairs played quite different roles. Dr. Al Davis was a much need champion of the A. Sophie Rogers Laboratory Preschool where the study took place. His encouragement of qualitative inquiry was critical at a time when engaging in it was viewed as a risk for an untenured faculty member. The late Dr. C. Ray Williams had the wisdom to provide his faculty with the freedom to "think big" and to create their own vision of professional paths and identities. The Research Foundation at Ohio State provided Seed Grant funding of about $20,000 that got us started and involved in the work. Ruslan Slutsky, a graduate research assistant and now a new faculty member at the University of Toledo, spent endless hours attending to the details of the book chapters, and we thank him for his diligence. We gratefully acknowledge the children, teachers, and parents of the Lab preschool for their cooperation and engagement with learning, and for allowing us to tell this, their unique story of life in a preschool.

Research projects do not become books without the guidance and assistance of key individuals along the way. As we discuss in the first chapter, we owe much to Judith Green, the Hampton Press Language and Social Processes Series Editor, for her personal mentorship and friendship over the years. In addition, we are grateful to her Series Co-Editors Ginger Weade and Carol Dixon for their guidance and feedback, and owe a special thanks to Hampton Press Publisher Barbara Bernstein for her faith in this work and her almost infinite patience.

Finally, we thank our spouses, Reed Martin and Linda DeStefano, for the ongoing support and gentle insistence that we finish this volume during times when it seemed impossible to coordinate and, in general, for sharing the fun that our two families have had over the years.

Rebecca Kantor   David Fernie

Series Preface

LANGUAGE AND SOCIAL PROCESSES

Judith Green, Editor

University of California at Santa Barbara

Associate Editors

Ginger Weade
Ohio University

Carol Dixon
**University of California
at Santa Barbara**

Language and Social Processes provides a forum for scholarly work that makes visible the ways in which everyday life is accomplished through discourse processes among individuals and groups. Volumes will examine how language-in-use influences the access of individuals and culturally, ethnically, and linguistically diverse groups to social institutions, and how knowledge construction and social participation across diverse social settings is accomplished through discourse.

Studies in education and other social institutions are invited from a variety of perspectives including those of anthropology, communication, education, linguistics, literary theory, psychology, and sociology. Manuscripts are encouraged that involve theoretical treatments of relevant issues, present in-depth analyses of particular social groups and institutional settings, or present comparative studies across social groups, settings or institutions. Send inquiries to: Judith Green, Series Editor, Graduate School of Education, University of California, Santa Barbara, CA 93106.

1

Becoming Ethnographers
of an Early Childhood Classroom

David Fernie
Rebecca Kantor
The Ohio State University

In modern U.S. society, it is increasingly typical for young children to encounter their first school experiences in an early childhood setting—a neighborhood preschool, a child-care program, a Head Start, or public school program. In the United States today, approximately 13 million preschoolers (three out of every five) spend substantial amounts of time in some kind of early childhood program (Children's Defense Fund, 2000). This is more than triple the 1965 rate; and, with increasing numbers of working mothers, fewer two-parent families, and more children qualifying for publicly funded educational and social services, one can expect to see increasing numbers of children in U.S. early childhood settings.

Even if a child experiences only a half day early childhood program of some sort as a 3- and 4-year-old, he or she will have logged more than 2,000 hours in an educational setting before the first day spent in kindergarten. Thus, it is in early childhood settings that these children will all encounter a first place to call "school," the first adults to call "teacher," their first curricular experiences, their first daily schedule, the first set of expectations for appropriate "school behavior," and the largest group of peers they have yet to encounter. Despite noteworthy differences across types of early childhood settings, all are first schools to children, and each is a complex world in which young students must learn the knowledge, behavior, and expectations appropriate to participate in the social and academic life of that classroom.

In our view, the importance of these first settings cannot be overemphasized; in these first school years, strong impressions are gleaned by impressionable young minds. First school experiences inevitably constitute an initial direction in young children's learning and "studenting" (Fenstermacher, 1986), a direction that only can be reinforced or contradicted, not replaced by later experience. First schools, are important both in their own right and as the framework that children bring to their subsequent school experiences (Fernie, 1988). Despite the prevalence and importance of this formative experience in society, there is little in-depth knowledge and insight into the "life world" (Corsaro 1985, 1997) created by child and adult participants in early childhood classrooms. Much of the extant research focuses on long-term developmental and academic "outcomes" of early educational experiences. For example, one body of research focused on the long-term effects of program models has been prominent in the public discourse about the usefulness and effectiveness of publicly funded early education "interventions" (Lazar, Darlington, Murray, Royce, & Snipper, 1982; Schweinhart, Barnes, & Weikart, 1993; Westinghouse Learning Corporation, 1969). A second, major line of outcome-oriented research compares center-based child care to early experiences in the home and has evolved toward issues related to quality of care (Phillips, 1987), and to critique of the notion of quality in child care itself (Dahlberg, Moss, & Pence, 1999). Although these lines of research are important, especially within the policy realm, they leave many questions unanswered for teachers, and for researchers who are interested in understanding classroom and curricular processes. On a daily basis, teachers seeking to make sense of their experience with students in their classroom and to improve their practice are faced with issues such as how to help children make friends and resolve problems with their peers; how to support young children in their initial explorations and uses of reading and writing; what to do for children who struggle to speak, read, and write because of their hearing loss; defining the teacher's role in helping children overcome gender stereotyping; how to help children learn to be cooperative in a small-group setting; and how to balance the play interests of the children, like superhero play, with personal concerns for order and safety? Teachers searching for answers to these questions will find little of direct relevance in these literatures.

The desire to address questions such as these, related to the processes of daily life in the early childhood classroom, was the driving force behind the research presented in this volume. This book is the culminating product of long-term collaborative research focused on understanding the daily life of a single preschool classroom (with one addition from C. Williams whose research was conducted in a classroom for children with hearing impairments). But in common across the chapters, all researchers used ethnographic approaches to reveal the social processes and educational possibilities that take place in classrooms for young children. Throughout the book, we reveal how diverse aspects of this daily life are socially constructed by teachers and children together. These descriptions of life in a high-quality preschool setting should not be seen as a prescription for "best" practice, but as a resource and a challenge to readers reflecting on their own classroom practices. We believe teachers may see the ethnographic lens we used in the research as useful in making sense of the complexity of their own classrooms, just as it proved useful to our research team as we sought to make sense of this classroom through a more formal inquiry process.

Our collaboration began in 1985 in the early years of our respective tenures at Ohio State but our respective individual histories led to the collaboration. We had each experienced a basic early childhood doctoral training in individual psychology/child development and constructivist early childhood education but had distinctive specializations—Rebecca's in language and literacy development and David's in children's play. Over the course of our graduate and early research experiences, we separately, but similarly, evolved toward a more social set of research questions:

> **David:** My research interests have always been very connected to my own experiences as a teacher of young children, to things that I saw and wondered about when I was teaching—things that seemed important to children and had special and complex meanings for them. Much of my work as a graduate student was in Piagetian theory and its implications for the curriculum, which had the effect of complementing and focusing my work toward children's cognition. As a consequence, my research on superheroes and later game play were interests provoked by my teaching experiences but researched in a task, interview format, similar to clinical interview method developed by Piaget.
>
> This well-accepted method, however, took me away from how these interests were played out by children in the classroom and to more controlled circumstances to conduct the interviews. Although the initial methods I used were well-suited to examining children's thinking and perceptions, I continued to gravitate toward how play was accomplished in more natural contexts; for example, I was curious about who children would choose for partners in game play, and how this partnering would relate to the friendship, game expertise, social status, and past histories among the players. These were questions that could only be answered by watching naturally occurring behavior over time in the appropriate setting.

Rebecca: I experienced a master's program in early childhood education and a doctoral program in applied developmental psycholinguistics while teaching in various early childhood classrooms in Boston during the mid- to late-1970s. My master's program gave me a theoretical perspective on classrooms and curriculum in the progressive tradition of Dewey, and my doctoral studies were about the acquisition of language in the biological and cognitive traditions of such theorists as Chomsky and Piaget. Although Piagetian constructivism provided a link between these two fields, the task/interview method was unsatisfying for me, as it was for David, because it did not bring me closer to the questions that emerged in the course of my teaching experiences with young children.

By the time I entered the dissertation phase of my doctoral program, I was searching for a way to bring these two streams of preparation and interests together. At the same time, the field of psycholinguistics was broadening from a cognitive and experimental focus to include research about language and social processes, especially between mothers and their children, the now famous "motherese" model of development. Guided by my mentors to explore an area of mother–child interaction, I worked as an early childhood classroom teacher by day, and videotaped in the homes of young deaf children on the weekend to collect dissertation data on mother–child social and language processes. Eventually, I realized that what served my interests best was to take this social orientation on language process to the classroom: My experiences had led me to question the role of language and communication as it is situated in the curriculum, and in the social world of students and teachers.

Thus, we each arrived at Ohio State with complementary "training" typical of graduate education at the time, and with similar dispositions to be interested in the context of the classroom, to pursue questions of a social nature, and to search for a methodology that would better fit the nature of these questions. A colleague, Elisa Klein, shared and explored these interests with us and participated in the beginning of the ethnography project; subsequently, she moved to a faculty position at the University of Maryland.

At the time of our initial meeting, we each had been hired into separate early childhood roles in different colleges within the university. Within the Department of Educational Theory and Practice in the College of Education, David faced a set of diverse and separate demands; these included teaching responsibilities, primarily at the master's and doctoral level, supervision of undergraduate certification programs, the press to create a tenureable research record and the call to serve the wider campus and public communities. At the time, he had traditional relationships with community programs (i.e., "visitor researcher" roles with limited involvement in the ongoing daily life of any particular setting). Rebecca had multiple but separate roles linked to the early childhood program in her Family Relations and Human Development Department within the College of Human Ecology: she was hired into a tenure-line position with the usual assistant professor responsibilities including creating a tenureable research record. Also, Rebecca had part-time responsibility as a lead teacher in the department's lab school, the A. Sophie Rogers Laboratory for Child and Family Studies. This professor/practitioner configuration was the department's strategy to "model" from within a new way of doing preschool, with the specific goals of introducing more constructivist-oriented programming and creating a more visible research program in the lab.

As faculty at a research-based yet large and comprehensive university, the reality of these multiple demands led us both to search for ways to create integration within our academic lives. As we came together to discuss the potential of collaborative inquiry as a way to create coherence in our faculty roles, our early dialogue as researchers centered around our common interest in how the classroom functioned as a social group. We shared a belief that classrooms are inherently social places, and that the field's dominant emphasis on individually oriented child development knowledge as a guide to practice was inadequate to describe and explain the classroom as a social place. As we socially constructed our ideas and formulated our questions about life in the preschool, we searched for a paradigm that would allow us to explore our interests.

Simultaneous to the researchers' search for a new mode of inquiry, the lead teachers in the lab school were conducting their own inquiry about the classroom and the process of undergraduate teacher apprenticeship. Led by Rebecca, the lab school staff worked to articulate their practice in a formal curriculum document (Kantor & Elgas, 1986) to share with their undergraduate practicum students, who spend a 10-week quarter in the lab school prior to a full-time student teaching field experience.

As part of this task, they too were struggling to find the language within their existing constructivist framework to better capture and make visible to students the more social aspects of a curriculum—what happens "between the heads" as opposed to "within the heads" of the children and teachers as they engage in curricular experience. The teachers were searching for the framework that both researchers and teachers would later call *social constructionism* (Gergen, 1985; Rizzo, Corsaro, & Bates, 1992). A passage from the foreword to this curriculum document illustrates this search:

I truly believe that our curriculum is the result of a negotiated process—teachers and children construct and negotiate the curriculum together. . . . Thus, we can only share with the reader some beginning ideas, basic guidelines, examples, anecdotes, and ways to choose activities, experiences and materials that match our curricular framework. From there the children take over, take the curriculum content in unforeseen, unpredictable directions which the sensitive, skillful teacher must go along with, carefully guiding, facilitating, probing and exploring. . . . In our program, the teachers value the children's ideas above their own or those of the manufacturer of materials. The motto of our program is "Working from the Ideas of Children." (Kantor & Elgas, 1986, pp. 1-2)

At this point, we met two colleagues who were expert in sociocultural theory and ethnographic methods and were pivotal in our transition to taking the an ethnographic perspective on classroom life in our research and teaching practices: Judith Green (Green & Harker, 1982; Santa Barbara Classroom Discourse Group, 1992), a pioneer in applying ethnography to reveal the nature of language processes in educational settings, and William Corsaro (1985, 1997), a sociologist developing a model of childhood socialization around the central idea of children's peer culture. As we came to understand ethnography as a method and theory, we were excited by its potential to make visible the social aspects of daily life and the emergent aspects of curriculum, and to provide a complementary perspective to developmental theory as a guide to child-centered/appropriate teaching practice.

WHAT IS A PRESCHOOL ETHNOGRAPHY?

Located in wider traditions most often associated with anthropology and sociology, ethnography is also a perspective increasingly evident in classroom-based research at various levels of schooling (Green, Kantor, & Rogers 1991; Green & Meyer, 1991; Heras, 1993). In common across disciplines, ethnography typically involves prolonged participant-observation, extensive interview, and interpretation. Yet, ethnography is more than a set of field methods and analysis strategies. Ethnography has multiple identities: It is an orienting theory, a methodology, and a research product or text (Zaharlick & Green, 1991).

To speak of ethnography as an "orienting theory," we mean that ethnography involves "a way of looking at things"—a perspective or framework that ethnographers bring to the research context. The central concept of what is called an *ethnographic* (or alternately a sociocultural) *perspective* is *culture*, the notion that a group of people in prolonged interaction within a particular setting will construct a patterned way of conducting life together:

To be able to interpret what occurs within any given classroom requires an understanding of that classroom as a "mini" society with norms and expectations, rights and obligations and, roles and relationships for its members. In other words, a classroom must be conceived of as a social system in which life is constructed over time by members interacting and building on each others' actions, intentions, and messages (Gumperz, 1981). Such life becomes patterned over time as routines and rituals develop, events recur, norms become established, and a common set of expectations and a common language develops for "doing" life.

This patterned way of being in a social group is referred to in cognitive anthropology as the "culture" of the group (Goodenough, 1971; Spradley, 1980). From this perspective, the culture of each classroom is constructed by participants as they work together to meet the expected goals of schooling. This perspective on classroom culture does not negate the existence of larger social groups which have their own culture (e.g., the school, the community, the nation) or social groups that transcend the classroom and school (e.g., the peer group, the family).

Thus, the ethnographer enters a particular group setting with the orienting expectation that groups construct culture and with an interest in revealing the specific and distinctive cultural patterns (rituals, routines, norms, etc.), which are locally constructed there. From a sociocultural perspective, topics as broad as learning, and as circumscribed as storybook reading, all are viewed as embedded within a classroom's culture where they are given meaning in relation to that culture. As a consequence, topics are investigated as they relate to and have meaning in classroom life, as opposed to as singular, decontextualized topics.

Ethnography as a methodology provides ways of revealing a group's patterned life and the processes through which such life is socially constructed by its participants. In order to do so, researchers must spend prolonged time within a setting of interest. This overtime involvement is necessary in order to become a relatively unobtrusive and unintrusive part of the setting, to gain access to the "emic" or insider perspectives of the participants, and to make sense of the complex and dynamic nature of life in such settings. Using multiple sources of data such as fieldnotes, interviews, audio- and videorecordings, and collected artifacts, this sense-making process is usually an inductive and recursive one, moving back and forth between more global questions to more focused questions generated and informed in the course of the research. This inductive process of progressive understanding is well described by Gumperz (1986), who observed that ethnography tends to move back and forth between a general understanding and more focused analyses which in turn inform the whole. In the specific analyses discussed in the chapters of this volume, we have been guided further by the procedures suggested in Spradley's (1980) developmental research sequence, an inductive approach based on cultural theory. Additionally, for each focused analysis we were also guided by the existing theory, method, and research relevant to that topic.

Finally, in addressing ethnography's multiple meanings, we must address ethnography as a research product. In its most literal sense, the result of conducting an ethnography is a written text that presents a "thick" description and interpretation of life in a cultural setting (Denzin, 1989). In addition to sharing these meanings of ethnography with other educational ethnographers, we also share with them the general goals of educational ethnography—to understand the educational issues, classroom processes, and developmental phenomena that are yoked to the daily life of children and adults in educational settings.

WHAT IS THE VALUE OF A PRESCHOOL ETHNOGRAPHY?

Beyond these shared meanings, it is also important to define the special focus, benefit, and appeal of this ethnography from the perspective of early childhood education. As ethnographers within a preschool, our interest is in how the general themes just mentioned are manifested in distinctive ways during the period of early childhood. For example, relevant classroom processes include those school formats that children are introduced to in the preschool, such as large-group circle times and small-group activities. An example of a germane educational issue is how children's beginning literacy learning is approached in the preschool classroom. And developmental phenomena such as children's growing social competence, too, are captured as children participate in both the peer-initiated play and teacher-initiated school formats of the preschool.

Although each reader will make his or her own assessment of the benefits of this ethnographic text, we anticipate at least three contributions that such a text can make to theory and practice in early education. First, it can serve as a detailed example of the patterns of daily life in a high-quality classroom, allowing teachers to "see" another's classroom, to envision new educational possibilities as they are described there, and to use it as a reflector illuminating one's own customary and sometime habitual ways of doing things. Second, it provides theory grounded closely in data, in other words, revealing what actually occurred within the setting. Thus, it contributes to "grounded theory" about curriculum, development, and classroom life that is generated from what is actually occurring within these settings of interest. Third, such a text adds to a growing body of educational ethnographies that describes life in various early childhood educational settings (Corsaro, 1985; Hatch, 1995; Leavitt, 1995; Lubeck, 1985; Tobin, Wu, & Davidson, 1989). If one looks across a growing body of ethnographies, it may be possible to identify recurring cultural themes and elements of life in early educational settings, as well as those that are unique to particular contexts.

It has been our experience that teachers within the early childhood community (and preservice teachers) relate well to ethnography as a perspective and methodology, perhaps because ethnography "bears a close resemblance to the routine ways in which people make sense of the world in everyday life" (Hammersley & Atkinson, 1989, p. 2). Making sense of the early childhood classroom has often meant having a "child-centered" philosophy (Kessler, 1991; Weber, 1971). To us, this means that children's needs, interests, and growth patterns are used as reference points for creating responsive curricular practices and a supportive classroom life. By revealing participants' perspectives (children's and adults') through ethnography, researchers and teachers can get a clearer vision of how children's needs, interests, and growth relate to the accomplishment of everyday life. By taking adults into children's play worlds, ethnography helps adults to see how children produce, talk about, and interpret their play. In these ways, ethnography is a powerful new resource for teachers to broaden the meanings of being child-centered in approach, complementing traditional sources of information such as child development theory and research.

Relatedly, ethnographers' use of prolonged observation of daily life in the classroom fits well with the tradition of early childhood teachers as "child-watchers." Early childhood education has a long history of using observational methods (e.g., anecdotal or narrative records) in order to document and understand children's growth and behavior (Cohen, Stern, & Balaban, 1997; Genishi, 1992). Although ethnographers also make use of (long-term and contextualized) observations, they distinctively interpret what they see in cultural terms. So, one child's actions get interpreted in relation to the actions of others, to the evolving history of the group and its ways of accomplishing ordinary daily life. Most importantly, one moment is never understood in isolation; rather, each moment of life is seen as belonging to patterns constructed and identified over time, with both stable and dynamic aspects, which define customary ways of conducting group life and interpreting its meanings.

Thus, ethnographers' ability to identify cultural patterns, offers a distinctive contribution to our understanding of classrooms. This search for and identification of cultural patterns fits teachers' need to clarify and "get a handle" on the sometimes overwhelming complexity of group life. From the distance gained through systematic analyses, ethnographic texts such as this one may provoke insights that are difficult to gain from the close and involved perspective of "online" teaching.

Furthermore, we believe that the words *evolving* and *inductive* apply equally well to the inquiry processes of ethnographers and of reflective teachers. In our teaching within the university and wider community, one of the gratifying revelations is that the sense-making of ethnographic research connects easily to the ongoing and evolving sense-making of both novice and experienced teachers in their classrooms. Because ethnography describes real classrooms, it is research related to practice rather than research that needs to be translated into practice.

A SOCIAL HISTORY OF THE RESEARCH TEAM

In 1987, we began our educational ethnography in the lab school. As we described in the opening of this chapter, it was our hope that the ethnographic project would serve an integrative function in several ways: (a) to bring together different aspects of our respective professional lives at the university; (b) to combine two goals, the development of grounded theory and informed practice regarding early childhood settings; (c) to facilitate the goal of transforming the lab to one more active in research, in tandem with the goal to better understand the social construction of emergent curriculum. Necessarily then, the research collaboration brought together a diverse group of participants—undergraduate, masters, and doctoral students, faculty from our respective departments, and the teachers, practicum students, and children in the lab school. Within this volume, the chapters represent contributions from this diverse group but are authored by the following team members who took the lead in exploring specific topics: Peg Elgas, then a doctoral student and now an associate professor at the University of Cincinnati; Donna C. Williams, formerly a lead teacher in the A. Sophie Rogers Lab School and now a kindergarten teacher in Indiana; James Scott Jr., a doctoral student at the time and now a program enhancement specialist with the Great Lakes Head Start Quality Enhancement Network (Q-NET); Paula McMurray, a doctoral student at the time and now associate professor at Iowa State University; Sandra Miller, also a doctoral student in the project and now an early childhood consultant with the Early Childhood Division of the Ohio Department of Education; and Cheri Williams, a doctoral student then, who now also holds an associate professorship at the University of Cincinnati.

Within the research team, a commitment to collaborative inquiry not only expanded the number and type of participants, but forged some new roles as well. For example, we envisioned something different from the traditional combination of lead professors charting the whole of a research project, junior doctoral researchers conducting subsidiary analyses, and teachers serving as subjects rather than as participants in the research. We were looking for a more collaborative and less hierarchical set of relationships between senior and junior researchers. Given these aims, we invited the doctoral students to bring their own topics of interest to explore within the ethnography. As a result, the students introduced the broad topics of literacy, gender, friendship and rejection by peers as initial foci within the project; each topic became shaped overtime by the inductive examination of classroom life and by the constructive, interpretive processes of continuing discussions within the group and ongoing individual and collective analyses.

Simultaneously, we were exploring new researcher-teacher configurations that promised special yield in terms of insight into the classroom: Rebecca served in an unusual dual role, as one of the co-principal investigators in the research and lead teacher in the laboratory; and, Donna, also a laboratory teacher as well as a master's student, conducted an analysis of her own daily small-group format. Thus, the lines so often drawn between teachers and researchers (and between research and teaching) were softened as researcher-teachers conducted research in their own classroom, participated in the interpretation and triangulation of data, authored writings, and cycled new research findings into the curriculum of the laboratory school. Because these "insiders" were both classroom and research team participants rather than the subjects of the researchers, their perspectives and interpretations was easily forthcoming and invaluable to the research process. Conversely, their participation in the research process and the insights of fellow team members provoked, informed, and contributed to their evolving understanding of their own classroom.

Both to forge a group identity and to accomplish a deeper and shared understanding of ethnography among the research team, we collaboratively designed and co-taught a series of seminars for doctoral and masters students from both of our departments. Over several years, seminar topics included theory, method, and empirical literatures (both ethnographic and other) related to school socialization, friendship, children's play, social competence, curriculum, and "developmentally appropriate practice" (Bredekamp & Copple, 1997). Typically, the master's students included lab school lead teachers and experienced practitioners from a variety of preschools and elementary schools in the community. As result of this mix, the seminars remained firmly grounded in both practice and theory.

In true seminar fashion, these courses were designed to encourage students and professors alike to explore new literatures together, not as a forum for professors to transmit their "expert" knowledge to students. Because this purpose put professors and students on a more equal footing, these seminars resembled, though in a higher education version, the guided collaborative inquiry witnessed among teachers and students that Donna Williams describes in chapter 3. These seminars ultimately served us all well: They allowed the professors to model and reinforce the less hierarchical roles we wished to establish with teachers and students; they allowed all participants (professors included) to explore and/or to revisit pertinent research literatures and issues; and they created a context to begin to mentor the doctoral and master's students who were also members of our research team.

But the commitment to collaborative inquiry did more than create a different social network for the research: It also provided a social structure that made the in-depth study of this setting possible. Through collaborative inquiry, our research group was able to conduct numerous "linked" analyses in distinct but related aspects of life in this classroom, far beyond what would be feasible for one or two researchers working independently. By *linked* we mean that each new analysis was provoked by the understanding gained in previous analyses and that each new analysis both informed and was informed by the interpretation of data in the others. Although individuals often took the lead in pursuing a particular topic and analysis, the research group met in weekly meetings to turn our collective attention to various aspects of the process—conceptualizing topics, analyzing data, and critiquing and contributing written text to manuscripts and to presentations. Students worked collaboratively with other students and with classroom teachers to triangulate data, to inductively develop research strategies and coding categories, to code data, and so forth. Thus, the original impetus to collaborate felt by us as individuals evolved into the creation of a wider collaborative inquiry group and in socially constructed knowledge. This process, we are convinced, is synergistic—making the interpretation of all participants more broadly and critically informed.

CHAPTERS AND THEMES

In the chapters that follow, each author presents a discussion of his or her early childhood education topic of interest. In each chapter, the uniqueness of a sociocultural/ethnographic perspective and the yield of a data analysis is highlighted through a comparison with a traditional early childhood literature on that topic. Because all but the C. Williams investigation were conducted within our preschool ethnography, certain salient and pervasive "cultural themes" characterizing this setting emerged across analyses. As we now introduce the individual chapters, we also present a first introduction to these three overlapping and recurrent themes within the volume:

1. *Peer culture and school culture*: theoretical frameworks for capturing two distinctive domains of activity within this and other classrooms.
2. *Social construction*: a theoretical construct to describe the accomplishment of diverse aspects of school culture and peer culture social processes.
3. *Educational possibilities*: demonstrations of what can be accomplished in high-quality classrooms when teachers have the disposition to go beyond traditional child-centered practice to explore diverse sources for the curriculum, and when such efforts are broadened to include and benefit from a sociocultural perspective.

In chapter 3, Peg Elgas describes how a cohesive and "popular" friendship group (dubbed the "core" group) emerged within the classroom as they socially constructed and regulated play in the service of their friendship. As the first analysis conducted within our research group, it benefited greatly from Corsaro's (1985) work on preschool *peer culture*. In this study, Corsaro defined the peer culture realm as including "a set of common activities or routines, artifacts, values, concerns, and attitudes" constructed and shared by a group of children (Corsaro, 1985, p. 171). In Elgas' analysis of this salient core group, she creates a window to the peer culture at work—or rather at play—and in doing so occasions a new look at the meanings traditionally ascribed to various aspects of preschoolers' play: What objects and routines signify to the group and how they are used to serve social dynamics important to children; how leadership is recognized and exercised within a classroom; and how children gain and protect access to their play—issues well-studied in our field but, in our view, not yet fully understood.

In chapter 2, Donna Williams presents her analysis of a *school culture* curricular format—the creation of the collaborative small group. The school culture realm, as we have defined it in parallel to Corsaro's notion of the peer culture, is "a common set of activities, routines, events, values, concerns and attitudes shared by classroom participants, related to the broad educational mission and demands for group living inherent within classroom life" (Fernie, Kantor, Klein, Meyer, & Elgas,

1988). In contrast to such elements in the typically child-dominated peer culture, school culture activities and events (e.g., large-group circle time and clean-up time), routines (e.g., daily transitions to the playground), and concerns (e.g., beginning literacy) are largely influenced by the teachers. They are responsible for the "game plan" to promote school culture goals with their novice students.

The D. Williams chapter details the creation of the small group format, showing its evolution over time as these novice students and their teachers first learn to "look" like a group and then to act like one. In particular, she shows the unique contributions that both socially competent 3-year-olds and their sensitive, aware teacher make to this way of experiencing collaborative artwork, shared storybook readings, and group membership. She reveals, through narrative example and data presentation, the manner in which consensual norms and knowledge develop and become an implicit and underlying structure that guides group action. Because educators are often skeptical of young children's ability to work in groups, even in the primary grades, this chapter analyzes an important educational possibility and describes how it evolved.

Each in its respective realm then, these two chapters also demonstrate how experiences as child-dominated as play and as adult-initiated as curricular formats are social constructions of all the classroom participants. By this, we mean that they are constructed in the moment-by-moment doing, through the face-to-face interactions among participants. And although we find it a useful heuristic and teaching tool to distinguish the child-dominated peer culture from a teacher-dominated school culture, it is important not to dichotomize these two realms because they co-exist within the same classroom and because both necessarily are co-constructed with varying involvements of both adult and child participants. Through the ethnography, we have come to view the social construction processes within this classroom as bringing together the realms of school culture and peer culture in mutually supportive ways (Fernie et al., 1988). Furthermore, we learned in the course of our investigation that many of the classroom topics of interest, for example, literacy and social competence, were more fully and better understood when examined across both realms.

The following three chapters present analyses conducted later in the chronology of our ethnography in which particular topics are explored as they are situated across contexts or realms of peer and school culture. In chapter 4, James Scott explores how two children experience difficulty and become "outsiders" or rejected children in the classroom. With a sustained look across peer culture and school culture realms, this ethnographic analysis revealed the outsider status to be a dynamic and differentiated social construction, one that evolved in somewhat distinctive ways for each of the two children. Furthermore, the chapter demonstrates the impact of this social construction process at both the individual and whole group level. This detailed picture contrasts with the traditional view that such status relates primarily to certain enduring personal attributes and problematic social behaviors and, thus, the Scott analysis implies different strategies for the classroom teacher.

In chapter 5, Paula McMurray also details the individual experiences of (two) children, but with a focus on how each constructs a place for himself within the social world of the classroom as a gendered person, a student, and a peer. These two interesting children negotiate flexible, highly individual, and distinctive roles across the range of their interactions with teachers and peers. For teachers interested in supporting children 's development of nontraditional gender roles, McMurray's moment-by-moment interactional analysis lends guidance for how this educational possibility can be accomplished and supported. The last two chapters concern literacy; one reports another linked analysis within our ethnography, whereas the other provides a unique look at literacy development in the special case of children with hearing impairment. In Sandy Miller's linked analysis within our ethnography, literacy is located and demonstrated across four different classroom contexts, serving diverse purposes in children's peer culture play, their exploration of art materials, and in the structured small-group collaborative activity (the latter is described by D. Williams in chapter 3). By taking this context-by-context look, we see how literacy is replete and differentiated across life in this preschool classroom, and how the educational possibility of literacy is conceived by teachers as a multifaceted phenomenon.

In chapter 6, Cheri Williams explores how literacy develops in tandem with other language processes (spoken and signed) in three children with profound hearing loss. Looking across home and school settings, the cases of three children with dramatically different verbal language experiences document the diversity of language experience typically found in this population of children. Moreover, C. Williams' finding that children with hearing impairment experience initial pathways to literacy similar to other children, despite not having a fluent verbal language, contradicts the traditional assumption that verbal language necessarily precedes literacy development. Although the C. Williams and Miller analyses were conducted in very different settings and with children with very different profiles, both analyses similarly interpret beginning literacy processes and practices in cultural terms. The final chapter is our opportunity to relate the analyses to cross-cutting cultural themes, to extend our understanding of a single classroom to broader implications for theory and practice, and to reflect on lessons learned during the course of doing this ethnography. Although each analysis has independent meaning as an exploration of a topic, collectively they tell a more comprehensive and integrated story of this classroom and its participants. And this was the overriding goal of the project—to "see" the whole of the early childhood classroom through the ethnographic lens. Thus, in the last chapter, we address questions that emerge when the analyses are linked together, for example: How were educational opportunities accomplished by children and teachers in this classroom? What do we gain as teachers and researchers through this understanding of the fabric of everyday life in an early childhood classroom? What have we learned about classrooms, children and their development, research, and teacher education within higher education? In order for one to understand the path we took to find answers to these questions, it is necessary to return to the starting point, the classroom setting and program that we sought to understand more deeply. Spradley (1980) suggested that observers take a "grand tour" to locate the basic dimensions of a cultural setting: elements such as the physical space, the actors, activities, events, time sequence characteristic of the setting. Here we describe the basics of this classroom, giving the reader a grand tour of those things that might be easily discerned or learned by someone when first entering the setting.

A GRAND TOUR OF THE CLASSROOM

The lab school is a spacious room set up for both the early childhood and the teacher education that takes place there. The adult students can observe the daily life of the group from a raised deck that runs along the long wall of the room. From that vantage point, an observer can see most of the activity centers in the long rectangular room. In addition to the main classroom there are separate rooms for food preparation, toileting, and music.

The preschool is located in an older university building, and has been in operation since 1925. Although a recent renovation created some updated features, like the bathroom and kitchen fixtures, the charm of the room lies in the older architectural style such as the oversized windows, high ceilings, and wood trim. The layout of the room is largely open and invites child exploration and play. Boundaries for separate activity centers are marked by shelving, furniture, rugs, and plants and the areas are well stocked with materials appropriate to each area.

At one end of the room, there are tables for lunch, snack, and planned art activities on a large tiled area as well as smaller areas created for water and sand play and carpentry; at the other end, there are ample, carpeted areas set aside for large hollow and unit block building, a pretend play area, and the cubbies near the entry to the room. In between, a large taped circle on the rug indicates the location for daily meeting times for "circle" and an alcove juts out behind the circle and is a place where books, puppets, and pillows suggest quieter interactions.

Because the lab school is situated in a research-oriented university, the room is equipped with 8 video camera stations and 20 locations for suspended ceiling microphones. Observations were conducted by students and researchers either from the observer deck or from the floor of the room by sitting unobtrusively near the activity of the children and adults.

The program at the time provided preschool experience scheduled for morning and afternoon sessions, 3 hours a day, Monday through Thursday. The program ran for 9 weeks, each of three quarters during an academic year. (Since then, the lab school has become a full-day, full-year child-care program.) The ethnography focused on the afternoon session in which Rebecca Kantor and Donna Williams were the co-teachers. Because of the student teachers and observers in the room, the children were used to extra adults in the setting facilitating an easy entry and acceptance for members of the research team.

With the image of the physical setting and program, the social histories of the members of the research team, and the original goals of the ethnography in mind, we turn now to our story.

REFERENCES

Bredekamp, S., & Copple, C. (1977). *Developmentally appropriate practice in early childhood programs* (rev. ed.). Washington, DC: NAEYC.

Children's Defense Fund. (April, 2000). *Child care and early education basics.* Washington, DC: Children's Defense Fund. www.childrensdefense. org/childcare/cc_facts.html.

Cohen, D., Stern, V., & Balaban, N. (1997). *Observing and recording the behavior of young children* (4th ed.). New York: Teachers College Press.

Corsaro, W. (1985). *Friendship and peers culture in the early years.* Norwood, NJ: Ablex.

Corsaro, W. (1997). *The sociology of childhood.* Thousand Oaks, CA: Pine Forge Press.

Dahlberg, G., Moss, P., & Pence, A. (1999). *Beyond quality in early childhood education and care.* London: Falmer Press.

Denzin, N. K. (1989). *Interpretive interactionism.* Newbury Park, CA: Sage.

Fernie, D. (1988). Becoming a student: Messages from first settings. *Theory Into Practice, 27*(1), 3-10.

Fernie, D., Kantor, R., Klein, E., Meyer, C., & Elgas, P. (1988). Becoming students and becoming ethnographers in a preschool. *Journal of Research in Childhood Education, 3*(2), 132-141.

Fenstermacher, G. D. (1986). Philosophy of research on teaching: Three aspects. In M. Wittrock (Ed.), *Handbook of research on teaching* (pp. 37-49). New York: MacMillan.

Genishi, C. (1992). Framing the ways. In C. Genishi (Ed.), *Ways of assessing children and curriculum* (pp. 1-24). New York: Teachers College Press.

Gergen, K. J. (1985). The social constructionist movement in modern psychology. *American Psychologist, 40*(3), 266-275.

Goodenough, W. H. (1971). *Culture, language and society.* Reading, MA: Addison-Wesley.

Green, L., & Harker, J. (1982). Gaining access to learning: Conversational, social, and cognitive demands of group participation. In L. Wilkinson (Ed.), *Communicating in the classroom* (pp. 183-221). New York: Academic Press.

Green, J., Kantor, R., & Rogers, T. (1991). Exploring the complexity of language and learning in the classroom. In B. Jones & L. Idol (Eds.), *Educational values and cognitive instruction: Implications for reform* (Vol. 2, pp. 333-364). Hillsdale, NJ: Erlbaum.

Green, J.L., & Meyer, L. A. (1991). The embeddedness of reading in classroom life. In C. Baker & A. Luke (Eds.), *Toward a critical sociology of reading pedagogy* (pp. 141-160). Amsterdam: John Benjamins.

Gumperz, J. (1986). Interactional sociolinguistics in the study of schooling. In J. Cook Gumperz (Ed.), *The social construction of literacy* (pp. 45-68). New York: Cambridge University Press.

Gumperz, J. J. (1981). Conversational inference and classroom learning. In J. L. Green & C. Wallat (Eds.), *Ethnography and language in educational settings* (pp. 3-23). Norwood, NJ: Ablex.

Hammersley, M., & Atkinson, P. (1989). *Ethnography: Principles in practice.* New York: Routledge.

Hatch, A. (1995). *Qualitative research in early childhood settings.* Westport, CT: Praeger.

Heras, A. I. (1993). The construction of understanding in a sixth grade bilingual classroom. *Linguistics and Education, 5*(3 & 4), 275-299.

Kantor, R., & Elgas, P. (1986). *Curriculum document, the A. Sophie Rogers Laboratory for Child and Family Studies.* Unpublished manuscript, The Ohio State University.

Kessler, S. A. (1991). Alternative perspectives on early childhood education. *Early Childhood Research Quarterly, 6,* 183-197.

Lazar, I., Darlington, R., Murray, H., Royce, J., & Snipper, A. (1982). Lasting effects of early education: A report from the Consortium for Longitudinal Studies. *Monographs of the Society for Research in Child Development, 47* (serial no. 195).

Leavitt, R. (1995). The emotional culture of infant–toddler day care. In A. Hatch (Ed.), *Qualitative research in early childhood settings* (pp. 3-21). Westport, CT: Praeger.

Lubeck, S. (1985). *Sandbox society.* London: Falmer Press.

Lubeck, S. (1995). Nation as context: Comparing child-care systems across nations. *Teachers College Record, 96*(3), 467-489.

Philips, D. (1987). *Quality in child care: What the research tells us.* Washington, DC: NAEYC.

Rizzo, T., Corsaro, W., & Bates, J. (1992). Ethnographic methods and intrepretive analysis: Expanding the methodological options of psychologists. *Developmental Review, 12,* 101-123.

Santa Barbara Classroom Discourse Group (Green, Dixon, Lin, Floriana, & Bradley). (1992). Constructing literacy in classrooms: Literate action as social accomplishment. In H. Marshall (Ed.), *Redefining student learning: Roots of educational change* (pp. 119-150). Norwood, NJ: Ablex.

Schweinhart, L., Barnes, H., & Weikert, D. (1993). *Significant benefits: The High/Scope Perry preschool study through age 27.* Ypsilanti, MI: High/Scope Press.

Spradley, J. (1980). *Participant observation.* New York: Holt.

Tobin, J. J., Wu, D. Y. H., & Davidson, D. H. (1989). *Preschool in three cultures: Japan, China, and the United States.* New Haven, CT: Yale University Press.

Weber, L. (1971). *The English infant school and informal education.* Englewood Cliffs, NJ: Prentice-Hall.

Westinghouse Learning Corporation. (1969). *The impact of Head Start: An evaluation of the effects of Head Start on children's cognitive and affective development.* Report to the Office of Economic Opportunity. Washington, DC: Clearinghouse for Federal, Scientific, and Technical Information.

Zaharlick, A., & Green, J. L. (1991). Ethnographic research. In J. Flood, J. M. Jensen, D. Lapp, & J. R. Squire (Eds.), *Handbook of research in teaching the English language arts* (pp. 205-225). New York: MacMillan.

2
Complexities of Learning in a Small Group

Donna Williams
Ball State University

A small group meets on a regular basis and shares an identity or sense of purpose. Thus, each small group has a character of its own and is a recognizable social entity to its members and to outsiders. This is what distinguishes a group from a simple collection of people. Six strangers in an elevator are not a small group.

—Ridgeway (1983, p. 3)

As Ridgeway's definition suggests, a "small group" of people is a unique social unit. The characteristics and qualities of a small group distinguish it from a "collection" of noninteracting people assembled in the same space. Just what these characteristics are, however, have been defined differently by researchers from various disciplinary perspectives. Sociologists (Ridgeway, 1983), psychologists (Lewin 1947a, 1947b; Leary, Robertson, Barnes, & Miller, 1986), business researchers (Cooper, 1979) as well as educators (Johnson & Johnson 1987; Sharan & Sharan, 1992; Slavin 1987) have all produced a substantial literature on small-group structure, skills, and process within their respective literatures, as well as a body of work that is interdisciplinary in nature. The intense interest in small-group interaction stems from the reality that such group experiences are typical throughout life in our culture as school instructional groups, friendship groups, committees, a corporate board, families, the lunch group at work, city council, and a teenage gang (Ridgeway, 1983).

In terms of small-group work within schools, interest has been most strong at the elementary, secondary, and even higher education levels (Barnes & Todd, 1977; Merrit & Humphrey, 1979; Weinstein, 1976; Wilkenson & Dollaghan, 1979), and has not been directed toward the early childhood small-group experience. This is despite the popularity of such a curricular format; frequently, in preschool classrooms, there is a point in the day when the entire classroom breaks into subgroups for the delivery of curriculum in smaller contexts, or when children form small groups of peers for play.

Of note, early childhood educators such as Katz and Chard (1989) and the Reggio Emilia researchers in Northern Italy (cited in Edwards, Gandini, & Forman 1998) have renewed the call for curriculum formats that are focused on the collaborative efforts of small groups of children—what has come to be called "project work." Here, the emphasis is not only on small group as a context for interaction, but on the potential for learning through collaborative small-group projects or longer term investigations in the tradition of Dewey's progressive education and the British Infant Schools (Katz & Chard 1989). Such learning relates to the topics that are pursued (topics that emerge from the interests of the children or ones that are introduced by the teachers) and the learning of participation in such a group effort, what Katz called the "disposition" to be a group participant.

In Katz and Chard's book, *Engaging Children's Minds: The Project Approach*, the research cited as support for such a return to group formats is diverse, but only indirectly related to group work with young children. The researchers invoke notions of children's active construction of knowledge and their intense need to understand their experiences (Katz & Chard, 1989) to support the facilitation of active project work on topics engaging to children. They also argue that early childhood is a time for teachers to be especially concerned with children's social and communicative competence, and that small-group project work sets a context for such interaction and thus, the development of such competencies. They turn to Nelson's work in script theory (Hudson & Nelson, 1983; Nelson & Gruendel, 1981) and suggest that "the variety of backgrounds that children bring to the group enriches the sources of information about how different people enact familiar events and what they do often" (p. 25).

In Reggio Emilia, the theoretical and empirical literature that has provided guidance and inspiration for their work is broad-based and diverse as they believe that "a unifying theory of education that sums up all the phenomena of educating does not (and never will) exist" (Malaguzzi 1998, p. 84). Instead, this community of researchers has looked to such important thinkers as Dewey (1902, 1916), Vygotsky

(1978) Piaget (1957, 1962, 1971), Hawkins (1966), Bruner (1986), Gardner (1983), and others within progressive education, and sociolinguistic, social constructivist, and symbolic interactionist perspectives.

Adding a voice from educational ethnography, Kantor, Elgas, and Fernie (1993) argued for more group-oriented research as an additional source of developmental and curricular guidance in the early childhood classroom. Specifically, in their work they broaden development to foreground its social nature arguing that development is a social process, and that the classroom is a social place in which certain kinds of "group development," can be uniquely examined (Kantor et al., 1993). For example, the ethnographers have described how one group of children and their teachers developed the skills for group discourse with the collective learning and participation structure (Erickson & Mohatt, 1982) shifting from a struggle to literally arrange themselves in a circle to the accomplishment of a (relatively) coordinated group conversation (Kantor, Elgas, & Fernie, 1989). Thus, this is group development because it changes in qualitatively distinct ways, but unlike individual development the accomplishment resides with and describes the group rather than the individual.

This notion of group development coming out of the ethnographic work of Fernie and Kantor provided the framework for my own research described in this chapter. Specifically, I wanted to know more about group development within the small-group activity time that I planned and conducted daily with ten 3-year-olds. In the next section, both the historical context for my own set of questions and the ethnographic project within which I conducted my analysis is presented.

THE CLASSROOM EVENT

I was a lead teacher in the classroom in which the preschool ethnography led by Rebecca Kantor and David Fernie was conducted. I was also a master's student at the time and chose to analyze my small-group activity event as the basis for an action research thesis. At the time, the other teachers and I valued the small-group experience for young children even though there was little evidence within the child development literature that egocentric 3-year-olds could engage in collaborative group activity; in fact, there was accepted theory and research to the contrary (Parten, 1932; Piaget, 1957, 1962).

We knew that the children had never experienced small-group work in schools because they were having their first school experience with us. It would be unlikely at this young age that children would experience small-group action very frequently within neighborhood and home contexts. Yet, despite the children's apparent lack of experience and ability to engage in group interaction, the teachers believed strongly that to nurture children's cooperation and collaborative abilities within small-group formats would serve children well in this classroom, in later schooling, and in life beyond the classroom. The thesis was my opportunity to follow my intuitions and systematically study the small-group process.

Small group is a daily event in the preschool classroom under study. For this activity, the preschool class is divided, roughly by age, into two ongoing groups, each one consistently led by one of the two lead teachers. My group of mostly 3-year-olds met daily in a small room within the larger classroom. As their group teacher-leader, I would prepare materials each day for the group time and would prepare the room with small carpet squares to help the children find an "individual space" within the group. Reflecting the classroom's commitment to inquiry both as an individual experience and as group collaboration, children's ideas were elicited and acknowledged in small-group activity as the members explored diverse and open-ended materials and as they learned to represent their experiences with different media and symbol systems.

Because my group was the younger of the two groups in this mixed-age classroom, my focus was necessarily on the beginning aspects of "being" a group. In other words, I realized that before a group could accomplish joint projects, it must first "become" a group. In the early part of the year, as the children worked side by side in a group context, the teachers (myself and our student teachers) would make public comments about each student's ideas, ask students to describe their own work to others, and work alongside the children. In this incipient togetherness the focus was on experiencing "group," on learning how to share space, materials, ideas, and conversation.

During the early part of the school year, I facilitated the children's continuing progress as a group: I helped them choose a name for their group through a democratic process; I suggested and created group displays of their individual art products; and I used conversation to help the children become aware of each other, of their responsibilities to the emerging group, and of their individual rights within the group.

Eventually, the children's guided progress enabled them to engage in true collaborative activity. When I sensed their readiness, I introduced materials that produced a joint product such as group murals and group wood constructions as the focus for collaborative inquiry. Although I (and the student teachers) had activities and goals in mind as starting points for the daily group time, my priority was to follow the lead of the children, which often takes the group in unexpected directions. For example, once I brought in a variety of construction materials (e.g., toilet paper rolls, cardboard, wood, industrial junk), with the idea in mind that the small group might want to create a "city." But, after my deliberately neutral introduction of the materials ("I thought we could use these to build something today"), the children worked together to build a "teenage mutant ninja turtle sewer," following their intense interest at that time in these popular media characters.

Although my co-teachers and I believed the development and accomplishment of small group to be a complex and gradual process, we were primarily guided by our collective intuitions. The ethnography being conducted in our classroom provided an opportunity to conduct a systematic inquiry into the development of small-group social action and, in turn, to further inform my own practice of this curriculum format.

THE ANALYSIS

My analysis began with the assumption that the whole of the preschool classroom can be conceived as a culture defined by its "system of standards for perceiving, believing, evaluating and acting" (Goodenough, 1971, p. 41). These patterned ways of constructing and conducting "life together" in a group are established overtime through the face-to-face interactions and actions of the members (Green & Harker, 1982). Within the larger classroom, there are many contexts such as small-group time that have their own patterned ways of acting, or participant structures that guide the flow of interactions. For the 3-year-olds, contexts like small group are brand new. These beginning preschoolers are facing viewpoints other than their own, participating in tasks and interactional situations that they have not yet experienced or given meaning. Their tasks and conversations may seem deceptively simple and informal, but indeed they are interactionally complex.

For the analysis described here, the complexity of group interaction was captured in several ways. First, a wall-mounted video camera placed in one corner of the room captured audio/visual recordings. Following the schedule of the "parent" ethnography, videotapes were made over three 2-week periods (autumn, winter, and spring). Additionally, a few extra tapes of small group were made at times when we felt there were shifts in interaction. A participant-observer from the research team attended each group time across the year and documented the event with fieldnotes. I kept weekly reflection notes in a journal to capture my "impressions" of the group's progress and as the basis for my decisions regarding curriculum.

All of these data sources were reviewed to begin to understand the nature of group interaction and the change in group process overtime. This initial cycle of review led to the assertion that change could be analyzed at a more microanalytic level by sampling an event from each of the three 2-week taping cycles. Three ordinary days, one from each quarter's 2-week taping cycle, were chosen for to analyze with a "mapping" process developed by Green and her colleagues (Green & Wallat, 1981; Green, Weade, & Graham, 1988), a technique I learned in a qualitative research course. In this sociolinguistic analysis, a verbatim transcript for each event is created, and a visual "map" of the interaction is constructed to show the links between units of meaning. Additionally, for each event, categories are created to capture the underlying communication strategies of participants (in my case, those of the teacher). A final step was to look across events to identify similarities (showing a stable pattern over time) and differences (showing group development over time). Thus, analysis consisted of three steps: transcription, mapping and category development, and pattern identification.

REVEALING THE COMPLEXITY OF THE EVENT

To explore the nature of patterned interaction within this event, a social action rule analysis was conducted (Green et al., 1988). Social action rules are patterned, explicitly stated or implicitly operating norms for participation (e.g., expectations, rights and responsibilities, limits, and so forth). They are derived from an examination of the moment-by-moment interactions as captured in the maps of the events.

Within this event, these social action rules fell into two broad categories: group-oriented rules (see Fig. 2.1) and individual-oriented rules (see Fig. 2.2). Group-oriented rules describe orientations, obligations, responsibilities of each child to the group. For example, the social action rule "All group members must come to group from a transition activity" was derived from a dismissal routine of the preceding activity. In this situation, the teacher might use a gamelike procedure ("If you are wearing red go to your group") to help children make the transition to their respective small groups. This was coded as a "group-oriented rule" because it describes all participants' collective responsibility to the group event.

Conversely, individual-oriented rules describe the group's orientations, obligations, and responsibilities to each individual child. For example, the social action rule "The group needs to accommodate individual member needs" was derived from the teacher's directive that the group "scoot back a little so William can get in our circle." This was coded as an "individual-oriented rule" because it describes each individual's rights within a group activity. Not surprisingly, group-oriented rules constitute the majority of all social action rules. This attests to the group nature of this event; that is, teacher messages about group are replete within all aspects of the event. This makes sense because "learning to do group" is the major purpose of this activity.

	Group does not proceed until all members enter the group space
	Group members must be seated before group time begins
	Group sits in a circle
	Group members need to be seated in such a way as to allow clear visibility for all group members
	All members of small group have red tags
Group	Group proceedings must not disturb the other group
	Materials owned by the preschool become property of individual small groups at the sanctioned times
	Teacher will build topic from student comments
	Teacher will build on nonverbal contextualization cues and create topic
	Entire group collaborates on some tasks
	Some materials have scheduled uses
	Some materials are for teacher use only
	Some materials must be shared by the group
	Materials need to be accessible to all group members (one person cannot hold them)
	Teacher's assistance is on a "first come, first served" basis
Group	Teacher's help is available on request
	Content of group activity changes
	Teacher will offer assistance if she is aware of student need
	Teacher may build topic from the activity itself
	Some activities in-group are repeated
	Teacher values collaborative behaviors
	When most members of the group are finished, only a few minutes more are allowed other members
	Those finishing first begin to clean up
	Group members leave the group together
	Some materials are for teacher use
	Small group room is only property of small group at designated times
	Teacher is the keeper of resources
Group	Teacher values collaborative behaviors
	Hands must be washed before snack
	Teacher will offer assistance if she is aware of student need
	Group members are responsible for the safety of group shared materials
	Group members are responsible for knowing expected classroom procedures
	Some materials must be shared by the group

Figure 2.1 Group-oriented rules.

Individual	Individual places are available for each group member
	It is acceptable to bring personal possessions into small group
	The group needs to accommodate to individual members
	Teacher values students ideas
	Once a student has claimed a material, it is his/hers as long as he/she wants
	Once a student has claimed a material it is his/hers as long as he/she wants
Individual	A student's name may be written on paper for identification
	Words of student's choice can be written by teacher
	Individual ideas within the group are acceptable
	Student may create rules for the use of their own personal possessions
	Look at books if you need to wait for other group members to finish
	Students are expected to articulate their needs
	Students' ideas may have the floor
	Teacher participates in activity and has her own ideas
	When a group member has the floor, other group members need to wait quietly for a turn
Individual	The decision for the fate of each student's product rests with the student
	All students are responsible for keeping their property safe
	Choice is available to students within an activity
	The group needs to accommodate to individual members
	Student individual ideas for activities
	Words of student's choice can be written by teacher on student product
	Group time is not brought to a close until all members are to a finishing point
	The group needs to care about each member's feelings
	The responsibility of some group tasks are determined by turn taking lists

Figure 2.2 Individually oriented rules.

On closer inspection of the sociolinguistic maps, the small-group event looked even more complex than originally thought. Specifically, small group turned out to be not a unitary event but one made up of three distinct phases marked by distinct social emphasis (individual vs. group) as well as distinct activity content: (a) an opening phase where the group gathered and readied themselves for the day's planned activity; (b) a middle phase of involvement with the day's curricular materials; and (c) a closing phase for clean-up and transition to the next part of the day.

Of course, the first task to be accomplished each day is for the participants to convene as a group. Thus, the opening phase is primarily related to the physical configuration or the "look" of the group ("Everyone must sit on a carpet square"), and to context-specific responsibilities (e.g., "Group proceedings must not disturb the other group"), with some attention also paid to group identity ("All group members have red name tags"), to social interactions ("An individual's idea that is distracting to the group is not acceptable") and to interactions with materials ("Materials owned by the preschool become the property of small groups during small-group time"). As these examples demonstrate, group-oriented rules (70%) predominate in this opening phase (see Fig. 2.3). At the same time, there are (30%) individual-oriented rules. Some provide individuals with choice in the group's physical configuration (e.g., "Each individual can choose among the places to sit"); in others, the group is asked to accommodate the individual (e.g., "The group needs to care about each member's feelings"); individuals' ideas are valued (e.g., "It is expected that students will have ideas for activities" and "Teachers value students' ideas"); and, individual's rights are established (e.g., "Once a student has claimed a material, it is his or hers as long as she wants").

The middle phase is when the day's planned activities are carried out. Here, interactions with materials and verbal interactions with others are prevalent as compared to the first phases' emphases on physical configuration and group responsibilities. In the middle activity phase, the dominant social action pertains to materials and their possession by individuals. An example of social action related to materials use is "there must be enough materials for everyone" and one related to verbal interaction is "An individual's time 'on the floor' (as speaker) may be limited by the group's needs." Furthermore, in contrasting the social emphasis in the middle phase to the opening phase, there is more individual-oriented rules as compared to group-oriented rules (56%/44%). Specifically, the acknowledgment of individual's ideas, the requirement that the group accommodate to the individual, the rights of individuals to have choices within the activity, and turn-taking comprised the social action rules in the middle activity phase.

In the closing phase, the group turns to the rituals related to bringing the activity to a close and leaving the group space to transition to the next part of the day. Thus, the group returns to physical tasks and group responsibilities as the dominant content of social action rules. For example, characteristic rules in this phase included "Group members are responsible to clean-up where they play"; "When most members of the group are finished, only a few more minutes are allowed for the others to finish"; "Those finishing first begin to clean-up"; and, "Group members leave the group together." As with the first phase, most of these social action rules (62%) are group-oriented emphasizing each

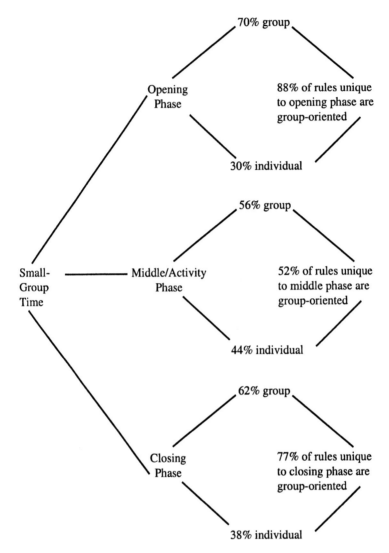

Figure 2.3. A taxonomic representation of small-group social action.

child's responsibilities to the group. With respect to individual-oriented rules (38%), individuals have choices (e.g., where to store their products), and the right to teachers' assistance in the closing phase.

The social action rule analysis provides evidence in both its content and social emphases for the interpretation that there are three distinct phases within this event. In each of these phases, about half of the rules are distinct to that phase. When all the rules operating across the phases are considered, the flow of social action within the small-group event can be seen in the type of rule that operates within different phases, from predominantly group-oriented rules in the opening phase (70%/30%), to a majority of individual-oriented rules in the middle phase (56%/44%), and back to a predominance of group-oriented rules (62%/38%) in the closing phase.

When the phases of the event are viewed from a group perspective, we see that the group-oriented social action rules create a physical and social structure that allowed productive interactions among group members and with materials to take place. From this group perspective, this small-group event required the concerted effort of its members in order to obtain and maintain a normative consensus that would allow the group to accomplish the following: arrive in a setting; achieve a consistent physical configuration; interact with group members and group materials; return the setting to its original state; and leave in an orderly fashion. These are complex demands for a group of 3-year-olds and its members to meet on a daily basis.

When the phases of the event are viewed from the individuals' perspectives, we see a variety of social action rules that describe an individual's rights, choices, and boundaries related to their activity and interaction within the group. Thus, the individual within the group has needs, the group will accommodate to the individual, and the individual has rights and choices concerning materials uses. In all, this social action analysis left us all feeling impressed with the abilities of a small group of 3-year-olds to produce such concerted and coordinated action.

Finally, it is important to point out that both kinds of norms and expectations are learned in tandem, in the doing, and not as self-conscious teaching but as a negotiated, co-constructed process. In other words, these are not rules that exist in the usual way in early childhood classrooms posted on the wall as "Dos" and "Don'ts." Instead, they represent a network of shared and emergent understandings that develop over time and serve to help accomplish the broader goals and purposes of the classroom event. These are not rules that I knew I was putting into place nor ones that I could see without engaging in the systematic and reflective process of research.

LEARNING TO BE A GROUP OVER TIME

Having accomplished the analyses just described, my interests then turned to the learning goal of the curriculum; that is, with the nature and structure of the group event revealed and represented concretely through the social action rules, it was then possible to examine the flow of social action over time, to compare three ordinary days, one each from the taping cycles in the fall, winter, and spring quarters to document how the children were learning "to do group".

In the beginning of the year, the children's inexperience children with this format made it necessary for me to often verbally suggest and state norms that could operate for the group. Intuitively, I sensed that as time went on the group norms became established and the need for me to explicitly negotiate or state them diminished. As the group developed shared knowledge, a social structure for doing collaborative activities came to guide the actions and interactions of both teachers and children. In the theoretical language of the sociocultural framework, I expected the children to internalize the norms and expectations that had been constructed by and for the group.

How could I explore and demonstrate this kind of learning— learning that paradoxically becomes less visible as it becomes more known? In order to explore this intuition, I compared the ratio across three quarters of explicitly stated rules with those that were operating implicitly and evident in behavior. Specifically, I expected the ratio to shift over time in the direction of more implicitly guided action.

In Table 2.1, a display of explicitly stated and implicitly operating social action rules by phase and by quarter demonstrates this change over time. In all phases, the proportion of implicitly operating norms grows overtime as more social action rules become constructed, accepted, and internalized by the group members.

By spring, consensual norms and ways of doing things are largely in place and guide behavior without a lot of explicit work and negotiation. So, for every time a social action rule is overtly stated by a teacher, there are between 9 and 15 rules operating as shared and unspoken knowledge held by the members of the group.

Looking at the distinct phases over time shows that the most challenging aspect of learning to do group is the middle phase, the actual doing of activity versus the physical coming together as a group, or the closing routines for leaving as a group. In the closing phase, for example, there is much explicit "work" being done in the autumn to establish norms for leaving the activity, but in winter the leaving is easily accomplished, guided by implicit norms. On the other hand, in Table 2.1, in the middle phase, we see in the fall and still in the winter continuing explicit work on the balance of rights and obligations. And it is not until the spring that many of the norms guiding collaborative work have come into place. This makes sense in light of the nature of the tasks in the middle phase as compared with the tasks in the opening and closing phases. The opening and closing phases tend to be more ritualized and consistent in their nature from day to day, whereas in the

Table 2.1. Total Occurrences of Explicit and Implicit Social Action Rules Across Quarters and Phases

Opening Phase

	Autumn		Winter		Spring	
	Explicit	Implicit	Explicit	Implicit	Explicit	Implicit
Group	10	24	6	20	5	24
Individual	0	16	0	9	0	21
Total Occurrences	10	40	6	29	5	45
Ratio/Explicit:Implicit	1:4		1:5		1:9	

Middle/Activity Phase

	Autumn		Winter		Spring	
	Explicit	Implicit	Explicit	Implicit	Explicit	Implicit
Group	23	43	1	51	3	84
Individual	22	97	28	96	7	71
Total Occurrences	45	140	29	147	10	155
Ratio/Explicit:Implicit	1:3		1:5		1:15	

Closing Phase

	Autumn		Winter		Spring	
	Explicit	Implicit	Explicit	Implicit	Explicit	Implicit
Group	25	6	5	56	1	25
Individual	12	16	8	40	2	15
Total Occurrences	37	22	13	96	3	40
Ratio/Explicit:Implicit	1:5 to 1		1 to 7.4		1:13	

middle phase, different activities introduce new issues to be negotiated by the group (e.g., new materials to be shared, new formats to be learned, and so forth).

Another way to show the learning of group over time is to examine the changing roles of participants, both teachers and children. Over time, the learning of group social action is evident in shifts in both teacher's and children's talk, and in the socially constructed products of the group. Thus, the teacher's talk shifts from group-oriented rules, that is, a focus on individuals' responsibility to the group (e.g., "William, we need you to be careful of your neighbor's work when you reach for the paint"), toward a focus on the social interactions of the group (e.g., "We will all have to work hard today to clean up the messy materials"). Children's talk shifts from an initial focus on themselves, their concerns, and their rights (e.g., "Where's my glue") toward a greater awareness of and interest in other group members (e.g., "What's William doing?") and in the group itself (e.g., "I know what we can do!").

DISCUSSION

Working and interacting in small groups is a common cultural practice— both in wider American culture and in the culture of schooling. Despite the tender age of its participants, the small group described in this study clearly has the characteristics articulated by Ridgeway (1983) in the opening quotation of this chapter: This group met on a regular basis, became a social entity recognizable to its members and to outsiders, developed an identity, a sense of purpose, and a character of its own over time. Throughout their lives, these children will participate in small groups; what is unique here is a description of how children and teachers are able to create such a social organization for the first time and at such a young age. It is the value of a sociocultural lens that it helps us to examine such a context for interaction and to gain insight into how it is established over time by the group. With this lens, I was able to see that children, with the help of their teachers, can form a meaningful group and collaborate long before we might expect, thus contradicting the commonplace assumption that young children are unable to cooperate and collaborate in small-group contexts.

The analysis provided me with a way to be reflective about my practice and to see the nature of the event in a way I could not possibly have seen in the online course of my daily teaching, involved, myself in these thousands of fleeting moments of interactions. I was able to answer my questions about the nature of the event itself: What is its structure? What are the social demands on its members? How does such a group become established? How does the nature of the work of the group and about the group shift with time?

A central feature of what I found is the yoked nature of group responsibilities and individual rights within a group. Groups are often thought of as essentially social, downplaying the individuals' contributions and places within it; on the other hand, teachers working with groups are often focused on problematic individuals—how to deal with individual children who disrupt or refuse to participate in the group. This perspective and the accompanying analysis revealed that the interplay and tension between individual rights and group responsibilities is crucial and productive, both to each child's sense of him or herself as a participant and to the group's evolving sense of identity.

What has been learned from one intensive look at group development in a single classroom that might be helpful to others? Many of the innovative curricular formats being discussed currently in educators' circles are the social and group-oriented ones—project work accomplished in ongoing small groups like the ones described here and in ad hoc groups such as those described in Reggio Emilia (Edwards, Forman, & Gandini, 1998), as well as cooperative learning activities (Johnson & Johnson, 1987; Sharan & Sharan, 1992) experienced in small groups in elementary schools. But innovation cannot be introduced into classrooms without infrastructures to support them—student and teacher roles and classroom norms that are necessary in order for the new curriculum format to be successful. Thus, group work is not goals and content alone, but also social structure inextricably tied to curricular goals and content. The finding that the event had three phases— progressing each day from the gathering of its participants to the doing of an activity to the disbanding of its participants—can help others see where they need to focus their own lens to establish an infrastructure that works for their own groups. In other words, the content of the social action rules will not be the same from classroom to classroom, but the need for a social participation structure to be co-constructed, explicit, and working well before productive projects can be accomplished is essential. Perhaps our history with failed innovations in American schooling is the failure to attend to the supporting social structures that must be in place (Kantor & Whaley, 1998). What my experience also taught me is the importance and the power of conducting teacher-action research (Burnaford, Fischer, & Hobson, 1996) and the benefits that conducting such research have for understanding and informing my classroom practice. My teaching was transformed by this experience—I was better able to see the group's social structure and dynamics and, thus, better able to support its positive growth and development. Often in education, we move from theory to research to practice to evaluation. This kind of work suggests a different helpful route, from researching our practice to building new theory, and then looping it back into our practice and further theory-building. I realize that I won't always have the opportunity and time to explore my intuitive theories in systematic research. But the support and refinement of my ideas about children's collaborative potential gives me reason to trust more of my intuitive theories about children and the desire to pursue more action research.

REFERENCES

Barnes, D., & Todd, F. (1977). *Communication and learning in small groups.* London: Routledge & Kegan Paul.

Bruner, J. (1986). *Actual minds, possible words.* Cambridge, MA: Harvard University Press.

Burnaford, G., Fischer, J., & Hobson, D. (1996). *Teachers doing research.* Mahwah, NJ: Erlbaum.

Cooper, M. G. (1979). Verbal interaction in nursery schools. *British Journal of Educational Psychology, 49,* 214-225.

Dewey, J. (1902). *The child and the curriculum.* Chicago: University of Chicago Press.

Dewey, J. (1916). *Democracy and education.* New York: The Free Press.

Edwards, C., Gandini, L., & Forman, G. (1998). *The hundred languages of children* (2nd ed.). Greenwich, CT: Ablex.

Erickson, F., & Mohatt, G. (1982). Cultural organization of participation structures in two classrooms of Indian students. In G. Spindler (Ed.), *Doing the ethnography of schooling: Educational ethnography in action* (pp. 102-132). New York: Holt, Rinehart & Winston.

Gardner, H. (1983). *Frames of mind: The theory of multiple intelligences.* New York: Basic Books.

Goodenough, W. H. (1971). *Culture, language and society.* Reading, MA: Addison-Wesley.

Green, J., & Harker, J. (1982). Gaining access to learning: Conversational, social, and cognitive demands of group participation. In L. Wilkinson (Ed.), *Communicating in the classroom* (pp. 183-221). New York: Academic Press.

Green, J. L., & Wallat, C. (1981). Mapping instructional conversations. In J. L. Green & C. Wallat (Eds.), *Ethnography and language in educational settings* (pp. 161-208). Norwood, NJ: Ablex.

Green, J. L., Weade, R., & Graham, K. (1988). Lesson construction and student participation: A sociolinguistic analysis. In J. L. Green & J. Harker (Eds.), *Multiple perspective analysis of classroom discourse* (pp. 11-48). Norwood, NJ: Ablex.

Hawkins, D. (1966). Learning the unteachable. In L. Shulman & E. Keislar (Eds.), *Learning by discovery: A critical appraisal.* Chicago: Rand McNally.

Hudson, J. A., & Nelson, K. (1983). Effects of script structure on children's story recall. *Developmental Psychology, 19,* 625-635.

Johnson, D., & Johnson, R. (1987). *Learning together and alone.* Englewood Cliffs, NJ: Prentice-Hall.

Kantor, R., Elgas, P. M., & Fernie, D. E. (1989). First the look and then the sound: Creating conversations at circle time. *Early Childhood Research Quarterly, 4,* 433-448.

Kantor, R., Elgas, P., & Fernie, D. (1993). Accessing cultural knowledge for membership in preschool friendship groups. *Early Childhood Research Quarterly, 8*(2), 125-147.

Kantor, R., & Whaley, K. (1998). Existing frameworks and new ideas from our Reggio Emilia experience: Learning at a lab school with 2- to 4-year-old children. In C. Edwards, L. Gandini, & G. Forman (Eds.), *The hundred languages of children* (2nd ed., pp. 313-333). Greenwich, CT: Ablex.

Katz, L. G., & Chard, S. C. (1989). *Engaging children's minds: The project approach.* Norwood, NJ: Ablex.

Leary, M. R., Robertson, R. B., Barnes, B. D., & Miller, R. S. (1986). Self-presentations of small-group leaders: Effects of role requirements and leadership orientation. *Journal of Personality and Social Psychology, 51*(4), 742-748.

Lewin, K. (1947a). Frontiers in group dynamics: Concepts, method and reality in social science, social equilibria and social change. *Human Relations, 1,* 5-42.

Lewin, K. (1947b). Group decision and social change. In E. Maccoby, T. Newcomb, & E. Hartley (Eds.), *Readings in social psychology* (pp. 197-219). New York: Holt, Rinehart & Winston.

Malaguzzi, L. (1998). History, ideas, and basic philosophy: An interview with Lella Gandini. In C. Edwards, L. Gandini, & G. Forman (Eds.), *The hundred languages of children* (pp. 49-97). Norwood, NJ: Ablex.

Merrit, M., & Humphrey, F. (1979). Teacher, talk and task: Communicative demands during individualized instruction time. *Theory Into Practice, 18*(4), 298-302.

Nelson, K., & Gruendel, J. (1981). Generalized event representations: Basic building blocks of cognitive development. In A. Brown & M. Lamb (Eds.), *Advances in developmental psychology* (Vol. 1, pp. 231-247). Hillsdale, NJ: Erlbaum.

Parten, M. (1932). Social participation among preschool children. *Journal of Abnormal Social Psychology, 27,* 242-269.

Piaget, J. (1957). *The language and thought of the child.* New York: Meridian Books.

Piaget, J. (1962). *Play, dreams, and imitation in childhood.* New York: Norton.

Piaget, J. (1971). *The construction of reality in the child.* New York: Ballantine.

Ridgeway, C. L. (1983). *The dynamics of small groups.* New York: St. Martin's Press.

Sharan, Y., & Sharan, S. (1992). *Expanding cooperative learning through group investigation.* New York: Teachers College Press.

Slavin, R. (1987). Developmental and motivational perspectives on cooperative learning: A reconciliation. *Child Development, 58,* 1161-1167.

Vygotsky, L. S. (1978). *Mind in society.* Cambridge, MA: Harvard University Press.

Weinstein, R. (1976). Reading group membership in first grade: Teacher behaviors and pupil experience over time. *Journal of Educational Psychology, 68*(1), 103-116.

Wilkinson, L. C., & Dollaghan, C. (1979). Peer communication in first grade reading groups. *Theory Into Practice, 18*(4), 267-274.

3

A Peer-Culture Perspective
on Social Group Play

Peg Elgas
University of Cincinnati

Bob and Lisa are wearing Batman capes and sitting in the climber together surrounded by blocks and red rhythm sticks. They "fly" around the room gathering stuffed animals, which they bring back and arrange on the floor pillows. Nathan approaches and tries to enter. Bob blocks the entrance and holding a magnet like a gun says: "Get out!"

Lisa uses a block as a gun to shoot Nathan and stands behind Bob blocking the entrance.

Bob and Nathan push each other as Lisa screams in the background: "You can't get in. It's our Batman house."

After Nathan retreats, Bob and Lisa gather blocks. They pile blocks on top of one another attempting to build a door, but the blocks continue to fall. After a series of unsuccessful attempts, they stuff their pockets with sticks and fly off around the room using small rectangular blocks as guns.

This opening anecdote represents a common occurrence in preschool classrooms and should sound familiar to teachers of young children. It also highlights concerns related to children's play, their friendships, and their participation in social groups. Teachers have concerns about exclusion and inclusion of children, marveling at the social successes of some children and worrying about the social difficulties experienced by others. They may be concerned both about the child who is without a companion and about others who are "too close" and play exclusively with each other.

Teachers want children to engage in cooperative play, to work toward common goals, and to negotiate roles, play themes, and solutions to problems. Teachers want all the children in their classrooms to fare well in such play and to experience opportunities for both leadership and "followership."

Because most teachers believe in the benefits of pretend play, they often encourage the creative use of objects in play themes, but we feel less comfortable when children creatively use these objects in aggressive ways, for example, pretending they are guns and swords. Relatedly, teachers want children's play themes to provide a way for children to work through feelings and provide a way for them to come to terms with social issues and concepts. However, teachers often feel uncomfortable if play themes revolving around power and control issues involve aggression, intimidation and mock killing, as often happens in war play and superhero play.

With respect to this, there is a traditional literature and prevailing perspective concerning each of these issues that has influenced teachers and guided how they might react to such play. In this chapter, an alternative perspective, a peer-culture perspective, provides different insights into the meaning of social group play, themes and roles, object use, and individuals within the group. It begins with a review of traditional literatures on many of the issues just discussed. Then an alternative peer-culture perspective as a framework for both interpreting and acting on children's play is discussed, with special attention given to the play-related findings of our ethnographic study of this preschool classroom. Finally, implications for classroom practice and the teacher's role are discussed.

TRADITIONAL LITERATURES

Sociodramatic Play

Sociodramatic, pretend, or thematic play has been studied in relation to the numerous benefits (cognitive, emotional and social) children derive from their engagement in it (Garvey, 1977; Isaacs, 1933; Rubin, 1980). Through interaction with others, children learn social skills, such as negotiating and cooperating with others. In the process, they are given the opportunity to work through social issues: Children create contexts for establishing interactions and rules, themes and roles are mutually negotiated and communicated to each other (Garvey, 1974). They engage in social interaction and gain practice in communicating, negotiating, and social problem solving.

Isaacs (1933) and Piaget (1962) both viewed play as a pathway from egocentrism to social feeling. It is here that two or more children start exchanging services or objects (i.e., they play at being cooperative).

Children move from harboring rivalries to discovering the benefits of the social world. They gain independence from adults as they learn to work cooperatively with peers.

Denzin (1977) suggested play is an important aspect of social development for children and an important place to gain information on this development. Society is viewed as a negotiated, social order and the social world is comprised of special symbolic gestures and language. Language becomes the medium for social interaction and it is here that selves, personalities, roles, and perspectives are created.

Lewis (1975) supported these findings and further defined play as a social domain. In play, children construct knowledge concerning interpersonal relationships. Children learn that there are social exchanges in which each partner continually affects the other. The child must learn to develop consistent strategies of interaction through which this reciprocal, mutual exchange can be maintained.

Roles and Themes

In order for pretend play to be successful, children need techniques for communicating the roles, the action plans or themes, and transformation of objects (Garvey, 1977). The arena of play is also a dynamic one and the system of meanings and interactions are created and negotiated among players. Children adopt roles and create themes or scripts that serve as blueprints for how social action is accomplished.

These social benefits, however, are sometimes questioned when the themes revolve around war play or superhero play. This is often a dilemma for preschool teachers because many adults view the themes as too violent or aggressive and they are uncomfortable with children enacting mock sword fights or karate-kicking solutions to problems (Carlsson-Paige & Levin, 1987). Recent literature suggests this type of play does in fact serve a social purpose and does provide benefits to children's social and emotional development as they work through issues of violence, power, and control (Carlsson-Paige & Levin, 1987; Paley, 1984).

Children are drawn to the superhero theme for many reasons. The characters have many characteristics that are appealing to children. They are endowed with powers and qualities that are the best of human nature; they are good, wise, and fearless. They possess powers that children wish they had, such as strength or speed or the ability to fly. They are able to overcome every obstacle, solve every problem in their constant quest for the triumph of good over evil (Carlsson-Paige & Levin, 1987; Kostelnik, Whiren, & Stein, 1986; Levin, 1995).

Children who take on the role of a superhero also take on the role of a powerful adult, moving from the somewhat powerless role of child. They are in control of the entire situation and, therefore, never make a mistake. Through this role, they have access to power and prestige that is unavailable in their daily lives (Gronlund, 1992; Kostelnik et al., 1986). They have the opportunity to be someone they admire or to take on attributes of someone they fear. In the latter case, they are able to work through fears and triumph over them. With the clear dichotomy of good and evil and the concrete actions and relatively simple plot lines, the characters are easy to imitate. As they enact these roles, they develop a sense of mastery related to physical prowess, such as climbing and swinging upside down from the climber, and a sense of mastery over their own fears.

Carlsson-Paige and Levin (1987) also suggested that children are provided in this war play with opportunities to work through political concepts, such as enemy, ally, power, control, and conflict. These are concepts that children have been exposed to and, as with any area of development, they are trying to understand them and relate them to their lives. Through war play and the teacher's active involvement and mediation, children can come to terms with these issues and can construct their own understanding about them.

Object Use

Object use has been traditionally regarded as an important aspect of children's play, but largely from a cognitive rather than a social perspective. The majority of studies focused on children's transformation of objects or symbolic representation, with object use found to enhance a variety of cognitive skills (Fein, 1975; Pepler & Ross, 1981; Sylva, Bruner, & Genova, 1976).

Both Piaget and Vygotsky's theories address children's use of objects as symbols within sociodramatic play. For example, as children use a doll to represent a baby they are actually setting the groundwork for a later understanding of more abstract symbols, such as the use of the written word to symbolize actions and objects. In play, children create their own meanings by labeling ordinary objects with unusual names and ordinary actions often represent different, unusual behavior. These designations are made despite the fact that children are aware of the real or more typical associations.

Fein (1975) investigated the manner in which transformation of objects develops. She described a developmental progression of play with objects that ranges from simple to complex. Fein's work had great implications for the classroom. Her research suggests that young children cannot make simultaneous multiple substitutions, so realistic objects become an anchor allowing symbolic play to occur. Hutt (1976) also studied children's object use in relation to children's learning. She distinguished between children's use of objects as exploration (i.e., discovery of properties) versus play (which constituted new possibilities for use after object properties are discovered). Hutt's work helped to guide teachers in that ample time should be allowed for children to actively explore new materials before expecting children to use them in any specific way.

A second line of research studies examines the significance of play with objects within an evolutionary/anthropological perspective. In a landmark primate studies, Schiller (1975) and Birch (1954) found that play with objects promoted tool use and problem-solving ability. Subsequent studies of children support these results (Sylva et al., 1976). Children given the opportunity to play with objects performed significantly better on divergent problem solving tasks. The children who engaged in (play) transformation of the object (e.g., using the stick to represent a spoon) were found to be the best problem solvers. Tool use was enhanced by the play practice in a pressure-free environment. Children developed particular skills that later were combined to achieve specific goal and to solve problems.

The literature examining the social uses of objects is not extensive (Mueller, 1972; Mueller & Brennen, 1977; Ross & Goldman, 1979). Some studies suggest that infants and toddlers have used objects for a variety of social purposes (Mueller & Brenner, 1977; Ross & Goldman, 1979; Whaley & Rubenstein, 1994). Mueller and Brenner found that infants and toddlers appeared to use objects as concrete vehicles establishing social interaction given their limited communication skills. In another study, children were found to use objects as offerings (Ross & Goldman, 1979). Furthermore, Ross and Goldman observed toddlers using balls and other objects as offerings to facilitate social interaction with their partners. This traditional developmental literature, when, complemented by the peer-culture perspective (Corsaro, 1985) taken in the present analysis, provides a broader and more comprehensive framework to help teachers to understand children's use of objects.

Group Participation and Leadership

The study of social play and play group began with Parten's (1932) landmark study and this study has influenced the way play group are viewed in classrooms. Parten considered two aspects of social participation: extensity (or the number of social contacts) and intensity (or the kinds of groups participated in and the role of the individual in those groups). A scale of social participation was developed that measured both extensity and intensity and group integration. Play behaviors were ranked from the lowest (unoccupied) to the highest (cooperative). Cooperative play was defined as a group organized to attain some cooperative goal or dramatizing situations. The goal necessitated division of labor (assigning roles and development of scripts). Unoccupied, onlooker, and solitary play were considered negative indices of social participation, whereas parallel, associative, and cooperative play were considered positive indices.

Social participation was found to be related to the age of the children and to the extent of their nursery school experience: The oldest children played in more highly organized groups, as did children who had greater school experience. Most of the children favored same-gender partners and playing house was the most social type of play engaged in by them. Parten described children's cooperative play groups as children coming together momentarily to work toward some common goal, such as enacting a grocery store theme in the dramatic play area. Roles and scripts are negotiated and developed as a means to facilitate cooperation and to accomplish the play.

More recently, several researchers (Corsaro, 1985; Howes, Unger, & Matheson, 1992; Parker & Gottman, 1989) have studied young children's play and the formation of social groups. Both Parker and Gottman and Howes et al. found that children used social pretend play as a form of disclosure between friends. Younger children used play to signal and communicate things about themselves that they were unable to articulate verbally. For example, a child might use a play prop such as a stuffed animal to demonstrate and work through fears or psychic and social conflict. Parker and Gottman also found that play can provide opportunities for children to work through fears and concerns and to explore issues of intimacy and trust with their play partners.

Howes and her colleagues (Howes et al., 1992) expanded on Parker and Gottman's idea and examined the idea that play can fulfill several different developmental functions and that these functions change with development. Howes et al. described three distinct stages and functions of pretend play. These stages include:

1. Toddler's communication of meaning through mastery of social pretend forms.
2. Preschooler's exploration of issues of control and compromise and their negotiation of scripts.
3. Older preschooler's (ages 4 and 5) exploration of issues of intimacy and trust.

Pretend play does not function for exploring intimacy and trust with all play partners, but is reserved for special participants (Howes et al., 1992), in which partners mutually select each other and their play reflects a shared positive affect. Shared preference for certain play content and similar play interests, such as identification with superheroes, may be important in children's selection of friends and play partners. These common issues may be the basis for forming and maintaining friendships and results in more harmonious play than play between acquaintances (Parker & Gottman, 1989). Therefore, pretend play is important in helping children establish friendships and in providing them with opportunities for self-disclosure. They may have more harmonious play because they have what might be called a shared history: Roles and scripts have continuity across days and are replayed (with evolving variation) over time. As a result, more time is spent in play and less in negotiating roles and themes.

Relatedly, Howes (1983, 1988) found that children involved in long-term relationships engaged in more complex social play than those engaged in short-term relationships. Rubin (1980) also found this self-selection. Children may select friends with similar fears or concerns expressed in play, with common play interests and compatible play styles, and those whose company they enjoy and prefer.

Various researchers have studied children's individual experiences within social groups. Often, this has been conceptualized and studied in terms of children's leadership and followership behaviors (Parten, 1932; Sluckin & Smith, 1977). Parten distinguished between leaders and followers according to behaviors ranging from directing the group (leader behavior) to following another child's directions (follower behavior). This description assumes that, from a social standpoint, children are either leaders or followers. In several studies (Parten, 1937; Sluckin & Smith, 1977; Strayer & Strayer, 1976), children who demonstrated dominance (often physically) over others were rated as leaders (although neither prosocial behavior nor acceptance by peers were examined in these studies).

More recently, this traditional idea of leadership primarily through dominance has been challenged (Hatch, 1990; Smilansky, 1968; Stone & Church, 1984; Trawick-Smith, 1988). These studies expand leadership to incorporate following behavior, pro-social skills, and the idea of give and take. Although leaders were still viewed as children who initiated play and made novel contributions to play, these children also allowed and accepted other's ideas and problem-solved disputes. While often asserting their ideas, leaders in these studies typically did so in a nonaggressive manner. Trawick-Smith (1988) described children who use prosocial appeals that reflect social understanding. Hatch (1990) described another child as an organizer and recruiter who entices children to join by presenting attractive ideas or offering bribes. He also described one of the leaders as a regulator who responds to the demands of other classmates; helping a friend who has been unfairly treated in the estimation of his or her peers. Another interesting strategy, noted by both Hatch and Trawick-Smith is the leader who enthusiastically pursues his or her own interests and in so doing, indirectly entices children into his or her preferred activities. And finally, in each of these more recent studies, children identified as leaders demonstrated both leadership and followership behaviors.

The previous section outlined the traditional play literature focused on in sociodramatic play themes (including superhero play) and object use, and on children's participation in play groups and as leaders in such groups. The next section describes the perspective taken in this study and the findings of my analysis.

AN ETHNOGRAPHIC AND PEER-CULTURE PERSPECTIVE

Corsaro (1985) was the first to introduce the idea of a peer culture, a construct that provides a distinctive interpretive lens for viewing social groups in the classroom. Corsaro suggested that, beginning in late infancy, children come to view themselves as different than adults and develop a desire to share participation with other children. Aware of this difference and as a result of their activities with peers, children begin to establish relationships with peers. Over time, they produce a peer culture through their shared participation. In this peer culture, children share a common set of routines, artifacts, concerns, values, and attitudes they produce together (Corsaro, 1985). Peer culture is a joint attempt by children to gain control over their lives through the establishment of a collective identity.

Although young children may not yet have a stable sense of self, they do have a clear notion of adult expectations and of the restrictiveness of the adult world. Corsaro further suggested that a sense of who they are is strengthened through their active resistance and opposition to adult rules and expectations regarding their behavior. For example, if guns are banned from the classroom, children may construct their own out of classroom materials and conceal them from teachers.

In part through collectively resisting adult rules, children develop and maintain a group identity. Children develop this sense of "we-ness" and in the process learn more about the adult organization. The construction and maintenance of the peer culture requires the active cooperation of the members and is dependent on the members' construction and use of a number of shared interpretive procedures (Cicourel, 1974). Children accomplish this through communal production and sharing of social activities or routines with their peers. They generate shared behavior routines that may seem inappropriate to adults, but they are appropriate and real to children. These routines are recurrent, predictable, and reflect children's shared grasp of the peer culture's underlying knowledge structure.

Corsaro's empirical work supports his theoretical assumptions that a peer culture exists, even for very young children, and that children's play and social groups are strongly yoked to that peer culture and to the appropriation of and reactions and resistance to the adult culture. This chapter expands on those general points and includes discussion of how objects are used to sustain peer-culture play and how individuals participate within a prominent peer-culture group in this preschool.

In this chapter, I focus on the locally constructed peer-culture patterns of one particularly salient and cohesive group. My experience in this classroom differs from that of Corsaro, in that he discussed the peer culture at the whole-group level, whereas I found several distinct, stable, and enduring friendship groupings in the classroom (Elgas, Klein, Kantor, & Fernie, 1988).

Procedures and Findings

As one of several participant-observers, I entered the classroom on the first day of school and lived within the classroom setting, interacting with the children daily for the entire academic year. My objective was to become an adult who was different from the teachers, one with access to the children's peer culture. A central feature of ethnography is the prolonged use of "up close" observation and fieldnotes taken by participant-observers (Spradley, 1980). This and other methods of recording data (such as videotape and teacher interviews) were chosen based on the belief that to truly understand the children's peer culture, one must learn it from its members, their actions, and their words. Therefore, I would uncover the rules, expectations for behaviors, and important artifacts or objects used by its members by entering their group and being informed by its members.

Interested in children's play, I began my observations by situating myself in areas that seemed child-dominated during free-choice time, such as the block and housekeeping areas. I tried to take my lead from the children, entering play when invited and interacting with the children carefully, for example, not making suggestions that could alter their play themes. More importantly, I refrained from engaging in what I considered to be "teacher behaviors," such as settling disputes or setting limits, and intervened only when children's safety was an issue. I did, however, tie shoes or retrieve an object out of children's reach or perform other adult behaviors that seemed natural and in response to children's requests.

As might be expected, this non-teacher adult behavior was confusing to children in the beginning of the school year. Because I was neither a teacher nor one of the children's mothers, they had a difficult time understanding my role in the classroom (children of this age generally classify most adults into these two categories). They continually tested me during our play interactions, repeatedly eliciting "teacherly" behaviors from me. I repeatedly declined, forwarding such requests to teachers, as the following anecdote illustrates.

> Sarah and Steve are playing at the sand table. Steve grabs Sarah's shovel. "It's mine." She screams and looks at me and struggles with Steve over the shovel. Steve looks at me as he continues to hold and struggle over the shovel. I said, "Maybe we should get a teacher if you can't solve the problem. She can help us."

My entry into the peer group was accomplished over time and by playing regularly with the identified leader of the core group (Bob). By gaining entry, I became privy to interactions not readily seen by other adults.

> Bob: "Come here." (Bob and Ken yell jumping up and down with boards in their hands.)
> "C'mon but be quiet." (They motion again.)
> "Don't tell anybody." (They close the door.)
> "Watch this." (They both begin to hit a large wooden dollhouse sitting on the floor. They laugh as the furniture and house fly in pieces around the room.)

Although I discussed this incident with teachers after the school day, I did not make an adult comment or evaluation when it happened. It was through this method of cautious and responsive participation that I gained access and insight into the peer culture, and how these children viewed their play and friendships.

Early in the year, I began to take notice of a lively group of five boys and one girl who seemed to play together each day. This group became my primary focus, chosen for my analysis because they were more visible than other groups. This group was dubbed the "core group" because of its great cohesion, salience, and influence in the classroom.

This group clearly differed both from Parten's (1932) play group definitions and from Corsaro's (1985) descriptions. Although Parten described ad hoc groups, in which children come together and manage to play cooperatively through negotiating their scripts, it became apparent to me and other observers that over time, the core group's play became ritualized, patterned, and highly organized socially. Although Corsaro found a peer culture across a classroom as a whole, we found a subgroup with a locally constructed peer culture. This was also supported by subsequent findings of several other subgroups within the larger peer culture (Elgas et al., 1988; Meyer, Klein, & Genishi, 1994).

The core group seemed to epitomize the peer culture in that their superhero and action-oriented themes and values often conflicted with school culture norms, plus they regularly declined participation in school culture activities (such as circle time and small-group time).

This group ritualistically shared time, space, objects, and themes together. Everyday during free-choice time, they would gather in the block corner, choose objects as weapons and designate other props (such as metal washers as "treasure") to support their superhero play themes. They determined who would play, who would be excluded, and what they would play. Through these daily negotiations and affirmations, the core group created a shared definition of this group and what it meant to be a member, just as they created and maintained the social dynamics that sustained the group. The roles and themes created by these children were not momentary as described by Parten (1932), but enduring or even ritualistic.

These daily play interactions created shared understandings, a solid base from which to work and a shared history of being a group of friends. They did not have to continually spend time negotiating new roles or major scripts for play from day to day. Instead, they were able to come together each day and begin play by building on a recent history of already agreed on themes and roles. Slight variations, such as introducing a new object as a weapon or changing the location would not interrupt the flow of the play because important elements were stable. The familiarity they gained by playing together each day allowed them to "pick up where they left off" as they reunited in the block corner. Far from ad hoc in their composition, this group remained a core group the entire school year, with the same members playing together on a daily basis.

As researchers, our first task was to uncover and describe the type of players in the core group, to analyze what was unique about this group of players, in comparison to other children in the classroom. At first, we started with the assumption (gleaned from the traditional literature) that there are leaders and followers in classrooms, and consequently inferred that this core group was comprised of leaders; however, this did not adequately describe the players. What did emerge and better described the group was the idea of peer players. We created a domain analysis in which the core group members' play behaviors were categorized. The domain was divided into three play behaviors: teacher play, peer play, and solitary play.

Core group players did not regularly play with teachers, nor did they extensively participate in school culture activities. In fact, participation in peer group play required a separate and distinct set of behaviors that was often in direct conflict with school culture values and teacher involvement in play. In peer play, for example, superhero themes dominated and scripts featured domination over "bad guys" by using guns, swords, and other weapons. Disputes were often settled with these weapons and in somewhat physical ways. In the school culture, peaceful negotiations were encouraged, as well as problem solving and "using your words" to explain to the other person the nature of the problem.

Core group members excluded teachers from their play and only afforded teachers limited entry if they provided an adult service (e.g., by writing such signs such as "No girls allowed" or the "Batman House Do Not Enter," or by taking Polaroid pictures of their structures). However, if teachers attempted to change the theme of the play to a less aggressive one, their suggestions often were overtly rejected.

Non-core group members' play interactions were quite different. Often, these children engaged in teacher play more than play with peers or solitary play. Children who played regularly with teachers were not included in the core group, and those children who used teachers to help them try to join the core group were often rejected.

Because this first analyses took place near the beginning of the year, the frequent play of non-core group children with teachers is not especially surprising. Many times, children follow the teacher around during free-choice time, lacking the social skills or experience with large groups of children to either enter ongoing play episodes or to coordinate with other children to create play interactions. But what was rather surprising was the fact that this core group formed so early in the year and showed a clear and consistent preference for playing with each other over the school year.

An important part of what defined the core group as a group was their common interest in superhero and war play themes. The prevalent interest in such themes is a common issue for early childhood educators, for classrooms abound with this kind of play. Even in classrooms where war play or superhero and weapons are banned, children find creative ways to work around this limitation; such as transforming their fingers into guns and shooting offenders when the teacher is not looking.

It is important to look beyond the surface of such play in deciding, as adults, whether to merely acknowledge, negatively sanction, or facilitate it. Underlying such play is children's concern and interest in power, control, morality, and vulnerability—issues that are a part of daily life in our wider culture and a normal part of social and emotional growth. It is as valid and important for children to construct and reconstruct their understandings concerning these concepts and issues as it is to construct their understanding of family life and gender roles or their understandings of cause-and-effect relationships in the scientific realm. Here, instead of interacting with science materials, children interact with media materials and each other, and through that social interaction grow and develop socially and emotionally.

Following the psychoanalytic perspective on play, we would certainly agree that war play or superhero play provides a way for children to work through issues and fears (Carlsson-Paige & Levin, 1987). And we also found that, while engaged in social interaction, children were negotiating, problem solving, and coming to terms with important issues. However, probably the most important aspect of superhero play, in my view, was its connection to the peer culture. The superhero theme was really the "glue" that held this group together. It helped them form a collective identity or "we-ness" (Corsaro, 1985). The choice of the theme fits nicely with children's need to resist the adult world and its restrictions. It was their way of maintaining control not just over the play, but the group itself. The shared meaning created by the theme allowed them to come together each day as a group. The rejection of more sanitized themes suggested by teachers or student teachers, such as "firefighters," was another way of keeping control of child-initiated ideas and values.

Object Use

In addition to the importance of superhero themes for the core group (and for other children in the room), the core group's character was created and maintained also through the special uses they made of specific objects. Although we all had previous knowledge and understanding of objects being used symbolically as props in children's play, what surfaced as important and noteworthy in this classroom is that children used objects for social purposes more frequently than for traditional thematic or symbolic uses. Early on, two objects surfaced as important to the core group's social dynamics: superhero capes and red rhythm sticks. Capes were used for gate-keeping purposes, allowing the group to afford access to some players and to deny it to others. In contrast, sticks were often used as social markers to show solidarity and common membership among the core group members—carrying them around, hoarding them in cubbies, and wearing them in their belts. Use of sticks was classified as a "social marker" when possession of the object seemed important but where no other pretend or play use was apparent. Perhaps this is best illustrated by the following observed episodes taken from videotapes and fieldnotes.

Example 1

Bob runs into the block area wearing a cape and shooting with a bristle block gun.
Bob: "You guys are dead."
He continues running. In his belt loop are five red rhythm sticks. He is followed by Paul and Ken. Each of the boys is wearing several red rhythm sticks in their belt loops.

Example 2

Bob and Lisa are seated in the climber. They are wearing scarves pinned like capes. A large box of red rhythm sticks is stashed in the corner.
Bob: "You guard these. Don't let anyone touch these. Don't let anyone in."
He flies away to get them dinner. When he arrives back at the climber with a stuffed alligator Lisa is wearing two of the sticks in her belt loop. Bob nods his approval and repositions the sticks in her belt loop.

The sticks seem to identify the player as a member of this core group. They serve the function of both setting the person apart from nonmembers and identifying that person with others in the membership group. Their main function seems to be one of belonging. Over time, the large number of sticks available in the room (a material originally intended for musical uses) made it possible for many children to acquire and use them in similar ways, perhaps signaling their own solidarity with this popular group or their membership in the wider peer culture of the room.

Capes, however, had a different distinct social purpose. In order to enter the ongoing core group play you needed a cape. Core group members would leave their snack time early, often as a group, to grab the capes in preparation for the free-choice time to follow Core group members continually reminded those trying to gain entry "You can't get in here without a cape—only Batman allowed." Possession of a cape afforded access to some children and denied it to others.

Although others (notably, Paley, 1992) have expressed concern over children's gate keeping and exclusion, our data suggested a more complex and balanced view, in line with Corsaro (1985). In our study, use of these objects became highly standardized, serving as a stable communication pivot, making it possible for the core group to play with one another cooperatively. Ownership of a cape or stick was the first step in facilitating social interaction or structuring the group and play for the day, and allowed the core group to control the number and familiarity of play partners and thus, to protect their fragile interactive space (Corsaro, 1985).

These distinctly social uses of objects differ from the social uses identified in previous studies, for example, as vehicles to establish interaction (Mueller & Brenner, 1977) and as social offerings (Ross & Goldman, 1979), and with the prevailing notion of cognitive value in object transformation following Piaget's (1967) work. Here, we found that the meanings of these objects are social construction of this particular group and serve to signal group solidarity and to monitor access to the group's activities.

Leadership and Group Participation

Within any play group, it is typical for children to take different roles, as even Parten noted with ad hoc cooperative play situations. In this chapter, two children are discussed (Bob and Lisa) because of their interesting and noteworthy ways of participation and contributing to the core group. Bob was chosen for analysis because both peers and adults acknowledged him as the leader of the core group, and Lisa was the only female to gain access to this group. By studying Bob we could uncover important aspects about how memberships and status is accorded within such a group, and because Lisa was able to join what might be thought of as a typical "boy's" play group, we wondered what she did or what afforded her easy entry and full participation.

Although we had identified objects as important for group membership, we also knew that possession of those objects alone was not sufficient. Some children gained procured objects such as the red rhythm sticks (and occasionally the capes), but they were still unable to gain membership to the group or its play. Through our study of Lisa what surfaced as important or critical in becoming a member was cultural knowledge. Cultural knowledge can be defined, in this case, as knowing how this peer culture is enacted (through a set of actions, attitudes, values and artifacts or objects). In other words, what is important to this group? How is it demonstrated? What kinds of roles and themes do they like to play? Which objects have significance for them? What values are evidenced and promoted by group members (Kantor, Elgas, & Fernie, 1993)?

Lisa was able to access and participate in the construction of the cultural knowledge created by this core group. By playing with Bob consistently early in the school year, she was naturally seen as a member of the group. Additionally, Lisa's cooperative and flexible interactions with children certainly contributed to her social success. The following anecdotes describe Lisa's behavior and illustrate her ability to access the cultural knowledge created and shared within the core group.

Bob, Paul, and Lisa are running through the block area shooting with lego made guns.

Ken enters and says "You gotta get a weapon."
I have a weapon." Paul shows his gun.
"I have one, too." Lisa says.
Bob and Lisa run to the climber.
"This is our house." Lisa says to Bob.
They have a box of red rhythm sticks on the floor of the climber and several in their pockets.
"Yeah, but c'mon. Let's get more weapons."
They fly away together to another part of the room.

Lisa was very skillful at identifying the core group's social expectations and applying her knowledge and understanding in appropriate contexts. Lisa was also successful in other friendship groups within the room, as well as in school culture activities. She related well to all members of the classroom with an easy disposition and a tendency toward social adjustment (Mandell, 1986).

Bob's leadership style would certainly challenge the early, traditional definition as a bully type who controlled the players by forcing them into submission through directing, threatening and intimidation (Parten, 1937). Bob could not be described as the typical leader who used aggressive or overt behavior to unify the group or exclude others (A. Hatch, 1987). His leadership seemed to revolve around his creative use of objects and related play interactions.

Bob's leadership status was evident in several ways. First, children regularly identified Bob as the leader. For example, children said "I wanna be a part of Bob's witches" or "I wanna be on Bob's team." On another occasion, a teacher had been asked by the core group to write a sign for the climber. She asked the children who they wanted to be (i.e., what pretend roles). Several children answered before Bob, giving names such as Batman, the King, and Superman. Bob said "the strong one." All of the core group members then asked the teacher to cross out their previously chosen names and to write "the strong one."

Second, Bob never had to seek access or ask to enter the play (as most children did); instead, he either initiated the group's play focus or was given automatic access by members. Although he would designate the trends or themes for the core group during play periods, he would abandon the group if a teacher organized the play to include nonmembers and/or too large a group of children. Often, he would choose solitary play over having to compete or to defend his territory or play theme. He was frequently observed playing by himself in close proximity to the larger group, and with one of the objects coveted by the peer group.

Bob's leadership style is more in keeping a more prosocial and flexible style of leadership described by Trawick-Smith (1988) and Hatch (1990) but with some distinct differences. Bob certainly set the tone and often introduced unique contributions to the play theme. He most often accomplished this through modeling and indirect influence, enthusiastically pursuing his own interests and drawing the core group members to him (Hatch, 1990). Bob did entertain some play suggestions from others (Hatch, 1990; Trawick-Smith, 1988), but was very selective in this process. Other core group member's ideas were accepted diplomatically on occasion, but ideas from non-core group players were often summarily rejected. If his ideas were challenged by a student teacher (e.g., trying to limit the aggression by changing the play theme), Bob would either overtly reject the student teacher's idea or leave the group, then play by himself in the general vicinity. It is here we would often see his unique style and this style, his leadership and his interactions centered around this use of objects.

Although Bob did use self-promotions on occasion to advance and signal his leadership, it was really his object use that set him apart from the other children, both in the quantity of different types of objects used and in the ways in which they were used. During free-choice time, Bob used more objects than anyone else in the classroom. On a given day, he used up to 22 different objects, with the highest daily (5.2) and weekly average (14.5). He often used these diverse objects as weapons. Using objects as weapons was not confined to sticks and Lego constructions (as with other core group members), but extended to many of the objects he used. These included using a curling iron as a pincher, a plastic lion as a gun (holding it by its back legs), and a curved piece of wooden track as a gun. One of the more creative ideas was to use plastic packing "bubblesheets" as bombs, which he popped in children's faces.

Bob introduced his important objects to the core group and modeled their use. For example, Bob was observed using a stick the first day of school. Importantly, he was the first to use the stick as a social marker, so that those who carried or wore them were following his lead. He continued to use the sticks everyday after their introduction, both as social markers and as weapons. Bob used a curved piece of train track as a weapon and this use was imitated by several children. He also introduced the use of silver washers as money during the second week of school. These then became popular with other core group members and were used periodically throughout the school year. During the second week of the winter quarter, Bob introduced ropes and a new use for the red rhythm sticks that provoked an abundance of cowboy play throughout that quarter. In this play, the ropes were used as lassos and the sticks as arrows with plastic hangers serving as bows.

In terms of being assertive or aggressive, Bob's efforts toward social dominance were more often directed at student teachers rather than at other children (although he would protect their space and possessions from peers when necessary). Often, he used the objects as weapons to intimidate student teachers, as the following example illustrates.

Teacher: "Time to clean up Bob and Paul. You need to put these blocks away."

Bob: "No way!" We're not gonna do that and you can't make us." He points a Lego gun at her as he says this.

Teacher: "You sure like to make guns, Bob." Can't you make anything else with those Legos?"

Bob: "You're mean. I'm gonna kill you with this. Kill you dead. You're mean."

This behavior preserved and protected the peer culture. By its oppositional nature, it distanced the core group from the school culture and challenged the authority of the adults (Corsaro, 1985). Conversely, Bob's behavior served to unify the group in it opposition to aspects of the adult culture (and school culture elements promoted by adults). Some of the other core group members were observed using the objects as weapons to challenge teachers' authority, but not as overtly nor as aggressively. So, Bob's behavior clearly stands out in this regard, as he served as "point person" or spokesperson for the core group valuing of opposition to adults.

The core group members also viewed him as someone who would help other members if they needed assistance, as in the following situation:

William is building with blocks. Ken and Jack want blocks and take them from William's pile.
"NO" screams William.
"I need some blocks." Ken replies, pushing William.
"No I need them!" William struggles with Ken.
"Let's push his down." Ken suggests to Jack.
"No I won't let you do that" a student teacher replies.
"Let's get Bob. He'll do it."

Both Ken and Jack are reluctant to defy the student teacher, but they believe Bob will challenge her by destroying William's block structure. They seem to view Bob as the peer who will help them when they are in conflict with school culture figures. Similar scenarios were observed often during the year. An interesting postscript to this anecdote is that Bob was called and he did "hang around" the area, walking back and forth, but he did not tear the structure down nor did he verbally challenge the teacher in this instance. This did not seem to matter to Jack and Ken. Eventually, the three members left with smug smiles on their faces whispering to each other. They proceeded to play superheroes throughout the entire classroom, sometimes "flying" back to the block corner.

Clearly, Bob had a special status within the core group and in the wider peer culture. He was viewed as the leader by both members and nonmembers, and by adults. His style is in some ways similar to the leaders described by both Hatch (1990) and Trawick-Smith (1988); however, Bob's creative object use, which in many ways defined and held the group together, was a salient and unique feature of his leadership. His introduction of objects and both their pretend and (more importantly) their social uses, helped to unify the group and to define membership within it.

CONCLUSIONS FOR TEACHERS AND RESEARCHERS

Experiencing the classroom for the first time not as a teacher but from a perspective more inside the children's world provided new insights in to the life world of the preschool. First, by taking the group perspective, one can see that some children create a very complex social world, in the center of which lies the phenomena of play. Play is what helps define and create the group and play is what the group comes together for and accomplishes.

Adopting a peer-culture perspective changes how teachers view children's play groups, their use of objects, and their interests in superhero play, and provides an important complement to the traditional research concerning these topics. For in each of these aspects of pretend play has been the salience of issues related to power, status, and social hierarchy.

Superhero play means something different to children than it does to adults. Children deal with issues of power (such as triumphing over bad guys) and control (through inclusion of some children and exclusion of others). Our research shows that a complex social hierarchy is created and maintained by these play groups and around these themes. Such group play provides a format to help children deal with developmental issues centered around political concepts, as suggested by Carlsson-Paige and Levin (1988), but also it provides a theme that is familiar, appeals to them, and makes sense to them. Because of this, these themes help to unite children as a group and to form a collective identity (Corsaro, 1985). The superhero theme is a representation of children's wider (media) world and offers the opportunity to react to and resist the restrictions and boundaries of reality, the adult world, and the classroom. From an adult or teacher's perspective, firefighter play might seem to be an alternative as it seems to provide exciting possibilities; yet, from a child's perspective, it is not an equivalent to superhero and war play as it does not provide the same opportunities for them to deal with issues of control, power, and social hierarchy.

Related to this, object use seen through an ethnographic lens also takes on a whole new meaning. Using objects in play is more than practice at symbolization (Fein, 1975). These peers used objects to achieve a common identity and to regulate participation in their play activities. For example, although the sticks were transformed into guns and swords a significant percentage of the time, they were used for social purposes, to mark affiliation, or to control group membership the majority of the time. These objects played an important social part in this culture, although of course, other peer cultures might not construct these particular object use associations.

Children's differential social participation can also be viewed differently from the perspective taken in this research. Social participation is embedded in a complicated social hierarchy that is created and maintained by the children. Successful participation requires that children learn to be socially competent within the particular group and situation. The complex, cultural knowledge (the values, objects, and behaviors) that are shared and of importance to the group are locally constructed. Leadership, too, was distinctive and situated, as Bob's profile reveals (Kantor et al., 1993). However, in this particular group, certain objects were identified as important. Bob's introduction and unique uses of objects contributed both to the importance of these objects and to his social success and standing in the peer culture of the classroom.

These findings and the peer-culture perspective should encourage teachers to make different decisions regarding children's social play and their role in the classroom. First, and foremost, it is important that teachers learn to live with the peer culture, to support the valid interests, concerns, and values expressed within it, and to negotiate reasonable solutions to potential conflicts between peer culture and school culture purposes. In any case, it implies working with the peer culture rather than ignoring or oppressing it in the classroom. A closer attention to the peer culture and its values shows its importance, and thus, justifies a more accommodating reaction to peer-culture play in the classroom. For example, understanding that superhero play provides a format for children to work through developmental issues as well as form a collective social identity, helps teachers change their adult feelings about this play.

Certainly, further research is needed to provide greater insight into the peer culture. However, from this study and in this chapter, children's peer-culture perspective regarding play, objects, and group participation has been explored. Possibly, this example will provoke opportunities for reflection and observation of children's play behaviors in other classrooms and help to make teachers' decision making regarding teacher–child interactions, peer interactions, and curriculum both more informed and more sensitive to the peer culture that is ever present in early childhood settings.

REFERENCES

Birch, H. (1954). The relationship of previous experience to insightful problem-solving. *Journal of Comparative Physiological Psychology, 38,* 367-383.

Carlsson-Paige, N., & Levin, D. (1987). *The war play dilemma: Balancing needs and values in the early childhood classroom.* New York: Teacher's College Press.

Cicourel, A. (1974). *Cognitive sociology.* New York: The Free Press.

Corsaro, W. A. (1985). *Friendships & peer culture in the early years.* Norwood, NJ: Ablex.

Denzin, N. K. (1977). *Childhood socialization.* San Francisco: Jossey-Bass.

Elgas, P. M., Klein, E., Kantor, R., & Fernie, D. (1988). Play and the peer culture: Play styles and object use. *Journal of Research in Childhood Education, 3*(2), 142-153.

Fein, G. (1975). A transformational analysis of pretending. *Developmental Psychology, 11,* 291-296.

Garvey, C. (1974). Some properties of social play. *Merrill-Palmer Quarterly, 20,* 162-180.

Garvey, C. (1977). *Play.* Cambridge, MA: Harvard University Press.

Gronlund, G. (1992). Coping with ninja turtle play in my kindergarten classroom. *Young Children, 48,* 21-25.

Hatch, A. (1987). Status and social power in a kindergarten peer group. *The Elementary School Journal, 88,* 79-93.

Hatch, T. C. (1990). Looking at Hank, looking at Ira: Looking at individual four-year-olds, especially their leadership styles. *Young Children, 45,* 11-17.

Howes, C. (1983). Patterns of friendship. *Child Development, 54,* 1041-1053.

Howes, C. (1988). Peer interaction in young children. *Monograph of the Society for Research in Child Development, 217*(53, No. 1).

Howes, C., Unger, O., & Matheson, C. (1992). *The collaborative construction of pretend and social play functions.* Albany: State University of New York Press.

Hutt, C. (1976). Exploration and play in children. In J. S. Bruner, A. Jolly, & K. Sylva (Eds.), *Play–Its role in development and evolution* (pp. 202-215). New York: Basic.

Isaacs, S. (1993). *Social development in young children.* New York. Schoken.

Kantor, R., Elgas, P., & Fernie, D. (1993). Cultural knowledge and social competence within a preschool peer culture group. *Early Childhood Research Quarterly, 8,* 125-147.

Kostelnik, M., Whiren, A., & Stein, L. (1986). Living with he-man: Managing superhero fantasy play. *Young Children, 42,* 3-9.

Levin, D. (1995). Power Rangers: An explosive topic. *Child Care Information Exchange, 102,* 50-51.

Lewis, M. (1975). The social determination of play. In B. Sutton Smith (Ed.), *Play & learning* (pp. 23-33). New York: Gardner Press.

Mandell, N. (1986). Peer interaction in day care settings: Implication for social cognition. *Sociological Studies of Child Development, 1,* 121-142.

Meyer, C., Klein, E., & Genishi, C. (1994). Peer relationships among 4 preschool second language learners in small group time. *Early Childhood Research Quarterly, 9,* 61-85.

Mueller, E. (1972). The maintenance of verbal exchanges between young children. *Child Development, 43,* 930-938.

Mueller, E., & Brenner, J. (1977). The origins of social skills and interaction among playgroup toddlers. *Child Development, 48,* 854-861.

Paley, V. (1984). *Boys and girls in the doll corner.* Chicago: The University of Chicago Press.

Paley, V. (1992) *You can't say you can't play.* Cambridge, MA: Harvard University Press.

Parker, J. G., & Gottman, J. M. (1989). Social and emotional development in a relational context: Friendship interaction from early childhood to adolescence. In T. J. Berndt & G. W. Ladd (Eds.), *Peer relationships in child development* (pp. 95-131). New York: Wiley.

Parten, M. B. (1932). Social participation among preschool children. *Journal of Abnormal Psychology, 17,* 243-269.

Parten, M. B. (1937). Leadership among preschool children. *A Journal of Abnormal and Social Psychology, 27,* 430-440.

Pepler, D. J., & Ross, H. S. (1981). The effects of play on convergent and divergent problem solving. *Child Development, 52*(4), 1202-1210.

Piaget, J. (1962). Play dreams and imitation in childhood (C. Gattegno & F. M. Hodgson, Trans.). New York: Norton.

Ross, H. S., & Goldman, B. D. (1979). Establishing new social relations in infancy. In T. Alloway, H. Krames, & P. Pliner (Eds.), *Advances in the study of communication and affect* (Vol. 3). New York: Plenum.

Rubin, K. H. (1980). Fantasy play: Its role in the development of social skills and social cognition. In K. H. Rubin (Ed.), *Children's play*. San Francisco: Jossey-Bass.

Schiller, P. (1975). Innate motor action as a basis of learning: Manipulative problems in the chimpanzee. In J. Bruner, A. Jolly, & K. Sylva (Eds.), *Play: Its role in development and evolution* (pp. 232-238). New York: Basic Books.

Sluckin, A. M., & Smith, P. K. (1977). Two approaches to the concepts of dominance in preschool children. *Child Development, 48*, 917-923.

Smilansky, S. (1968). *The effects of sociodramatic play on disadvantaged preschool children*. New York: Wiley.

Spradley, J. P. (1980). *Participant observation*. New York: Holt, Rinehart & Winston.

Stone, L. J., & Church J. (1984). *Childhood and adolescence*. New York: Random House.

Strayer, F. F., & Strayer, J. (1976). An ethological analysis of social agonism and dominance relations among preschool children. *Child Development, 47*, 980-989.

Sylva, K., Bruner, J., & Genova, P. (1976). The role of play in the problem-solving of children 3-5 years old. In J. Bruner, A. Jolly, & K. Sylva (Eds.), *Play: Its role in development and evolution* (pp. 244-257). New York: Basic Books.

Trawick-Smith, J. (1988). Let's say you're the baby, ok? Play leadership and following behavior of young children. *Young Children, 43*(5), 51-59.

Whaley, K. L., & Rubenstein, T. S. (1994). How toddlers "do" friendship: A descriptive analysis of naturally occurring friendships in a group child care setting. *Journal of Social and Personal Relationships, 11*, 383-400.

4

The Social Construction
of "Outsiders" in the Preschool

James A. Scott, Jr.
The Ohio State University

Example 1: Adjusting to Classroom Life
(10/01)—The First Day of School (Half the Children are Present)

Rebecca starts to sing the transition to circle song, "Come on everybody and find a seat." The children come to the circle and sit in front of Rebecca. Rebecca suggests that Don sit on the masking tape outlining the circle. Don moves to a position on the tape and sits down at circle.

Don: "We're going to make a big circle (inaudible)." He then leaves the circle and runs to play in another area of the classroom. Using hand gestures, Rebecca motions Don and Bob to join the other children for circle time.

Rebecca: "Could you guys come and join us, we're waiting for you to get started. Can you come and have a seat with us? We're going to have circle time and you guys can play over there later." Don returns to the circle.

Don: "How come I can't play with some other toys?"

Rebecca explains to Don that everyone remains in circle during circle time. Don immediately leaves the circle again. Rebecca continues to reinforce the importance of circle; then uses a puppet to dismiss children to small group. Don returns to circle just as Rebecca dismisses Jill to the music room. She tells Don to come with her for small group.

Most teachers know a child like Don who stands "outside" the group. He requires much more than his share of her attention. He disrupts the flow of the group activity and may be too aggressive with peers. At the beginning of the year, the teacher worries if her small-group and whole-group activities will ever "come together" because she is "pulled out" of these groups so often to deal with him. When a child like Don is in her classroom, the teacher feels like whole days are dominated by her attempts to cope with that single personality and his impact on others. Days when the child is absent feel like a reprieve. Communicating with the child's parents creates a lot of anxiety.

Example 2
(10/06)—William's Aggressive Behavior Toward Peers

Today is the first day when all of the children are present. William, Don, Bob, Peg (participant-observer), and Donna (teacher) are all playing at the water table. The three boys are eagerly pouring water from the jars into funnels, filling containers, and pumping water into containers. William walks around to the other side of the water table and attempts to get a water pump from Don. William tries to grab the pump from Don and a struggle begins. Donna intervenes and talks with both about using the pump. Don drops the pump into the water and begins to play with another toy. William retrieves the pump from the water and returns to his spot. He stays for 14 seconds, then leaves.

He returns 45 seconds later and attempts to grab a water pump from Nate and successfully grabs one from Don. Don reaches toward William and tells him that he wants it. Donna grabs the pump from William and explains that Don was still using it. William listens to Donna while holding on to the pump. Donna explains the waiting-and-asking procedures during water play. William drops the pump and again attempts to grab a water toy from Nate and Don. William tries to grab another toy from Nate. Donna intervenes again and William begins to cry loudly. Donna comforts and holds William; then leads him away from the table.

Most teachers also know a child like William. He experiences difficulty playing, negotiating, and communicating with other children. The teacher must constantly monitor his activity during free play. She must also intervene when necessary to try and curtail his aggressive behavior and mediate disagreements between him and other children.

In addition to these concerns about how children like Don and William are affecting the group and the flow of life in the classroom, there is also the teacher's genuine concern for them. What can the teacher do to support the development of these children? How can the teacher give such a child the needed help? How can the teacher keep this type of child from a path leading to social rejection, failure, and isolation?

At some point during the year, teachers worry about the effect this type of child is having on the experiences of the rest of the children. Is it fair to devote such a large amount of attention to these children when others also need the teacher's time and attention? Also, at some point during the year, the teacher must address the concerns of the other children's parents, who are likely to hear of and react to the child's aggression. In the extreme case, the ultimate question the teacher struggles with is, "Should the child be asked to leave the program?" She is likely to strongly resist this decision because it may be devastating to the child and parents and is an admission of "failure" for her.

Children like Don and William not only have an impact on the actions, planning, and decisions of their teachers, but also on other individual children in the classroom as well. In some instances, children express fear of such a child to the teacher, who then must provide assurances that allay those fears (even when such fears may be well-founded). In coping with children like Don and William and their impact on classroom life, what guidance can teachers find in the traditional research literature?

TRADITIONAL LITERATURE

Of course, many children experience positive peer relationships and are viewed and described as *popular, well-liked,* or *accepted* (Roopnarine & Honig, 1986). In contrast, children who experience social difficulties and negative peer relationships are referred to variously as *outsiders* or as *unpopular* or *rejected* children.[1] According to Oden (1986) and Roopnarine and Honig (1986), rejected children are those whose bids for social interaction are often refused and with whom most classmates prefer not to play. The term *outsider* has been used in other sociocultural research (Hatch, 1988) and is the term used in this study.

The characterizations of children just described are most often found in sociometric assessments of how children, as individuals and as a group, feel about and perceive each other socially. Sociometric assessments are derived using either a "nomination" method or a "rating-scale" method (Roopnarine & Honig, 1986). In the typical use of the nomination method, each child is shown a board with photographs of classmates. Each is asked to name each child and then to choose a limited number of pictures of children they would most like (or least like) to play or work with, or sit next to at circle, and so on. Reasons for these selections are also typically elicited.

---

[1]The label of *neglected* refers to children who are unpopular but are ignored rather than actively opposed by peers (Roopnarine & Honig, 1986). Such children, who are often depicted as shy or withdrawn, have been labeled *invisible children* (Byrne, 1985) and *omega children* (Guarnica, 1981) in research descriptions. In this chapter, the focus is on children whose behaviors are more socially salient and problematic for peers and teachers. Thus, we spend little time discussing the traditional literature dealing specifically with neglected children.

The rating-scale method provides an indication of a child's attitude relative to each and every member of the group (Hymel, 1983; Oden & Asher, 1977; Schofield & Whitley, 1983). This technique requires children to answer questions by choosing a response along a particular dimension or continuum. For example, children are asked, "How much do you like to play with this person in school?" and to choose a face along a continuum ranging from a frown to a smile.

The outcome of both methods is an assessment and quantification of individual children's popularity or unpopularity in the classroom and to so label them. In observational research using sociometric judgments as a starting point, children identified as popular display behaviors and levels of social competence that are different from those associated with unpopular children. Following developmental research such as that of Parten (1932), teachers often expect young children to advance naturally in their ability to create and extend their play within peer groups; yet popular and unpopular children use different strategies to enter and access peer groups and with different results. Popular children have been found to enter the play of peers more quickly and after fewer bids, whereas unpopular children are more likely to be ignored or not accepted by the group (Coie, Dodge, & Kupersmidt, 1990; Putallaz & Gottman, 1981). Moreover, popular children behave as if they will be accepted rather than ignored or rejected by peers, an attitude that is both a reflection of past experiences and a harbinger for future social successes.

Because unpopular (and especially rejected children) are widely characterized as *at risk* for later academic, social, and occupational problems (e.g., Asher & Coie, 1990; Howes, 1988; Roff, Sells, & Golden, 1972), a goal of this body of research is to help identify such children during the early years so that effective interventions can take place. Furthermore, such research may help us to identify behaviors and/or personality characteristics contributing to their negative social status, and thus to be better attuned to these factors when displayed in the classroom.

A related body of research focuses on helping to improve the social skills and, in turn, the social status of rejected children. Social skills training research evaluates the effectiveness of teaching various specific strategies to help children engage peers in play and social interaction (Cartledge & Milburn, 1986, 1995; Mize & Ladd, 1990). Other research focuses on what teachers can do as they assist children in context: Helping rejected children to observe and gauge peers' play before attempting to enter it (Bremme & Erickson, 1977); redirecting their attention to socially adept role models (Rogers & Ross, 1986); and "coaching" children about cooperation, sharing, and communication (Asher, 1985; Hendrick, 1992; Oden & Asher, 1977). However, teachers should not assume that the skills children learn are easily applied or even useful across the different subcontexts of the classroom (circle, small group, free play). Indeed, knowing when and where to use specific social strategies is itself a complex process, and "reading the cues" to produce situationally appropriate behavior may be especially difficult for some children (Kantor, Elgas, & Fernie, 1993).

A final line of traditional research on children experiencing social difficulties takes a broader cognitive-developmental perspective. The underlying assumption of this position is that cognition plays a major role in directing behavior, thus, the child's adverse behavior may be indicative of inadequate social experience or immaturity. Thus, teacher interventions are broad, attempting to foster social problem-solving skills in children through techniques such as co-playing, role-playing, and mirroring (Cartledge & Milburn, 1995; Krogh, 1982; Scarlett, 1986).

Although these lines of research on unpopular and rejected children have contributed to researchers' and teachers' understanding of peer relations and social competence or incompetence, there are inherent problems and limitations with these approaches. One major problem concerns the unintended consequences of labeling a child's social status. If teachers and other adults view such a social status as enduring and unchangeable, they may easily accept the prospect of continuing social difficulties for children thought of as rejected. With such expectations (by adults and perhaps internalized in children), the negative label can become a self-fulfilling prophecy as others lower their expectations for such children and anticipate social problems.

Sociometric and associated methodologies are limited in that they cannot reveal how such a status evolved for a child within the classroom, or how other children contributed to this situation and what experiences were particularly problematic. Another limitation of this research is that it focuses on others' perceptions of a rejected child, missing the child's own perspective on his or her status and experiences. Moreover, such research rarely ventures into the everyday contexts of children's lives; thus, it misses the diversity inherent in the subcontexts of settings and the potential that children may experience different levels of success within them.

ETHNOGRAPHIC QUESTIONS

Because it is contextualized and focused on the "doing" of everyday life, the sociocultural perspective necessarily focuses the researcher on the dynamic and over time social construction process through which a child becomes an outsider. Reciprocally, it provides a unique venue to explore the impact of this social construction process on the larger life of the group. Because the goal of ethnography is to understand the whole of life in a setting, exploring phenomenon such as outsider status is assumed to involve examination of the entire social group across both peer culture and school culture subcontexts. Thus, the ethnographic perspective addresses distinctive and important social questions, ones complementary to and unanswered by other bodies of research.

Although these are the orienting issues typically addressed by ethnography, specific questions have to evolve and be located inductively within a particular research project. As the examples at the beginning of the chapter demonstrate, the first days of classroom life for this group of teachers, children, and researchers were marked by the significant challenges posed by and for Don and William. Quite naturally, the teachers responded to the difficulties these children experienced during small-group, free-play, and large-group sessions with a variety of strategies and techniques intended to help them be more successful; the teachers expressed great concern to one another and to the research team.

The research team was also very aware of Don and William, in part because of their salience in the classroom, and in part because they worried that their disruptions would "mask" the wider process of establishing life in the classroom. Early on in the research process, the discussion of these two children dominated our research meetings, creating the additional concern that the team would not move on to other aspects of their research agenda.

My own research interest in the outsider phenomenon evolved during these ongoing discussions within the research group and my participation in an analysis conducted by the senior researchers on the opening 3 days of school (Fernie et al., 1990). The analysis from the first 3 days provided initial indication of the unique positionings of these two children within the early life of this classroom. Over the course of these days, both children appeared to be inquisitive explorers who often left group activities and wandered around the classroom, disrupting the nascent group activity at hand. Both also displayed various types of behavioral "stretches" (defined as when children diverge from, or go beyond the teacher's stated expectations while most of the group conforms), largely during the new group events of circle time and small group that the teachers were trying to establish. Some stretches included refusal to participate in such school culture activities and verbal and/or physical conflicts with peers. In fact, these two children were responsible for the large majority of such stretches within the first few days of school.

Intrigued by Don and William, I began a systematic examination of their outsider status. With an orienting focus on the social exchanges among such children, their peers, and adults or teachers, I aimed toward a broader description of the construction of outsider's social status over time and an interpretation of its cultural meaning for this classroom.

During the first 3 days of analysis, the following specific questions evolved to guide my outsider analysis:

1. What is the genesis and course of the process of becoming an outsider?
2. Is this co-construction process unique for each outsider?
3. How do teachers respond to outsiders during social interactions? Do these responses vary by context?
4. What is the mutual influence of outsiders on the group and the group on outsiders? How does this mutual relationship look at different points in time?

PROCEDURES

In order to address these questions, I selected five daily activities within which to examine the outsider phenomenon. These activities (two daily circle times, two small-group times, and the free-choice time) represent a range of both small- and large-group contexts across both school culture and peer-culture domains of the classroom. Multiple sources of data were used in the analysis to get the fullest possible picture of the outsider phenomenon: I analyzed 40 days (148 videotapes) of classroom activity, fieldnotes written by various participant-observers from every day of the school year, retrospective notes written each week by lead teachers, child interviews conducted during the year, and individual retrospective interviews with lead teachers. The 40 days of videotape covered at least 3 weeks of each season (fall, winter, and spring).

Data Analysis

Spradley's (1980) Developmental Research Sequence was used to guide the data analysis. Guided by the questions cited earlier about the genesis and influence of the outsider phenomenon in this classroom, the data analysis was conducted in four phases, with knowledge gained in a prior phase guiding the investigation in a subsequent phase.

The Phase 1 of data analysis entailed a review of videotapes and fieldnotes from the first 5 days of school. This review consisted of creating written narratives or episodes that broadly described the interactional participants (both children and teachers), the interactional events, and the outcome of the episode. Phase 2 consisted of a systematic review of all fieldnotes and teacher's retrospective notes gathered over the school year. I coded each fieldnote and documented any interaction involving either Don or William.

In Phase 3, I used what Spradley (1980) called a "domain analysis" to discover the cultural domains of meaning for both target children, across the five events and over the three quarters. Spradley used what he called "semantic relationships" to organize and interpret meaning within a cultural domain. For example, in my case I adapted the general relationship he called "means-end" (which he expressed as "X is a way to do Y") to describe Don and William's outsider interactions with others. Thus, my episodes were organized to reveal (a) X is a way to become an outsider, and (b) X is way for teachers to respond to an outsider.

In effect, this yielded a set of categories (also called a *typology*) of "ways to become an outsider" and "ways for teachers to respond to outsiders." A final layer of analysis consisted of reviewing each videotape, categorizing the outsider behaviors displayed by the target children throughout the course of the year. This information was organized by quarter and by context, to detail and cumulatively illustrate the frequency patterns of outsider behavior and teacher responses. The frequency of "ways to be an outsider" and "ways teachers responded" for Don and William, are shown in the tables, appendices, and figures. The figures are in light and dark shapes; the light shapes represent behaviors that occur two or more times, and the dark shapes represents behavior that only occur once.

The following comparative descriptions of both children provide a balanced picture of both the positive and negative characteristics of their behavior and interactions with others, as it evolved over fall, winter, and spring quarters in both school culture and peer-culture events. Their comparative stories show that being an outsider does not always mean the same things for different children; their stories told with an over-time perspective shows the changing and socially constructed nature of these social roles, and that outsider status is more broad than its usual definition as difficulty with peers. The stories are told as quarter-by-quarter phases and separated into school and peer culture domains.

FALL: DON AND WILLIAM EXPERIENCE COMMON DIFFICULTIES ACROSS SCHOOL CULTURE AND PEER-CULTURE DOMAINS

School Culture

The social construction of Don and William as outsiders began with the first days of fall quarter and occurred in both school culture and peer-culture domains of the classroom. Somewhat to our surprise, because outsiders are often portrayed in the traditional literature as experiencing their social difficulties mainly in peer play, there were many examples of how the incipient outsider role developed during the school culture events of the fall quarter.

During many circle times throughout the fall, Don chose to wander and play in different areas of the classroom rather than participate with the rest of the children and teachers. The anecdote that began this chapter illustrates Don's refusal (from the first day onward) to accept group norms for participation. During the first week of school, Rebecca noticed Don's refusal to attend circle and provided him with options (Fig. 4.1). In the following fieldnote, a participant-observer describes Don as he sits in his cubby.

Fieldnote Entry (10/09)—Sitting in Cubby

Don won't join group and he goes to the locker area and sits in a cubby. He leans out of the cubby toward the circle area and watches through most of the singing and discussion. As circle time nears the end, he calls out to the group at large: "I'M GETTING THIRSTY!" He repeats this many times. A student teacher goes and gets him to get a drink. Rebecca has talked with Don on the playground about circle time, and told him that if he doesn't want to join the circle, he will need to stay in the cubby, rather than wandering around the room.

Both teachers expressed concern about Don's behavior.

Rebecca: "My immediate concerns about Don were that he was withdrawn, disruptive, and wanted nothing to do with school events. As a teacher I felt frustrated because one person was constantly taking us away from the group, which made it difficult to maintain the progress of the group activity and manage Don at the same time."

Donna: "The structure of the day was difficult for Don. While Rebecca lead the group during circle, I was constantly responding to Don, in the group and outside the group."

A legitimate and widespread concern of most teachers at the beginning of the school year is to get the flow of daily events established. In this classroom, events are co-constructed by participants. In the co-construction of circle time, for example, teachers seek to introduce and facilitate group time in partnership with children, supporting their participation and incorporating their interests. Teachers get anxious and concerned when one or more children decide not to participate in group activities. In handling this kind of situation, a teacher's role can become overwhelming when attempting to create "group" while simultaneously attempting to meet the needs of children who opt out or have only marginal or fleeting interest in the group activity.

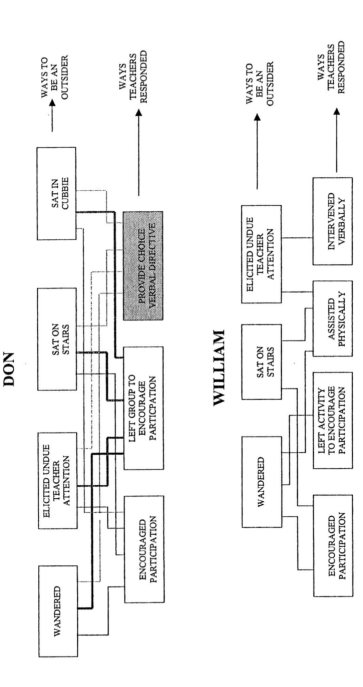

Figure 4.1. Fall: Ways to be an outsider and teacher responses in Circle Time I.

Table 4.1. Fall: Way to be an Outsider in Circle Time I

Ways to be an Outsider	Don	William
Whining	1	1
Wandering	7	8
Eliciting undo teacher attention	3	3
Sitting on stairs	3	5
Sitting/playing in cubby	4	1
Inappropriate or unusual behavior	1	1
Sitting/playing in the "story corner"	3	
	22	19

The tables and figures illustrate Don's difficulty in adjusting to most of school culture events (both circles and Small Group I). Throughout the quarter, his inability to deal with these more structured events increased, as did his aggression toward peers during free play. He preferred not to be part of school events where he was expected to become an active participant and to contribute to the group's social construction of the event. His nonparticipation consistently placed him literally outside of group events, set apart from participation with his peers. As a consequence, Don did not participate in many circle-time discussions, where group concerns were discussed and group interests were explored, simultaneously establishing group identity and norms; with Don's nonparticipation in this group process, his separateness was intensified and made salient to both classroom and research team participants. Don's behavior became a central focus of discussion during research meetings and staff meetings, as the adults attempted to interpret and deal with it.

Like Don, William also played elsewhere or wandered during circle time. The domain analysis in Table 4.1 (see also Appendix B) shows that out of his 19 "ways to be an outsider," the majority (13) consisted of wandering, and sitting on the stairs or in his cubby. The following episode is typical of his wandering and exploratory behavior.

Episode (10/09)—Wandering

Rebecca begins to sing "Come on everyone and find a seat, its circle time." The children come to circle and sit on the masking tape. Many of the children sit close to Rebecca and sing along with her.

Rebecca: "William why don't you come over to Mary (student teacher) who will help you take off your jacket and come to circle."

William decides to keep on his jacket. He continues to walk around and through the circle while simultaneously participating in the group discussion. Rebecca explains how to care for the pet turtle in the classroom. The children ask and answer questions about handling and feeding the turtle. After the discussion, Rebecca leads the children in song.

Rebecca: "William if you don't want to be in our circle, you can sit quietly, but we can't have you playing."

Donna leaves the circle to get William who is playing in another part of the classroom. William eventually takes off his jacket and joins the circle. He leaves again, just before Rebecca involves the children in a dismissal game.

The options to spend circle time sitting on the stairs or in the cubby were socially constructed alternatives. The teachers respected (and began with) Don and William's need to opt out of group participation but needed to balance it with the group's need to focus on their event without distractions. By creating options for William and Don who kept them close by, the teachers continued to work, over the course of the year, toward the ongoing goal of involving Don and William in school culture activities. Thus, we trace the beginnings of one aspect of the outsider role for both boys to their inability to participate (for whatever reasons) in formative school culture events. With their stances literally outside of the group, they established themselves as different, as disruptive, and as special cases requiring accommodations and undue public attention from the classroom teachers.

Peer Culture

Although William's (and Don's) social difficulties were first apparent during school culture events such as those just described, all was not smooth sailing for them in their peer interactions. William displayed many aggressive behaviors during free play as he attempted to interact with peers. He experienced difficulties when he attempted to initiate activity or enter the ongoing play of peers, and had many conflicts with peers when he was involved with them. It soon became evident that, without teacher support and intervention, William lacked the communicative skills for independently resolving disputes with peers.

As in the following example from the first week of school, William's interactional style set up a negative social history with Ken, Lisa, and other peers who would become members of the core group described in chapter 3:

Episode

Ken is playing alone at the sandbox with trucks and dinosaurs. William enters: "I have a big shovel." Ken ignores him. Lisa walks up to the sandbox, too, pulls up a chair and begins to play quietly. William offers a small dinosaur to Ken and he accepts it, but doesn't say anything. William (to Lisa): "I am a sand monster and I'm going to eat you up." Lisa ignores him. William: "I'm going. Don't take my dinosaur!" but he doesn't leave and then he sticks his dinosaur in front of Lisa, who briefly feeds it. William (to Ken): "My lion is going to eat your dinosaur." Ken ignores him. William then makes his lion "eat" Ken's dinosaur. Ken: "Don't." William pulls back but continues to make noises. Lisa tries the same idea, pulls her animal back when Ken shouts, and then plays quietly.

Those involved in conflicts with Don and William during the fall quarter were often members of the dominant core group. This was true because both boys, and especially William, were so persistent in trying to join the play of this emerging and socially powerful social group.

Like William, Don also experienced difficulty participating with peers. As his nonparticipation in school events consistently placed him "outside" of the social context and highlighted his absence from the ongoing activity of the group, his aggressive behaviors during free play is an interaction in the peer culture that also magnified his position as an outsider. Don's aggressive behavior toward peers became problematic for him because it occurred during the early weeks of autumn, a time when children are establishing relationships, and a disproportional number of children involved in the conflicts involving Don were also members of the dominant core group that he tried to access.

To summarize the social construction of outsider status for Don and William during fall quarter, they often failed to meet the shifting social demands of both school culture and peer-culture events. Although these social demands undoubtedly challenged all of the new students, William and Don were unable to sustain positive social attention and to accommodate to the agendas of others, whether those of teachers or peers.

WINTER: THE PATHS OF THE OUTSIDERS DIVERGE

School Culture

Although the general experience of both boys were similar during fall quarter, their experiences within the classroom diverged during the winter quarter, making each child's outsider status more distinctive.

In winter quarter, Don's adjustment to circle time became more difficult. His nonparticipation continued, made more obvious when contrasted with the group's longer and more productive circle times. His elicitation of undue teacher attention increased in frequency, as teachers attempted to involve him and meet his needs. The following fieldnote entry demonstrates how Don's disruptive behavior in a single circle time displayed multiple "ways to be an outsider."

Fieldnote Entry (1/13)—Cubby, Whining, Eliciting Undue Teacher Attention

---

The group sings the song about Alice going upstairs to make a bath and she goes down with the bath tub water. Just as the song ends, Don cries out:

Don: "You sang it wrong, not up; down, not up."

His face gets a worried look, intense . . . and the speed of talk picks up. Rebecca and the rest are surprised by his loud outburst. Attention focused on him, as he became more upset, as people didn't seem to understand. He was holding a brush with a long handle, which he threw to the center of the circle with a frustrated look accompanying the fast motion. Rebecca verbally reprimands him for throwing, but his attention is still on the song . . . and the fact that it wasn't sung right. He said something about people singing it wrong and getting him mixed up. Someone suggested they sing it again so that Don can point out the problem, as no one understands his complaint. The whole classroom starts singing "Alice, went up the stairs. . . .

Don: "No, not up, not upstairs, downstairs!"
Rebecca: "Oh, the bathroom is downstairs." Don nods and the singing picks up again.
William: "No upstairs."
Rebecca: "Well this time it will be the downstairs bathroom."

The song is sung with "downstairs." Don stops crying and settles down a moment, but then gets restless. Donna goes to him as he gets up and walks over to the cubby area. He stays there awhile. Donna returns to circle. . . .

In Don's whining, his trip to the cubbies, and his continual eliciting of the teachers' and group's attention, we see that Don signals his outsider status in multiple ways throughout this very public event.

At the same time, the aggressive throwing of the brush is an example of a new problem that emerged for Don during winter quarter (i.e., a tendency to be aggressive toward peers and adults in such school culture events; see Fig 4.2). His aggression toward adults is especially noteworthy because Don stands out as the only child who displays aggressive behavior toward them. The teachers and researchers believed that such aggression toward adults would be seen as very unusual and even upsetting to his peers, perhaps further marking him as different from them. The following fieldnote entry demonstrates this aggressive behavior.

Fieldnote Entry (2/02)—Aggressive Behavior Toward Adults

Jack, Ken, Paul. and Linda are sitting around Rebecca. Nate is sitting on Rebecca's lap. Don is turning the knobs on the stereo. Rebecca looks at him.

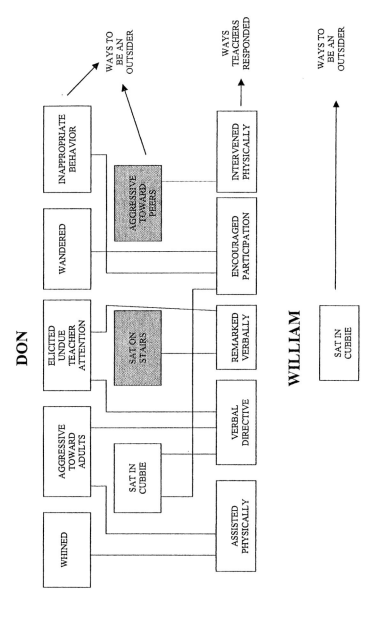

DON

- WHINED
- AGGRESSIVE TOWARD ADULTS
  - SAT IN CUBBIE
- ELICITED UNDUE TEACHER ATTENTION
  - SAT ON STAIRS
- WANDERED
- INAPPROPRIATE BEHAVIOR
  - AGGRESSIVE TOWARD PEERS → WAYS TO BE AN OUTSIDER

- ASSISTED PHYSICALLY
- VERBAL DIRECTIVE
- REMARKED VERBALLY
- ENCOURAGED PARTICIPATION
- INTERVENED PHYSICALLY → WAYS TEACHERS RESPONDED

WILLIAM

- SAT IN CUBBIE → WAYS TO BE AN OUTSIDER

Figure 4.2. Winter: Ways to be an outsider and teacher responses in circle.

Rebecca: "That's the teachers stereo, please move away from it."

He looks at her and smiles and continues to turn the knobs. Rebecca calls again, "Don I'm worried you'll break it." A student teacher gets up and Don darts to the game area. Don is playing with toys in the game area directly behind where Rebecca is sitting. She gets up and takes the toy away. She walks to the pillows and tells him he needs to sit there or come to circle.

Rebecca sits back down at her place and Don jumps on her back. He jumps on Rebecca's back again. Donna takes him by the hand and leads him to the cubby area. Everyone at the circle is talking. Mira is wandering around the circle sucking their thumb.

Comparing William to Don in winter quarter makes us aware that the path to outsider status is not a singular or unchanging one. In contrast to Don's escalating problems in school culture activities, William did a dramatic turnaround during the winter quarter school culture activities. Increasingly, William began to remain at circle time and to participate in the group activities. He had more success when interacting with non-core group peers, and participated in songs, movement activities, and finger plays. William also contributed to group discussions, problem-solving sessions, and "sharing" activities.

In small-group activity described by D. Williams in chapter 2, William began to participate in every activity and truly became part of the group. In one small-group art activity, the children colored with markers and stencils. At the end of the activity, William put his picture in the classroom and helped to clean up the small-group area. This helpfulness became typical of William in winter quarter, much to the surprise of those who observed him during the fall quarter. His outsider behavior diminished and he became more cooperative with teachers and children and displayed many prosocial behaviors (Fig. 4.3).

Peer Culture

In order to understand the evolving meaning of Don and William's outsider status in the peer culture during winter quarter, it is necessary to briefly revisit the core group.

In a previous analysis of play and object use, Elgas (1988) found that the core group of six peer players solidified their friendship and daily play with each other during winter quarter. Some of their common sociodramatic play themes included firefighters, superhero play, and the construction of large block structures. Superhero play was the favorite theme in the block corner and core group members enacted this on a daily basis. Like many of the children in the class, Don found the core group's play appealing, and wanted to join them. His attempts are demonstrated in the following episode:

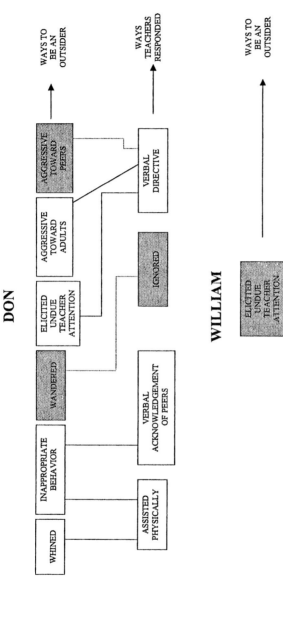

Figure. 4.3. Winter: Ways to be an outsider and teacher responses in small groups.

Fieldnote Entry (1/22)—Eliciting Undo Teacher Attention, Aggressive Behavior Toward Adults and Peers, Whining

In the block area Paul, Don, and Ken are wearing capes chasing each other. They run to the circle area and Bob runs over and tackles Ken to the ground. Don hides behind the ironing board in the house area. Ken lunges forward and tries to grab Don.

Rebecca: "Maybe if you feel like running you should go in the motor room. I'll get a teacher to go with you.

They go up to the motor room. Paul, Ken, and Don are swinging plastic hangers and baseball bats at each other. They run around the room chasing each other. They are yelling at each other and holding it like a gun. Ken yells. Don hits Ken on the shoulder. He screams.

Ken: "Stop it you dummy," Don corners Ken.
Don: "I never give up." Craig (staff) intervenes and takes the bat from Don.
Don: "My bat, give me my bat." He continues to cry and scream. "No joke, no joke." He kicks Craig in the shins. Donna comes in and puts her hand on Don's back. She asks him "What's wrong."
Don: "Craig took by bat."

Donna explains why he did so, and asked Don if he could use the bat in another way. He says, "Yes."

Elgas (chap. 3) describes the core group members as active children who favored play themes that involved mock aggression. However, their aggressive behavior, either pretend or intentional, was directed at non-core group members; aggressive acts within the core group were not sanctioned. The episode just presented demonstrates that when Don had access to the group's play, he either did not understand this implicit rule or was unwilling to comply with it (Fig. 4.4).

However, as Don himself would say, "he never gives up," and so continued to try to gain membership. He wore the capes they valued, used similar objects, and proposed superhero themes. As children played out these themes during winter quarter, Don's aggressive behavior prompted the core group to regularly exclude him from play. These conflictual interactions with peers often drew the attention of teachers.

Although Don's level of interaction with others increased, it was neither comfortable for peers or teachers nor successful—the access he so intensely sought still eluded him. Both teachers reflected on Don's difficulty and the experience they had trying to communicate his difficulties to his parents.

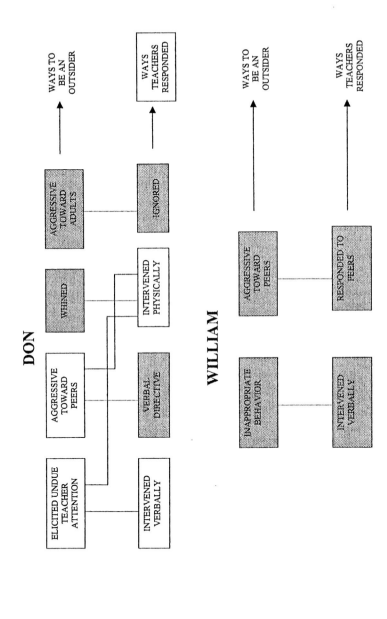

DON

WAYS TO
BE AN
OUTSIDER

WAYS
TEACHERS
RESPONDED

| ELICITED UNDUE TEACHER ATTENTION | AGGRESSIVE TOWARD PEERS | WHINED | AGGRESSIVE TOWARD ADULTS |

| INTERVENED VERBALLY | VERBAL DIRECTIVE | INTERVENED PHYSICALLY | IGNORED |

WILLIAM

WAYS TO
BE AN
OUTSIDER

WAYS
TEACHERS
RESPONDED

| INAPPROPRIATE BEHAVIOR | AGGRESSIVE TOWARD PEERS |

| INTERVENED VERBALLY | RESPONDED TO PEERS |

Figure 4.4. Winter: Ways to be an outsider and teacher responses in free play.

Donna: "In some instances, Don prepared for battle before he would enter into the core group play because he knew they would be in opposition to his access. He also battled with the core group over who would be in charge of the 'script'. After talking to his parents, I felt sad about their position and acceptance of Don's behavior."

Rebecca: "It was very hard to capture his parents' attention in understanding his behavior. His mother would vent, but never get involved in problem solving with us."

Why did Don's problems worsen? Perhaps the rest of the classroom group was developing at all levels (sharing, social problem solving, group conversations, community-building), foregrounding Don's inabilities to participate in more complex social interactions even more. As his social incompetence relative to his peers became more exaggerated and more obvious, and simultaneously as his aggression increased and was directed toward more children, a socially constructed "attitude" became manifested by the group that might be expressed as "We hate Don." For example, this attitude was prevalent in interview data gathered to assess whether children "saw" the cultural patterns we interpreted as developing. When asked the open-ended question, "What don't you like about school?," half of the 18 children mentioned "Don."

What could be done to help Don at this point in winter quarter? One strategy might have been to engage the core group in problem-solving situations that might have influenced them to consider Don's position in their group play. Perhaps they could have included Don in their discussion of themes or activities and roles identification process early in their play to avoid him "arriving" during their play and disrupting it.

By contrast to Don's "never give up" style, William made a dramatic turn, abandoning his previous attempts to gain membership in the core group in favor of social interaction with other children and teachers. He had become what Elgas called a "teacher player," simultaneous with his newly positive participation in school culture. The following field note entry about William contrasts with the earlier example at the same table during fall quarter.

Fieldnote Entry (2/10)—Sand Table

Mendy and William were at the sand table, which was damp and had several bowls in it with some sand in them. William was walking back and forth to the sink, carrying a little brown plastic bottle, filling it with water and taking it back to dump in the bowls. He switched to a smaller plastic bottle that he took from under the sink. Back and forth, carrying more water to the sand table. The bowl is nearly overflowing. I can see a brown plastic dinosaur standing in the sand next to the bowl. (I think it belongs to William; William's blue backpack is laying on the floor near the sand table). On one trip he carried both bottles. After about five trips, several bowls seem to be running over. Rebecca tells him there seems to be enough water.

As William played by himself, with teachers, and sometimes with other children, he very rarely attempted to gain access to the core group of peer players. The following reaction of the core group to one such attempt suggests that his pulling back may have been prudent.

Fieldnote Entry (2/23)—William and Core Group Play

Bob and Ken are walking around together carrying pretend bows and arrows (plastic hangers and smooth rhythm sticks). They are playing in the cube by the story area. Alexis and I are by the puzzle area. They approach us pointing the sticks at me very close to my face.

Ken:	"We're gonna shoot you, we're gonna kill you, shoot you dead."
Bob:	"Yeah shoot you." Bob very close to my face says "no girls, get out, get out, no girls." They push me. "Only boys."
Peg:	"So can any boy play?"
Bob:	"Yeah."
Peg:	"So can William play?"
Bob:	"No, he's old. Only boys that are not old."
Peg:	"Could Don play?" "No." They both shake their heads.

The comment about William being old is interesting because in actuality William is younger than Bob and Ken. Perhaps they invented this unfounded reason to justify their exclusion of William. This fieldnote also demonstrates the "mediator" role that teachers and sometimes participant-observers (Peg) assumed to help William access the play of his peers.

But, as the core group grew stronger and more cohesive and constructed complex shared knowledge of play themes, values objects, rituals, it became increasingly difficult for William to participate in their play because he lacked the cultural knowledge created within the core group play (Kantor et al., 1993). As William failed to access the core group, he began to rely on teachers as play partners.

William's withdrawal from peer play and shift to adults is interesting from the standpoint of social competence. Usually, withdrawal is seen as social incompetence. Our interpretation, however, is that William's shift should be regarded at the very least as socially adaptive. In making the shift, he evidently had assessed his social reality rather well— it's wise to stay away from a group that doesn't want you, and to seek out more flexible play partners who accept and even like you. At the same time, it is important to note, from an individual-within-group standpoint, that this choice may have been a "forced choice"—forced by the fall quarter's bad blood with members of the core group.

Both teachers shared their impressions of William's winter quarter turn about.

> Rebecca: "William's aggression ceased and he attended school culture events, but clearly he didn't have any friends. His parents were concerned that he sought out teachers and didn't have any peer players. We were concerned because even though he was doing better in school and peer-culture events, it appeared that he was giving up on friends."
>
> Donna: "William returned (for winter quarter), decreased his whining, and integrated into the group. I was surprised! He became so good at understanding the schedules and routines that he often repeated statements and modeled teachers. This shift helped him to understand the routines, but it was not popular with his peers. So William began to seek out teachers as players."

The different outsider paths taken by William and Don during winter quarter as compared to the fall quarter show the dynamic shifting nature of the process. Don experienced more problems across both school and peer culture domains, but William began to successfully participate in school culture events and opted out of peer culture by becoming a teacher player.

The example of William argues against the idea that a "problem child" will remain a problem child and cautions that a label may mislead one to believe that it represents only one kind of child. The example of William shows that children can adapt their interactive skills (Corsaro, 1985) and make social progress in different realms of the classroom.

SPRING: WILLIAM TAKES A "STEP BACK"; DON STEPS INTO A "TRAP"

School Culture

As William slightly regressed to outsider behaviors displayed during fall quarter, Don's interactions with the core group continued to evolve. In the course of the year, circle time was the most difficult context for Don to adjust to and to actively participate in. Each quarter, Don's "ways to be an outsider" became more frequent and more diverse as he consistently positioned himself outside of the circle, for example, by wandering and sitting or playing on the stairs, in the story corner, or in his cubby (see Table 4.2).

Table 4.2. Spring: Way to be an Outsider in Circle Time I

Ways to be an Outsider	Don	William
Whining	5	
Wandering	4	2
Eliciting undo teacher attention	13	
Sitting on stairs	1	3
Sitting/playing in cubby	8	2
Inappropriate or unusual behavior	1	
Aggressive behavior toward peers	3	
Aggressive behavior toward adults	1	
Sitting/playing in the "story corner"	5	
	41	7

In the spring quarter, William reverted back to the type of behavior that he displayed during the fall quarter. He began to leave the circle activity and wander around the classroom. William would also sit on the stairs and sit or play in his cubby. Even though William's behavior was similar to Don's, he did not display as great a frequency of outsider behaviors as he did during the fall quarter. When William sat on the stairs, the teacher invited him to circle, and when he sat in his cubby the teacher ignored him (see Fig. 4.5).

Peer Culture

In the course of shifting social interactions and positioning by Don, his outsider status made him an insider. In free play, Don's play with peers was similar to his interactions during the fall and winter quarter. His aggressive behavior toward peers warranted teacher attention and intervention. Don experienced many interactions with core group members. As he interacted and played superhero and cowboy and Indian roles, his outsider position shifted temporarily to "one of the group." I describe and analyze this phenomena in the following episodes and fieldnote entries. The following field note entries demonstrate Don's participation in core group play.

Fieldnote Entry (4/06)—Core Group Play

Bob remains seated on the climber, but Ken runs around the doll house, He says to me: "This is my Dr. Jones rope." Don standing nearby says: "I have a Dr. Jones movie. The Indian tears the heart out." Ken says. "My Dr. Jones movie is scary." They both repeat this in an arguing tone. Don waves several rhythm sticks and a plastic hanger he is holding in Ken's face. "I'm an Indian."

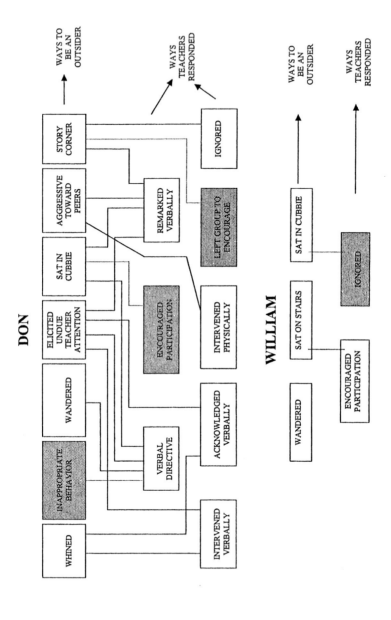

DON

WHINED — INAPPROPRIATE BEHAVIOR — WANDERED — ELICITED UNDUE TEACHER ATTENTION — SAT IN CUBBIE — AGGRESSIVE TOWARD PEERS — STORY CORNER → WAYS TO BE AN OUTSIDER

INTERVENED VERBALLY — VERBAL DIRECTIVE — ACKNOWLEDGED VERBALLY — ENCOURAGED PARTICIPATION — INTERVENED PHYSICALLY — REMARKED VERBALLY — LEFT GROUP TO ENCOURAGE — IGNORED → WAYS TEACHERS RESPONDED

WILLIAM

WANDERED — SAT ON STAIRS — SAT IN CUBBIE → WAYS TO BE AN OUTSIDER

ENCOURAGED PARTICIPATION — IGNORED → WAYS TEACHERS RESPONDED

Figure 4.5. Spring: Ways to be an outsider and teacher responses in Circle Time I.

Paul approaches carrying "camping" sticks and a hanger. Don asks: "Are you an Indian?" Paul shakes his head no. He smiles at me and puts his sticks in his belt loops. Don says: "Oh no you're the spear man. Those are spears." He points, Paul looks at him and smiles. Don gives me a piece of leopard skin paper and asks me to help him make an Indian head band.

Don is part of the core group's chasing and cowboy and Indian themes. He is involved and socially interactive with members of the core group and is striving to develop a friendship with them that is based on aspects of peer culture. However, it is still apparent that even though Don does access the core group and co-constructs play themes with members, he is still not considered part of the "group." This notion is described by a participant-observer on the first day of spring quarter.

Fieldnote Entry (4/06)—Core Group Play

Paul, Don, and Jack are all using familiar play items from last quarter—plastic hangers, rhythm sticks, and Don is wearing a headband. Don is starting to chase the others, they respond. Don is smiling, calling them names; seems to be happy. He is having contact with the peer group. He is not part of the "group," doesn't travel with them, but can chase them and is using some of the same equipment and wearing a headband, which they sometimes do.

This entry describes the dual perspective of Don and core group members who are an integral part of the social construction of Don's position in the classroom. Don's perception is one of an insider. Don wears the core group clothing, uses similar objects, and uses familiar sociocultural language during the interactive play. He runs, negotiates, plays, and laughs with the group.

He has clearly internalized his "bad guy" role as part of the core group play. Although he looks like the group, talks like the group, and walks like the group, he is not part of the group. The core group's perspective on him is that he is an outsider. When he does interact with the group, he is always in an oppositional role. If they are all Batmen and Supermen, he is "supergold"; if they are cowboys, he is the Indian; if they are the cops, he is the robber; and if they are the good guys he is the bad guy. In order to engage in their peer-culture play, the core group needs opposition, and because their group has developed strong friendships, the opposition must come from the outside. In a unique way, Don, the outsider, positions himself in the play as a "pretend outsider."

Interestingly, Rebecca was not aware of Don's access to the peer group.

> Rebecca: "I had no idea that Don had gotten into the core group play at any level. I only saw the aggression and conflict. I felt very frustrated with Don's behavior and had a real concern for the safety of the other children. We finally decided to insist with his parents that they seek counseling for Don and that we receive some guidance about helping him participate in the class. Sadly, his parents reaction was to dis-enroll him and send him to a different center for next year."

Don has always tried to gain access to the group; therefore, the group does not look far for opposition. Yet, another related factor that positions Don as an outsider is his aggressive behavior toward members of the core group (Table 4.3). His engagement in "bad guy" roles creates more opportunities for him to be aggressive. So as he becomes a member of the group, he also solidifies his outsider position in children's reactions to his aggression.

Episode (4/13)—Aggressive Behavior Toward Peers

Paul, Ken, Jack, and Don are playing on the climber. They are playing a "good guy/bad guy" theme and they are playing rather rough. Don is the bad guy. After a while they stopped playing at the climber. The core group members are angry with Don because they feel he plays too rough. The core group plays with the yellow rocket tube and take turns getting into it. They won't allow Don to get into the rocket. He gets angry and hits Jack in the face. The core group gets upset with Don and decide not to allow him access to the rocket.

Table 4.3. Spring: Way to be an Outsider in Free Play

Ways to be an Outsider	Don	William
Whining		1
Eliciting undo teacher attention	4	
Aggressive behavior toward peers	10	
Aggressive behavior toward adults	1	
Pretend outsider	7	
	22	1

Episode (4/14)—Aggressive Behavior Toward Peers

Ken and Paul are playing on the climber. They both have their Batman capes in their hand. A student teacher talks to both while they are playing on the climber. Don walks over to the climber and snatches the cape from Ken. He becomes very angry and screams for Don to return the cape. Don refuses to give it back to Ken but drops it on the carpet for him to pick up. Don returns to the climber and Ken and Paul tease him with their capes. Later in the same episode Ken is waiting in line behind Don. They are waiting to enter the plastic yellow rocket. Don thinks that Ken is trying to go before him and hits him in the chest. Ken hits Don back.

Interesting phenomena occurred as core group attitudes toward Don developed into themes and rituals. One such ritual was the setting of a "trap" (a block structure with some strategically placed boobytrap blocks) by members of the core group. The following fieldnote entry describes the "trap."

Fieldnote Entry (5/27)—Core Group Play; Trap

Don is playing at the sand table. Paul runs up to the sand table, smiling proudly. "Don we have a surprise for you." Don looks up surprised, and Paul turns about and runs back in the direction of blocks. Don continues to play with a tube in the sand. Once again Paul runs to Don, "We have a present for you . . . come" (smiling, sweet voice). He gestures for Don to follow him as he runs to blocks. Don drops his tube and runs off after Paul, saying something like: "What is it, what, what?" (smiling happily). I follow quickly behind and can see a huge construction in the middle of blocks. Walls of blocks and a table-shaped construction in the middle that is covered with foam. I can hear the word "trap" being mentioned by kids, Ken looks angry as Don approaches, yelling: "No, no, not yet." He yells at Bob who is smiling and watching, Don's approach. Jeff, a student teacher, stands nearby, with an exasperated frown on his face. Don runs into the area, looking around, and Bob and Paul gesture to the middle construction. Don stretches out his arms and flops into the center of the foam construction, which collapse on impact. He looks surprised, shocked, gets up again and then starts to kick at it and begins to kick the walls down also. His happy smile has now transformed to an aggressive face as he uses energy to kick hard.

As these phenomena emerged, so did the outsider behavior. To be a pretend outsider is a way to be an outsider. To be "supergold," a robber, a bad guy, or the Indian who steals the money is a way to be a pretend outsider.

In some episodes, Don's aggressive actions were interrelated. If you are the opposition you must display some kind of counteraction to retaliate. In other instances, Don became aggressive when his insider–outsider position shifted and the play or the group's acceptance of him broke down; thereby leaving him confused and angry.

Teachers responded in diverse ways to Don's outsider behavior. Responses included, physically and verbally intervening, and making verbal remarks and directives (Fig. 4.6).

Unlike Don, William displayed hardly any outsider behavior during free play. The only episode that involved him occurred on 4:9 in the block area. In this episode Ben, Ken, and Paul threatened to knock down William's structure. In the process of building their own structure Ken bumps William; who cries loudly and contends that Ken hurt him badly.

William played in many different areas during free play. He played in the block corner, at the sand table, at the activity table, and in the housekeeping area. In many episodes, William played by himself, near peers, or identified a teacher or student as a play partner.

William's social interaction was still a concern of teachers, the research team, and his parents. Although William was successful in identifying teachers as play partners, and he occasionally played casually with peers, his social progress with peers and the peer culture was still minimal. He practically gave up at trying to access the core group of peer players or any other group of peer players. William's small-group teacher provided the same conclusion.

Donna: "Even though he made strides and gains he was still an outsider at the end of the spring quarter. William was participating in the school culture, but he never really adjusted to the peer culture and experienced difficulty in this area up to the end of the school year."

DISCUSSION

This study described the social construction of two outsiders in a preschool classroom. Many teachers may know a child like Don or William, or have a child in their classroom with similar experiences.

In order for teachers to observe the actions of a child like Don, observations need to occur within the group. Somehow, teachers need to supervise the more child-dominated areas (such as blocks) in order to get close enough to know what is happening. How can we extend William's play with teachers to help him get success with peers?

A co-playing strategy (Scarlett, 1986) may be useful. In co-playing, the teacher joins the child's play and follows the child's lead. Co-playing is useful for encouraging social play, providing the child a play context to practice, and induces classmates to come over and play

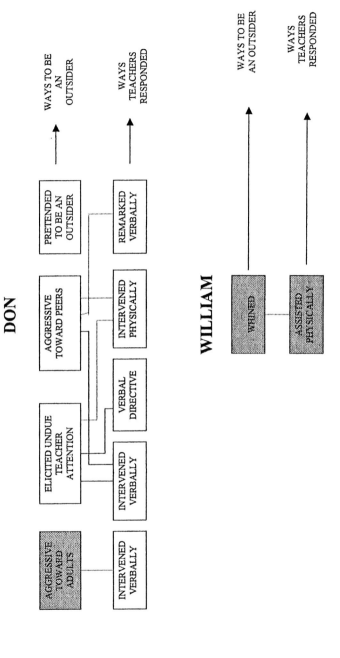

Figure 4.6. Spring: Ways to be an outsider and teacher responses in free play.

with the child. Once William has successfully played together with peers and a teacher, the co-playing strategy requires the teacher to decrease the social interaction and become an observer who now mirrors the relationship between the children. Consequently, William becomes increasingly aware of self as a partner in play.

Across contexts for Don and William, both experienced some difficulties in social participation that were not exclusively in free play or strictly related to peer interactions. The problems experienced by outsiders occurred across all contexts that required sustained social participation, attention to group activities and norms, including but not limited to play and friendship interactions. Thus, a basic argument implied in this study is that to fully understand the outsider phenomenon, one must look at how such status is constructed and how it influences all members experiencing the inherently social setting of the classroom.

Unlike some of the social skills training studies in the existing literature (Hartup & Coates, 1967; Mize & Ladd, 1990; Spivack & Shure, 1974), intervention strategies must be holistic (Carteldge & Milburn, 1995). You cannot just work with the child and his or her behavior, because it is a social construction by the group that has a social history that has to be undone over time. So the focus might be to work explicitly with the group. In retrospect, working with the core group and Don during spring quarter could have been a possibility. The combination of Don's aggressive behavior with the new pretend outsider roles, was likely to create more problems for the group, and for Don. Perhaps the interventions might have been about widening Don's positions so that he was not only the bad guy, about helping him to control and modify his aggression, and about helping the group change or diversify their narrow construction of him as an outsider.

We sometimes equate access and entry to play groups with success or "popularity" according to the traditional literature. But for William, becoming a teacher player was a form of success or at least an adaptation. At the same time, William's social adaptiveness and decision to seek out teachers as players in effect denied him access to the peer group. How could teachers have helped reintegrate William into the peer group? Providing him leadership in school culture events may have elevated his status with peers.

Don's access to the peer group play is a similar example. He gained access as a "bad guy" but an analysis of winter and spring quarters clearly suggest that he was not successful. It appears that he succeeded only as a "peripheral player." Once again, teachers need to understand that access and entry does not necessarily mean success.

The two different paths imply different interventions. For William, who had removed himself rather adaptively from peer interaction during free play, an attempt could have been made to reintegrate him into peer play. As Kantor et al. (1993) suggested, William lacked the cultural knowledge held by the core group, and this made it difficult for him to access the ongoing play. Perhaps intervention with the group and William would have helped him to read and produce the appropriate cultural knowledge during free play.

To conclude, let me note a couple of observations related to social competence from this negative case phenomenon.

The acquiring and use of social knowledge is an important aspect of social competence. This study showed that social competence is essential in the negotiation and construction of life in the classroom. Children who are able to use their cultural capital to read social cues, interpret social meanings, negotiate positions, and access play groups, will be viewed more positively and experience more success in group settings. This competence must encompass a diverse repertoire of social skills that are fluid enough to be utilized across diverse settings (Kantor et al., 1993). The relation between social competence and incompetence revealed in this study might be characterized as more like yin and yang, than like two discrete and separate sides of a coin.

Teachers need to be aware of the dynamic interpretation of social competence so they become informed and are more able to assist children who are lacking the interactive skills and the social knowledge (Corsaro, 1985, 1997) to actively interpret, negotiate, and read social cues during various classroom activities, across all contexts. The individual-within-group perspective implies that a close and contextualized look must be taken to determine whether actions often deemed relevant to social competence and incompetence in the traditional literature, such as withdrawal and entry, really have their traditionally ascribed meanings to the participants of the rich and dynamic social world of the preschool.

APPENDIX A: DESCRIPTION OF OUTSIDER AND TEACHER BEHAVIORS

Definition of Ways to be an Outsider

1. Whining
   - A high-pitched complaint, expression, or distressed cry
2. Wandering
   - Moving about the classroom during circle time or small group without a fixed chair or goal
3. Eliciting undue teacher attention
   - An inappropriate, unusual, or aggressive action or verbal message that induces a verbal or physical reaction from a teacher(s)

4. Sitting on stairs
   - An approved option for children who refuse to participate in a school activity
5. Sitting/playing in cubby
   - An approved option for children who refuse to participate in a school activity
6. Inappropriate or unusual behavior
   - An action or verbal message that is judged to be unsuitable, uncommon, or unsafe by a teacher(s)
7. Aggressive behavior toward peers
   - A forceful verbal action or physical attack on a child
8. Aggressive behavior toward adults
   - A forceful verbal action or physical attack on an adult
9. Sitting/playing in the "quiet" corner
   - Specific places in the classroom where children can go if they refuse to participate in circle (not an approved option like the stairs or cubby)
10. Tantruming
    - A fit of bad temper that requires physical assistance and removal from the activity

Definitions of Teacher Responses

1. Ignore
   - A conscious decision to refuse to take notice of or acknowledge a child's behavior.
2. Encourage participation (without leaving the activity)
   - Teacher or other adult makes inspiring remarks to persuade the child to join or return to the group.
3. Physical assistance
   - To physically escort, guide or support a child.
4. Physically Remove
   - Taking a child away from the group or a specific area.
5. Leave the Activity
   - Encouraging a child to return to the activity.
6. Verbal Intervention
   - Verbal messages used to resolve a conflict directed toward a child involved in a conflict with another child.
7. Physical Intervention
   - Coming between or separating two or more children who are involved in a conflict.

 8. Verbal Remark
    - A direct communication to a child about a specific behavior.
 9. Providing an alternative choice
    - Verbally providing the child with another option.
10. Verbal directive
    - A direct communication given to a child that serves to instruct or guide; without options.
11. Not present; unaware; no information about teacher's response
    - The teacher is not present; totally unaware of the child's behavior; or there is not enough or no information about the teacher's response.
12. Verbal acknowledgment of a child or teacher's feelings
    - A direct message that openly recognizes and identifies how a person is feeling.
13. Assistance to peers
    - A verbal response to peers who were the recipient of an outsider's behavior

APPENDIX B: DOMAIN ANALYSIS

According to Spradley's (1980) Developmental Research Sequence, a cultural domain is a category of cultural meaning that includes other smaller categories. These cultural categories consist of three elements; cover term, included terms, and the semantic relationship. The cover term is the name for a cultural domain and the included terms are the names for the smaller categories. The single semantic relationship links the two categories together. Spradley contended that the function of the semantic relationship "is to define the included terms by placing them inside the cultural domain" (p. 89). Spradley identified the following nine semantic relationships (pp. 103-105):

1.	Strict inclusion	X is a kind of Y
2.	Spatial	X is a place in Y
3.	Cause–effect	X is a result of Y
4.	Rationale	X is a reason for doing Y
5.	Location for action	X is a place for doing Y
6.	Function	X is used for Y
7.	Means–end	X is a way to do Y
8.	Sequence	X is a step in Y
9.	Attribution	X is a characteristic of Y

REFERENCES

Asher, S. R. (1985). An evolving paradigm in social skill training research with children. In B. H. Schneider, K. H. Rubin, & J. E. Ledingham (Eds.), *Children's peer relations: Issues in assessment and intervention* (pp. 157-171). New York: Springer-Verlag.

Asher, S. R., & Coie, J. D. (1990). *Peer rejection in childhood.* New York: Cambridge University Press.

Bremme, D. W., & Erickson, F. (1977). Relationships among verbal and nonverbal classroom behaviors. *Theory Into Practice, 16*(3), 153-161.

Byrnes, D. A. (1985). "Cipher" in the classroom: The invisible child. *Childhood Education, 61*(2), 91-97.

Cartledge, G., & Milburn, J. F. (1986). *Teaching social skills to children: Innovative approaches.* New York: Pergamon Press.

Cartledge, G., & Milburn, J. F. (1995). *Teaching social skills to children and youth—Innovative approaches.* Needham Heights, MA: Allyn & Bacon.

Coie, J. D., Dodge, K. A., & Kupersmidt, J. B. (1990). Peer group behavior and social status. In S. R. Asher & J. D. Coie (Eds.), *Peer rejection in childhood* (pp. 17-59). New York: Cambridge University Press.

Corsaro, W. (1985). *Friendships and peer culture in the early years.* Norwood, NJ: Ablex.

Corsaro, W. (1997). *The sociology of childhood.* Thousand Oaks, CA: Pine Forge Press.

Elgas, P. (1988). *The construction of a preschool peer culture: The role of objects and play styles.* Unpublished doctoral dissertation, The Ohio State University, Columbus.

Fernie, D., Kantor, R., Scott, J., MacMurray, P., Kesner, J., & Klein, E. (1990). School culture and peer culture influences on adult and child roles in a preschool classroom. In C. Genishi (chair), *Life in preschool and elementary school settings: Aspects of peer and school culture.* Symposium conducted at the annual meeting of the American Educational Research Association, Boston.

Guarnica, O. (1981). Social dominance and conversational interaction The omega child in the classroom. In J. L. Green & C. Wallat (Eds.), *Ethnography and language in educational settings* (pp. 229-252). Norwood, NJ: Ablex.

Hartup, W. W., & Coates, B. (1967). Imitation as a function of reinforcement for the peer group and rewardingness of the model. *Child Development, 38*(4), 1003-1016.

Hatch, J. A. (1988). Learning to be an outsider: Peer stigmatization in kindergarten. *The Urban Review, 20*(1), 59-72.

Hendrick, J. (1992). *The whole child: Developmental education for the early years.* New York: Merrill.

Howes, C. (1988). Peer interaction of young children. *Monographs of the Society for Research in Child Development, 53* (1, Serial No. 217).

Hymel, S. (1983). Preschool children's peer relations: Issues in sociometric assessment. *Merrill-Palmer Quarterly, 29,* 237-260.

Kantor, R., Elgas, P., & Fernie, D. (1993). Accessing cultural knowledge for membership in preschool friendship groups. *Early Childhood Research Quarterly, 8*(2), 125-147.

Krogh, S. L. (1982). *Encouraging positive justice reasoning and perspective taking skills.* Paper presented at the annual meeting of the National Association of Early Childhood Teacher Educators, Washington, DC.

Mize, J., & Ladd, G. (1990). Toward the development of successful social skills training for preschool children. In S. Asher & J. Coie (Eds.), *Peer rejection in childhood* (pp. 338-364). London: Cambridge University Press.

Oden, S. (1986). Developing social skills instruction for peer interaction and relationships. In G. Carteledge & J. F. Milburn (Eds.), *Teaching social skills to children: Innovative approaches.* Elmsford, NY: Pergamon Press.

Oden, S., & Asher, S. R. (1977). Coaching children in social skills for friendship making. *Child Development, 48,* 495-506.

Parten, M. (1932). Social participation among preschool children. *Journal of Abnormal Social Psychology, 27,* 242-269.

Puttalluz, M., & Gottman, J. M. (1981). An introductional model of children's' entry into peer groups. *Child Development, 52*(3), 986-994.

Roff, M., Sells, S. B., & Golden, J. M. (1972). *Social adjustment and personality development in children.* Minneapolis: University of Minnesota Press.

Rogers, D. L., & Ross, D. (1986, March). *Encouraging positive social interaction among young children.* Paper presented to the annual meeting of the National Association for the Education of Young Children, Washington, DC.

Roopnarine, J. L., & Honig, A. S. (1986). Research in review. The unpopular child. In A. Honig (Ed.), *Reducing stress in young children's lives.* Washington, DC: National Association for the Education of Young Children.

Scarlett, W. G. (1986). Co-playing: Teachers as models for friendship. In D. Wolf (Ed.), *Connecting: Friendship in the lives of young children and their teachers.* Redmond, WA: Exchange Press.

Schofield, J. W., & Whitley, B. E. (1983). Peer nomination vs. rating scale measurement of children's peer preference. *Social Psychology Quarterly, 46,* 242-251.

Spivack, G., & Shure, M. (1974). *The problem solving approach to adjustment.* Washington, DC: Jossey-Bass.

Spradley, J. (1980). *Participant observation.* New York: Holt, Rinehart & Winston.

5

Individual Pathways
Through Preschool

Paula McMurray-Schwarz
Ohio University Eastern

Most early childhood teachers would acknowledge that children's individual differences influence their teaching strategies, the children's learning experiences, and the overall classroom environment. However, understanding these differences and capitalizing on them is a complex issue and one that is often debated. Traditionally, educational trends have emphasized a generalized education so that all children receive and comprehend the same "academic" content regardless of individual characteristics and experiences (i.e., educators view the classroom as a group of children). To date, research has primarily focused on groups of children or individual children. Also, early childhood curriculum has typically been directed at groups of children instead of individuals, with the exception of programs for children with disabilities.

More recently, with the inception of the guidelines called Developmentally Appropriate Practice (DAP; Bredekamp, 1987; Bredekamp & Copple, 1997; NAEYC & NAECS/SDE, 1991), the education community, specifically those who adopt a child-centered approach to early childhood education, emphasizes the classroom as individuals within a group. DAP creators identified the need to develop early childhood curriculum and assessment that is age, individually, and culturally appropriate (Bredekamp & Copple, 1997; NAEYC & NAECS/SDE, 1991). Additionally, there is a national trend toward unifying early childhood education and early childhood special education practices in early childhood teacher education programs (NAEYC, DEC/CEC, & NBPTS, 1996). Thus, teachers attempt to explicitly respond to the individuals in their classrooms despite the large numbers of children typically represented in their groups. However, what help from research do educators have to guide and support their practice?

In this chapter, a research story (McMurray, 1992, 1998) is presented that describes two children as they experience themselves as individuals in an early childhood classroom—specifically, their journey toward becoming gendered persons, students, and peers. The ethnographic approach taken in this chapter allows one to examine the classroom as many individuals within a group.

GENDER DEVELOPMENT, THE STUDENT ROLE, AND PEER RELATIONSHIPS: THE TRADITIONAL PERSPECTIVE

To fully describe an individual is a complex and difficult undertaking. There are myriad of characteristics that could be used to describe each of us. In the research shared here, three salient dimensions of an individual—that is, gender, student role, and life as a peer—are emphasized to show how children begin to explore their individuality in their earliest classrooms. How has traditional early childhood research and theory influenced teachers as they seek to support or unintentionally inhibit individuals' gender development, student role, and peer relationships?

Gender Development

Early in the gender development research literature and psychological theory, sex-typed standards and behaviors were viewed as psychologically necessary for children (for literature review, see Ruble, 1988; for theoretical review, see Bussey & Bandura, 1984; Gardner, 1982; Kohlberg, 1966; Mischel, 1966, 1970). In the classroom, boys and girls are viewed as having distinct experiences (Paley, 1984; Sadker, Sadker, & Klein, 1986). Boys and girls differ, in relation to their sex, in their toy preferences, where they prefer to play in the classroom, classroom activities, themes of play, and play mates. Parents, peers, and teachers are some of the many social reinforcers of children's sex-typed play behaviors (Huston, 1983; Liss, 1986). Traditionally, teachers have encouraged children to feel comfortable with their gender by supporting and facilitating sex-typed behaviors which they thought were important for children's early gender development—often, maintaining sex-role stereotypes. Additionally, psychological theorists have characterized children as passive receivers of gender information. For example, adults have often said "boys don't play with dolls" or "girls don't shoot guns" with the intention of maintaining traditional gender behavior. Early childhood research has shown that children are aware of such socially shared standards of masculinity and femininity (Etaugh & Liss, 1992; Fagot, Leinbach, & O'Boyle, 1992).

More recent literature is guided by the implicit assumption that sex-role differentiation may place limits on the individual child's growth and flexibility (Bem, 1983, cited in Ruble, 1988; Eisenberg, Martin, & Fabes, 1996; Huston, 1985, cited in Ruble, 1988; Lamb & Urburg, 1978, cited in Ruble, 1988; Pleck, 1981, cited in Ruble, 1988). Children are now viewed as active in the process of becoming gendered as they come together and help create and challenge gender structures and meanings (Thorne, 1993). Progressive teachers have responded to this information by adopting curricula that is nonsexist (McCormick, 1994), gender sensitive (Diller, Houston, Morgan, & Ayim, 1996), and gender equitable (Bendixen-Noe & Hall, 1996). Children are encouraged to play in different areas of the classroom (e.g., girls are assigned to play in the block area and boys are assigned to play in the housekeeping area). Also, by varying play areas and toys, teachers have attempted to encourage individuals to broaden the range of gender behaviors that they are willing to accept. Early childhood classrooms are viewed by some as settings where children can question the usual male–female dualism (Fagot, 1975; Maccoby & Jacklin, 1985) and explore other possibilities for themselves.

The Student Role

To be successful in school, children must interpret much about school and its requirements, and experience a "student role" of appropriate behavior, knowledge, and expectations that will guide their participation in the academic and social life of classrooms (Fernie, 1988; Fernie, Kantor, & Klein, 1988). This student role is communicated in a variety of subtle ways (e.g., messages transmitted through the structure of the physical environment, curriculum, and the actors' roles within the structure; Klein, 1988). Often, what the teacher says or doesn't say tells the children about what is expected of them as learners and as participants in school (Klein, 1988). This process of learning how to be a participant in the classroom and in school is referred to as *socialization*.

The traditional perspective on socialization is that children are socialized to society through schooling. According to this perspective, children are passive and are viewed as the social product of schooling (Fernie, Kantor, Klein, Meyer, & Elgas, 1988). The purpose of schooling is seen to be the transmission of the larger culture (Bar-Tal, 1978; Bruner, 1982; Callahan & Long, 1983; Dewey, 1966; Elkin & Handel, 1972; Goslin, 1965; Hamilton, 1983; Himmelweit & Swift, 1969; Katz, 1979; Kutnick,

1983; LeCompte, 1978; Spindler & Spindler, 1987). Therefore, teachers have focused their teaching on the transmission of societal standards by narrowly defining the student role as a passive receiver of information.

Peer Relationships

School not only provides a setting where children experience what school is and how to become a participant, but it also provides a setting where children experience and build relationships with other children (i.e., peers). Traditionally, researchers have studied children's social competence as an indicator of peer relationships or vice verse (Asher & Renshaw, 1981; Pellegrini & Glickman, 1990).

According to Rizzo (1988), in order for children to build solidarity and similarities, they develop complex play themes. These play themes are often misinterpreted by teachers to be violent and aggressive; therefore, "bad" for children. Thus, teachers have avoided children's social worlds and peer friendships. For the most part, these relationships have been ignored and inhibited in the classroom while permitted to develop only outside the classroom, at home, or on the playground.

BECOMING AN INDIVIDUAL GENDERED PERSON, STUDENT, AND PEER: A SHIFT TO A NEW PERSPECTIVE

Traditional research and theory have positioned children as passive receivers of information, teachers as omniscient, ideas or knowledge that can be shared with teachers and peers, and schools as places where one learns how to become a citizen of society. Research conducted in contrived situations and settings assumes that day-to-day life is static, predictable, and unchanging. However, the reality of children's lives as dynamic, complex, and exciting new adventures every day is revealed as one teaches in or observes early childhood classrooms. Therefore, there is a need for new perspectives and methodologies for studying young children.

The Sociocultural Perspective

Researchers with a sociocultural perspective (Bloome, Puro, & Theodorou, 1989; Erickson, 1982; Green & Harker, 1982; Zaharlick & Green, 1991) assume that all members of an ongoing social group are cultural beings in that they share and have learned the customary patterns for engaging in everyday life. Sociocultural researchers view school as a social setting, and classrooms as group cultures where people construct and conduct daily life (Green & Kantor, 1988; Gumperz, 1981; Havighurst & Neugarten, 1975; Sarason, 1971). Furthermore, this classroom culture is co-constructed by teachers and children as they interact in daily life (Dorr-Bremme, 1982; Erickson, 1982; Fernie et al., 1990; Fernie, Kantor, & Klein, 1988; Green & Kantor, 1988; Kantor, 1988; Kantor, Elgas, & Fernie, 1989; Klein, 1988; Mehan, 1980; Philips, 1972; Weade, 1987). From this sociocultural view, children are socialized to schooling (Blumenfeld & Meece, 1985; Corsaro, 1988; Dreeben, 1967; Erickson & Mohatt, 1982; Gearing & Epstein, 1982; Gracey, 1975; Green & Kantor, 1988; Havighurst & Neugarten, 1975; Jackson, 1968; Mehan, 1980; Sarason, 1971).

Researchers have also focused on children's lives from a sociocultural perspective, led by Corsaro's (1985) peer-culture theory. Children are viewed as co-constructing their peer culture through affiliation and activities shared. Both the school culture and the peer culture in the classroom influence and shape the other (Kantor, 1988). The preschool peer culture and school culture accommodate to one another in a dynamic intersection (Fernie, Kantor, Klein et al., 1988). Therefore, children's first experiences with school involve the simultaneous entry into two important and emergent spheres which form the participation structures of the classroom—school culture and peer culture (Fernie, Kantor, Klein et al., 1988).

The Poststructuralist Perspective

In contrast to the psychological stance, proponents of the feminist perspective (Birns & Sternglanz, 1983; Curry & Bergen, 1988; Huston, 1983) and, more specifically, the poststructuralist perspective (Davies, 1989) view children as active agents in the acquisition of gender-role understanding.

Researchers with a poststructuralist perspective believe in a nonunitary, ongoing nature of self (Davies, 1989, 1993). According to Davies, children appear to learn maleness or femaleness as if it were an "incorrigible element" of their personal and social selves. They do so through learning the "discursive practices" in which all people are positioned as either male or female. "Correct" positioning is facilitated by the interactive others each child encounters. However, Davies contended that children should be able to "take up" a range of both masculine and feminine positionings if they have access to discourse that renders it acceptable. Therefore, gender positionings, as opposed to static, enduring, and well-defined roles, can be characterized as diverse, multiple, and fluid in nature.

Positionings

Walkerdine (1981) and Davies (1989) introduced the concept of positioning or positions. Davies (1989) defined this concept as "possible ways of being." In their interpretations, positionings are primarily related to power and dominance, and therefore, related to gender. That is, males are positioned as powerful, controlling, and dominant in our culture, whereas females are positioned as powerless and submissive. In the context of this study, the concept of positionings was broadened to include other types of positionings, such as those related to being a student and a peer, in addition to gender positionings. As people interact with others, they experience themselves and the others with whom they interact in various ways, "possible ways of being." These possible ways of experiencing oneself and others are self-selected as well as offered by others. They can be accepted, rejected, or negotiated. This all occurs at the margins of awareness and simultaneous with the interactions.

Ethnographic, naturalistic observation is a lens to explore individual children and experiences related to gender, school, and peer culture. In this study, specific positionings emerged in order to describe interaction in the data. Children exhibited certain behaviors or said certain things in relation to others that were categorized as positionings. The following example illustrates how positionings were identified throughout the data. Positionings are indicated in parentheses.

Example 1

Lisa enters the small-group room wearing a cape (Identifying with Peer Culture and Masculine). She gets a carpet square and lays it down on the floor, then sits on the carpet (Self-Sufficient). As the teacher reads the story, Lisa sits beside him (Attached) and looks at the book. Lisa responds to the teacher's questions about the story (Participating and Informing). When the teacher finishes the story, he asks the children to put their carpet squares away (Helping). Lisa picks up her carpet and puts it away, then goes to the door and everyone leaves the room. [1/14—L003]

In this interaction, Lisa positioned herself in many ways. By wearing a cape, an artifact with cultural importance in the classroom's peer culture, she positioned herself as "Identifying with Peer Culture." Additionally, wearing a cape was most often associated with being a boy (it was referred to as a Batman cape by a popular peer group of boys) so, by choosing to wear a cape, Lisa positioned herself as "Masculine" as well. When she got her own carpet she positioned herself as "Self-Sufficient" and by answering questions about the book she positioned herself as both "Participating" in the group activity and

"Informing," by expressing answers and her opinions about the book. She also positioned herself as "Attached" by sitting near the teacher. When the teacher asked the children to pick up the carpets, he positioned them as "Helping," which Lisa accepted as she picked up her carpet and put it away. It can be seen that the positionings in this example were fluid, shifting, and specific to the behavior exhibited by Lisa during the interaction as opposed to a role, which would be enduring and would be used to describe behavior in general throughout the interaction.

Thirty-eight positionings[1] were identified to describe of 6,280 actions of six children over 15 days of observation for each child. As can be seen in Example 1, one action, such as wearing a cape or giving answers to questions about the book, was coded as two positionings. However, if a behavior was more accurately identified as only one positioning, then the best, most descriptive, positioning was chosen. Note that the identified positionings were descriptive of the behavior and for the most part worded in active, present tense. The fluid and dynamic nature of positionings, as seen in Example 1, called for this way of labeling the children's behaviors.

As positionings emerged from the data, several initial observations were made about them, which guided the construction of specific questions for the study. A systematic analysis of the observations was designed by taking four "sweeps" through the data. These sweeps corresponded to four general questions of interest:

1. How do individual children negotiate subject positionings as they experience the daily life of the classroom?
2. How are positionings related to three domains of study, gender, student, and peer?
3. How do children negotiate positionings?
4. How are positionings influenced by specific contexts?

The first question is the focus of this chapter.

A Multiple Perspective

To capture the negotiation of positionings and understand the complexities of how a child becomes an individual with full social membership in the classroom, a multiple perspective approach to the data was necessary. Multiple perspective research can be accomplished in several ways, including bringing different theoretical and analytical

---

[1]Definitions of positionings can be obtained from Paula McMurray-Schwarz, Ohio University Eastern, 45425 National Rd., St. Clairsville, OH 43950.

perspectives to bear on different dimensions of a single event(s) (Green & Harker, 1982). In the context of this study, a multiple perspective was used to examine social processes, specifically, the simultaneous social construction of "gender," "student," and "peer" (Fernie, Kantor, Davies, & McMurray, 1993). The conceptual framework relating to the integration of these processes originated in the collaboration among researchers (Fernie et al., 1993; Kantor, Fernie, & Scott, 1989).

The following example illustrates how a multiple perspective reveals a child's work toward becoming a student, peer, and gendered person. This interaction occurred at the end of a circle discussion time in preschool. The children and teachers had constructed a "dismissal" routine for leaving the circle area to attend story time, the next activity on the daily schedule. The children introduced their peer-culture interests by requesting that the teacher call them by their favorite characters' names such as Big Bird, Batman, or She-Ra, or their favorite animal such as kitty cat or snake as she dismissed them.

On this particular day, the teacher introduced a modification by suggesting that the children become little balloons like the ones they just sang about.

Example 2

Lisa arrived at circle discussion time wearing a cape and carrying a stuffed animal. After the group sang three songs the teacher suggested that everyone pretend to be "little balloons."

T: How about everybody make themselves into little balloons. Tiny little balloons.

The children curled up on the floor and waited to be excused from the circle.

Bob: Tap me first.
Sally: I'm She-Ra! I'm She-Ra balloon!
Bob: I'm gunnerman!
T: Okay gunnerman balloon, you can go to your group (as she tapped Bob on the shoulder).

The teacher proceeded around the circle, excusing the children by their chosen name or character. Lisa was the second to the last child to be excused.

T: You can go to your group (as she tapped Lisa on the shoulder).
Lisa: I'm Batman!
T: You can go to your group, Batman (as she tapped Lisa on the shoulder again).

Lisa left the circle area holding her cape behind her. (11/3—K016)

This dismissal routine reflected much about participation in this particular classroom. From the school culture perspective, the co-constructed nature of the game (i.e., the fact that the game was shaped by both teachers and students) reveals the positionings related to teacher and student that are available to each other in collaboration. In other words, this was a classroom where children actively participated in the construction of school events and where teachers accommodated and supported the ideas of the children.

Taking a peer-culture perspective, it can be seen that children's ideas in this example were tied to their interests with peers. Superhero themes and roles in general were very salient in this classroom's peer culture and were introduced into this school culture dismissal routine by the children. Therefore, in supporting children's ideas, teachers supported the peer culture.

Finally, a gender perspective revealed the salience of gender in this example that the school and peer culture perspectives disregard. Lisa's request to be called "Batman," rather than "Batgirl," reflects a gender positioning that she is choosing for herself. Lisa is positioning herself with the boys, and more specifically with a prominent core group of five boys, and chose a male positioning rather than a female positioning.

A multiple perspective allowed one to see how in one context positionings related to being a student, a peer, and gendered were integrated and occurred simultaneously: the dismissal routine itself was part of participating as a student in school culture; the request to be called "Batman" was tied to peer culture; and Lisa's choice of "Batman," rather than "Batgirl," contradicted the dominant gender discourse by positioning herself in a positioning usually only available to males.

In the "Batman" example, Lisa showed how she regularly created her individuality in this classroom. It was characteristic of Lisa to align herself with a group using the right language, choosing the right artifacts, using them with the appropriate social action, and recognizing the theme of the moment. This example also shows that the subject positionings an individual chooses for him or herself might be different from those he or she is offered. Additionally, positionings experienced in one context, or in one moment, might dramatically contrast with those experienced in another context or moment.

It was the nature of this classroom and the teachers in this classroom that allowed this integration to occur. The teachers in this preschool had a child-centered approach to early childhood education, in fact, the motto of the program was "working from the ideas of children." The teachers built their curriculum around this philosophy by encouraging children to be active participants in the generation and construction of the curriculum. Therefore, teachers were open to children's ideas, peer culture, and gender flexibility, which supported children as they negotiated positionings in search of their individuality.

Lisa and Nate: Revealing Individual Pathways Through the Group

Six children, two girls and four boys, represented the target children for observation and analysis in the original study (McMurray, 1992, 1998). Two of these children, one girl and one boy, are described in this chapter. These children were purposely selected from the group of children enrolled in the school because of their diverse positionings as students, peers, and gendered persons, which were determined from previous studies and the ethnographic history of this classroom. For example, Lisa was chosen for her unique relationship to the salient boy's peer group in the classroom and her seemingly flexible gender orientation. But Nate was selected for his flexible gender orientation and opposition to the school culture. These children differed in their relationships to the school culture (i.e., one of the targeted children seemed comfortable in school culture activities whereas the other seemed uncomfortable).

A purposeful sampling technique was used to select 16 days of videotape, for a total of 96 hours of viewing, for analysis in this study. Fieldnotes, teacher retrospective notes, and interviews were used for clarification, on specific events and analysis verification. The classroom teachers, Rebecca and Donna, were interviewed throughout the collection of data and data analysis. Finally, I attended research meetings with two of the original investigators and other researchers where the classroom "reality" was constructed.

Individual Profiles

For all of the focus children, their subject positionings in the classroom were a negotiated process, however, the amount of control they exhibited over how they experienced themselves in this classroom differed as well as the content of their negotiations. Additionally, the diversity of experiences individual children encounter in a single setting was revealed. Individuals' positionings can be compared to gain insight into how they co-construct themselves as persons through their own actions and those of others.

One difference between individual children was the extent of their negotiations, that is, some children negotiated positionings more often than others. Another difference between individual children was the range of positionings that he or she exhibited (i.e., some children exhibited more positionings than others). Also, individual children differ in the total number of positionings that they exhibited and the amount of control they demonstrated over their positionings.

The following profiles of two of the six targeted children illustrate the similarities and differences between individual children as they negotiated positionings. How individual children experience becoming gendered, a student, and a peer, including the range and content of their positionings, is discussed for each child.

Lisa: At Home in School Culture and Peer-Culture Worlds

At the time of the study, Lisa was 3 years old and the youngest child in her family. She has one stepsister, who was 17 years old. Her mother and father live together and were 36 and 52 years old, respectively. Lisa's mother is a registered nurse and student; her father is a physician. This was Lisa's second experience in a group setting (she had previously attended a play group), but her first experience in a formal school setting. Lisa was one of two girls in the sample for this study.

Rebecca, one of the lead teachers, described Lisa in very stereotyped terms as "a pretty little girl, slender, quiet, quite compliant and easy going." Rebecca remembered that, as time passed, Lisa exhibited "a very funny, more outgoing, teasing sense of humor."

Lisa, unlike many other girls in an early childhood classroom, seemed extremely interested in the boys' peer group. It was exciting and interesting to watch her interact with the other children, and specifically the boys, in the classroom. It was unusual to see a female obtain a position in the peer group that did not compromise her chosen individuality, particularly as it relates to gender.

As an individual, Lisa showed diversity, multiplicity, fluidity, and range in the positionings she constructed for herself. Specifically, in terms of gender positionings, she constructed a place for herself that was not accessible to many of the other children. Lisa is a child who seems to be able to create and maintain positionings not available to or not desired by most of the other children. In this sense, she is an unusual child with a distinct profile in the classroom. She is competent in both the school culture and the peer culture and readily sought participation in both spheres of the classroom.

Lisa was the only girl accepted into the play of a lively group of boys known by the research team as the "core group" for their salience, power, and influence in the classroom (Elgas, 1988; Elgas, Klein, Kantor, & Fernie, 1989). The core group often incorporated peer-culture themes into their play as well as in school culture activities. They often created themes, such as "Batman" or "gunnerman," in which they were the only ones who knew the rules. The themes created by the group often involved aggressive play and Lisa's mother was uncomfortable with her daughter being involved in this aggressive play; however, Lisa appeared to thoroughly enjoy the rough and tumble play characteristic of the boys' peer group.

In the following example, Lisa negotiates positionings in the block area. This example illustrates Lisa's interest and involvement in the core peer group.

Example 3

Student
Teacher: You guys playing cowboys or something?
Bob: We're playing gunnermen [as he walked away carrying a stick and wearing a cowboy hat].

Lisa watched the boys for a long time and then found herself a stick. Paul ran past Lisa.

Paul: Bang, Bang!
Lisa: Bang, Bang!

Lisa turned to the student teacher and another child and pointed her stick at them.

Student
Teacher: Ah, Lisa's got one, too.

Lisa pointed her stick at Paul and Kevin.

Lisa: Bang, Bang!
Paul: Get out of here. Get out of here. You can't get me. Bang! Bang! Bang [to Lisa]!

Lisa pointed her stick at him and Kevin then turned and pointed her stick at the student teacher.

Lisa: Bang! Bang!
Student
Teacher: Bang [to Lisa]!
Paul: Bangleader? Leader [to Kevin]? Leader?
Paul: Banglady! Banglady [from the top of the climber while looking in Lisa's direction]!
Ken: Banglady [pointing his stick at another boy in the block area while laughing]!
Lisa: I'm a gunnerman!
Paul: Bang [as Lisa walks by]!
Student
Teacher: I'm a gunnerman, too. [10/15- L009]

Here, we see that Lisa was initially positioned by Paul as "Pretending" and "Feminine" when he called her "banglady." She rejected the positioning of "Feminine" and positioned herself as

"Masculine," "gunnerman." Additionally, Paul positioned Lisa as "Participating in Peer Culture" when he called her by a character's name related to the ongoing play theme and shooting her with stick guns. Lisa did not reject being positioned as "Participating in Peer Culture," she used her stick to shoot back at Paul and the other boys and seemed to be quite interested in their play. This episode was similar to others that were witnessed by teachers. As Rebecca remembered:

> She (Lisa) also became a pretend gun-toting member of the exciting group of boys in the room. She would play right in there with them, in the middle of their rough and tumble play in the block corner. It was funny to hear her shout things like "Quick! We need to save the ship!" (personal communication, November 1991)

For instance, another self-positioning that Lisa displayed in Example 3 was "Playing with Adults" because she was trying to engage the student teacher in shooting play. The teacher accepted Lisa as her play partner when she "shot" Lisa and when she indicated that she was "a gunnerman, too." This behavior from a teacher in another preschool might not be accepted, but the teachers in this preschool, as mentioned earlier, were willing to support children's choices in the kind of play themes and gender positionings in which they were interested.

However, teachers did not allow violent or aggressive behavior that would cause harm toward anyone. The philosophy in this preschool was that children use aggressive play themes (i.e., act aggressively) to work through developmental changes and as a way to define their peer culture. They felt that children need to vent their frustrations and aggressions, as well as experience power and control over their environments, through play. Also, teachers understood that if they did not allow this kind of play that it would go "underground." Therefore, they permitted this type of play with specific limits and ground rules. For instance, they permitted gun play but without realistically looking play guns; in other words, the children could only use classroom materials (they often used rhythm sticks or Lego guns). The teachers monitored play and set limits for safety reasons. Children were not allowed to hurt themselves or another child, and each child was respected if he or she did not want to participate (e.g., if he or she did not want to be "shot"). Additionally, teachers discussed aggressive play with individuals and with all of the children as a group to make them aware of how their actions affect others and how they are responsible for their own actions. In summary, these teachers established "classrooms as safe havens from violence" (Slaby, Roedell, Arezzo, & Hendrix, 1995) which complied with the position statement on violence (NAEYC, 1993).

What was more interesting about this example, and more relevant to understanding how Lisa constructed herself as an individual, was the salient gender issue present in the interaction. Peer culture and gender understanding intersected in Example 3. Lisa wanted to be accepted by the dominant peer culture, which was co-constructed by the boys. As it turned out, many girls were interested in this group of boys, but Lisa had regular access and membership. She used the right materials in the right way to gain access to this peer-constructed game. Lisa appeared to understand what was important to, what it takes to be a part of, and what positionings were important to the peer culture. Also, Lisa wanted to be seen as having equal power and status in the group and to be recognized as a "gunnerman." She did not want to be distinguished by her gender. This is evident from the interview with Donna, one of the lead teachers, who indicated that she remembered Lisa as a child who was comfortable both in traditionally feminine roles and traditionally masculine roles.

Lisa seemed equally adept in both peer culture, as discussed earlier, and school culture activities. She often participated during circle and small-group times. Lisa rarely needed to be positioned as "Socially Responsible" by the teachers, which indicates that she usually followed rules and caused little disruption during school culture activities. Donna stated that Lisa seemed to know the school culture well and was a competent member of the group. She also discussed Lisa's involvement with the boys' peer group and how she was able to obtain access to their play.

By being adaptable in both cultures of the classroom, Lisa showed real social brinkmanship. Although the boys' peer group was interested in being oppositional toward adults, Lisa was able to bridge the school and peer culture by not being oppositional to adults but still being involved and accepted in the boys' peer group play. Therefore, Lisa was competent in both school and peer-culture domains and her positionings indicated that gender was a salient issue as she constructed herself as an individual in preschool.

Interestingly, Donna remembered that in the following school year Lisa did not seem to be as interested in the boys' play themes but was frequently playing in the housekeeping area with other girls, something that she was not observed doing during the year that the data were collected for this study. This finding is important because it leads one to believe that not only would children appear different in another school setting but they may also look different in another year. Thus, children negotiate positionings differently and position themselves differently from one year to the next. In Lisa's case, it might lead one to speculate that the high salience and popularity of the core peer group might have motivated her to get involved in this particular school year, whereas in the following year the core peer group was not as prominent in the classroom; therefore, not as interesting to Lisa.

Nate: Negotiating with teachers

Nate is the third of five children in the family and was 4 years old at the time of the study. Nate's father is an architect, and his mother a music student. Nate's attendance in the preschool was his first school experience. Rebecca described Nate as "an adorable boy but very needy."

Nate was involved in many extended negotiations of positionings. Most of his negotiations involved school culture activities. Specifically, Nate's teachers had difficulty getting him interested in coming to group. In contrast to Lisa, who willingly joined and participated in group activities, Nate often rejected others positioning him as "Participating" and almost always had to be coaxed to join the rest of the children for circle, an activity, or story. Due to his initial aversive reaction to structured activities, Nate was not a participant during small group or circle time. He appeared to be attentive, once he came to group, but he did not always participate in singing or discussions. Nate was not a peer player, but was a teacher-player (Elgas, 1988). Although he spent some time with the core group, he was with teachers the majority of the time. Additionally, his positionings in peer culture, and school culture, were often rejected by others, as opposed to Lisa's positionings, which were accepted in similar situations. However, similar to Lisa, Nate showed a wide range and diversity of positionings, primarily related to gender.

As can be seen from the following interaction, Nate often exhibited noncompliance during school culture activities, especially at the beginning of the activity. It was difficult for Rebecca to get Nate to come to group. Rebecca recalled:

> One of his strategies for getting attention from me was to resist coming to group times, to be non-compliant whenever he could, and to need my help. (personal communication, November 1991)

The following example is a typical negotiation for Nate during the transition to school culture activities.

Example 4

Nate goes to group where everyone is waiting for Rebecca to come over to read the story for today. Instead of sitting down on the pillows with the rest of the group, Nate goes to the typewriter and begins typing.

Nate:　　Look what happened [as he taps the student teacher on the shoulder and points to the typewriter]!

Student
Teacher:　Come on and sit down Nate. [pause] Nate we're going to get ready for story time so why don't you come and sit down with all of us.

Nate continues to type on the typewriter.

Student
Teacher:　You can play with the typewriter tomorrow.

As the student teacher finishes her sentence, Rebecca enters and reaches out toward Nate.

Rebecca:　Nate, come on over lets talk about something. Come here. Come guys.

Nate continues to type. Rebecca begins talking to the other children, then:

Nate:　　Maybe the typewriter is broken [as he looks toward Rebecca who is now ready to start reading].

Rebecca:　Yes, there's no ribbon in there. Why don't you come over? We're going to read this story...

Nate looks toward Rebecca and the group but stays in the chair at the typewriter.

Student
Teacher:　Nate, come sit next to me and listen to the story. Come on.

Nate comes over and sits by the student teacher, then moves so that he is sitting opposite of Rebecca. He looks at the book as Rebecca reads and answers question and comments about the story. [1/13—H002]

Nate frequently had to be coaxed to come to group. In this interaction he positioned himself as "Not Participating" when he went to the typewriter instead of to the pillows. The student teacher positioned him as "Participating" by asking him to join the group. Nate rejected this other positioning by staying at the typewriter and positioning himself as both "Not Participating" and "Noncomplying" (5% of his positionings). This negotiation went back and forth with Nate and the teachers until he finally sat down to listen to the story, positioned as "Participating." Many of Nate's negotiations were similar to this one in length and content. He had more negotiations than the other children, and he had the most extended negotiations out of all of the targeted children.

Nate exhibited the highest number of student positionings, 76%. Many of these were positionings such as "Participating," "Socially Responsible," "Attached," "Attention-Seeking," and "Announcing," which were related to his difficulty in getting involved in a group activity. Sometimes he did not participate at all by sitting away from the group during circle or small group. The positioning "Not Participating" was accepted by the teachers if the child sat in the cubbies or on the stairs and did not disturb the group. Once Nate was coaxed to join the group, and if he was interested in the activity, he appeared to be quite competent in the school culture. Also, he frequently vied for a physical position at circle or small group that was next to Rebecca, often positioning himself as "Attached."

Nate seemed to be an occasional peer group player. He did not seem overwhelmingly interested in the peer group like Lisa. He was not always accepted by the core group. Rebecca recalled the following:

> He didn't have many friends in the class although he played with Maria sometimes. Maria and he had in common their intense interest in me! (personal communication, November 1991)

Nate would barge right into peer group activities in an intrusive and disruptive way, whereas Lisa would observe the group for long periods of time before trying to gain access to their play. Donna said that Nate was "in and out" of the peer group and that he did not seem overly concerned about being a regular member of the group and was satisfied exploring the other areas of the classroom.

Additionally, he tended to spend a lot of time with teachers. Donna remembered that Nate was very interested in adult contact especially with Rebecca. He was constantly positioning himself as "Attention-Seeking" (9% of his positionings) in relation to Rebecca. He would repeat her name several times from across the room until Rebecca answered his call. Rebecca remembered that he "called my name all day long and I admit it was frustrating for me at times."

Nate positioned himself in a wide range of gender positionings. In the next example in the housekeeping area, Nate accepts the positioning of "Mom," Bob became a hunter, and William appears to be the father as they constructed a play scenario in the housekeeping area.

Example 5

Nate and William were in the housekeeping area together.

William: What do you want for dinner?
Nate: Huh?
William: What do you want for dinner?

Nate goes to the refrigerator and opens it. William follows.

William: What do you want for breakfast?
Nate: We're having eggs. We just need two eggs and we need and we need some water and we need some (inaudible).

Bob: Hi Ma (pause) Hi Mom.
Nate: I I I'm the Mom.
Bob: Hi Mom. I've got a lot of guns, okay (carrying a bunch of sticks)?
Nate: Okay.
Bob: They're to shoot animals.
Nate: What?
Bob: I said they're to shoot animals so we can eat'em.
Nate: Thanks. Thanks a lot.
William: Put'em right here (to Bob as he points to the table).
Bob: I'll put them in the cart (pointing to the baby buggy).
Nate: Dinner's ready (walking over to the table)! Now the rabbit is going to eat cauliflower.
Bob: Well, I'm goin' huntin', okay (sitting on the floor, rearranging the sticks)?
Nate: What (while taking care of the bunny)?
Bob: I'm goin' hunting.

Bob leaves the area and Nate shakes his head in approval. After a short time, Bob returns with a plastic elephant in his hand and gives it to Nate.

Nate: Thanks (as he examines the elephant).

Bob walks away. Nate walks over to William.

Nate: He caught one elephant (pause) honey.
William: What?
Nate: He caught one elephant. (10/23—K012)

Nate's acceptance of the cross-sexed positioning of "Mom" serves the moment of play (i.e., there were no females in the area at the time). Children come together to share participation (Corsaro, 1988) and this play event needed someone to be the "Mom" to be accomplished. One wonders if a girl had been available, if she would have been offered the role of "Mom"; we can only speculate. In accepting the traditional female positioning in this interaction, along with various positionings Nate assumed in other interactions, Nate showed diversity, flexibility, and range in his gender positionings.

However, as opposed to Bob who offered a "Feminine" positioning and positioned himself as "Masculine," a "hunter," Nate was often observed doing and playing in traditionally feminine ways. For example, Nate liked Barbies and dressing up. The disturbing thing to the teachers about Nate's interest in dressing up was that he hid it from the others in the classroom, seeming to be ashamed of wanting to dress up in "girl's" clothing. Rebecca remembered:

His mom worried a little about his interest in trying on women's clothes. We tried to reassure her; we worried too, not because he tried on the clothes but because he had picked up a shame feeling about it. He would take the girls' dress-up clothes and hide in the bathroom or the climber to try them on. (personal communication, November 1991)

Donna also indicated that the most salient positionings that Nate exhibited were related to gender. She stated that she remembered that he hid when dressing up and that the teachers were very concerned. However, Nate was also observed participating in traditionally masculine activities.

Nate positioned himself in traditionally feminine ways (19 times) slightly more often than in traditionally masculine ways (12 times). In contrast, Lisa positioned herself in traditionally masculine ways (26 times) more often than in traditionally feminine ways (8 times). Thus, these varied positionings showed that Nate, similar to Lisa, had a wide range of gender positionings available to him. At the same time, although Nate did not exhibit a greater quantity of gender positionings than most of the other children, it was the content of his gender positionings that determined their salience.

A NEW PERSPECTIVE: IMPLICATIONS FOR EARLY CHILDHOOD CURRICULA

An ethnographic approach to exploring the early childhood classroom, reveals children actively constructing themselves as individuals within a group—as students, peers, and gendered persons. Additionally, children integrate student, peer, and gender domains through the complex interactions that they construct with adults and peers in the early childhood classroom. This ethnographic perspective has implications for early childhood curricula as discussed in the following sections.

Individual Pathways Through the Classroom

Children create, construct, and maintain themselves as individuals in distinctive ways. The social world of the classroom is complex and is by definition a group experience, and yet there are individual pathways through this world. Children create themselves in a variety of ways in relation to others, which can be captured in distinctive profiles.

Individual children find their place in the social world of the classroom in innovative ways as they choose subjectively different positionings. Children participate in the construction of the social world as well as create different pathways through these social worlds; thus, the negotiation of positionings is both social and individual. In other words, it is the interaction of an individual child with his or her social world that enables him or her to construct him or herself as an individual person.

Most research focuses either on the individual (e.g., in the case study tradition) or on the group and social world (e.g., in the ethnographic tradition). However, a situated examination of individual children as they interact within their social world reveals that focusing on just one, the individual, or the other, the social world, does not reveal the true complexity of the interaction between the individual and the social world. A multiple perspective allows this complexity of children's social development and individual development to be revealed.

Teachers need to understand that the classroom is created as a different place for each child; that is, children experience being individuals—students, peers, and gendered persons—differently. By understanding that individuals experience the classroom in different ways through interaction with the social world, teachers can support, facilitate, and encourage children to seek their individual pathways through school. Teachers need to see group life as well as individual life in relation to and within group. A child-centered, developmentally appropriate curriculum facilitates and supports children's chosen and constructed individual pathways through the group journey.

The Integration of Cultures by Individuals

Although the process of "becoming a student" and "becoming a peer" has previously been recognized as interpretive, constructive, and participatory and as a complex, ongoing, and active process on the part of children as well as teachers (Corsaro, 1988; Fernie, Kantor, & Klein, 1988; Gumperz, 1986; Kantor, Elgas, & Fernie, 1989), the integration of these processes with the process of "becoming a gendered person" is revealed in this research on positionings. School culture and peer culture, then, are not given entities, but are dynamic, unfolding, constructed products of patterned ways of perceiving, believing, acting, and evaluating that develop over time (Goodenough, 1970) in the classroom. The ethnographic perspective reveals these patterned ways of behaving as they are being constructed by children's creation, negotiation, and integration of school culture, peer culture, and gender positionings.

Early childhood teachers have continually recognized, either consciously or unconsciously, that children's development is integrated and complex. This is reflected in the movement toward more integrated curricula, and developmentally appropriate practices, for the early years (Bredekamp, 1987). Teachers need to constantly remind themselves of the complexity at which children function on a daily basis. Teachers need to incorporate children's individual and gender stances and interests into the school culture. Additionally, it is important for teachers to value peer culture by supporting children's peer interests that are constructed and integrated into school culture activities. By encouraging this freedom and opportunity, teachers can build children's self-confidence, social competence, and gender identities.

The Dynamic Nature of Individual Negotiations

In child-centered, developmentally appropriate settings, children are active and in control of how they experience their social worlds; that is, children actively construct their own positionings in the child-centered early childhood classroom. This active construction is consistent with related analyses of early childhood classrooms (Elgas, 1988; Fernie et al., 1990; Miller, 1991). The negotiation of positionings in the study, particularly self-positionings, or reflexive positionings (Davies & Harre, 1990) on the part of the children, shows one's active production of culture. It is impressive what children accomplish at such a young age in a complex social world such as the early childhood classroom.

Therefore, teachers need to prepare an environment that is adaptable to the dynamic nature of individuals as they construct and negotiate the cultures of the classroom. Additionally, the environment should facilitate individually appropriate curriculum. To do this, the teacher needs to expose children to a broad range of diverse activities, books, materials, pictures, role models, and visitors and to select these experiences through critical evaluation (Derman-Sparks, 1987; Derman-Sparks & the A.B.C. Task Force, 1989; Jones & Derman-Sparks, 1992; Leipzig, 1987; Saracho & Spodek, 1983; Swadener, 1988, 1989; Swadener, Cahill, Marsh, & Arnold, in press; Whaley & Swadener, 1990). These experiences should reflect an understanding of the individuals within the classroom recognizing their diverse and individual backgrounds (Whaley & Swadener, 1990) as well as their actively "created self," as revealed in this chapter.

The Co-Construction of Classroom Life by Individuals

The ethnographic perspective reveals that there are two broad spheres of activity within the classroom, that of the school culture and the peer culture, which children and teachers co-construct through daily interaction (Elgas, 1988; Fernie et al., 1990). Furthermore, these spheres appear to be overlapped and integrated (Fernie, Kantor, Klein et al., 1988; Kantor, 1988). The findings discussed in this chapter contribute to the line of research on socialization to schooling, as opposed to socialization through schooling. From this perspective, children and teachers co-construct the preschool culture.

These spheres are constructed and reconstructed over time. There is a link between positionings, at a microanalytic level, and the intersections of school culture and peer culture, at a macroanalytic level. As individuals position themselves and are positioned by others, they are simultaneously co-constructing with others the intersections of school culture and peer culture (Fernie et al., 1990). Each of these processes influence the other. Only by understanding the co-construction of school culture and peer culture and the intersections of these cultures can the true complexity of individuals be revealed.

In general, it is important for teachers to see the preschool classroom as a joint construction between participants. Teachers need to realize that children are active agents in the construction of their social lives and not just sponges ready to "soak up" any information that they have to offer. The culture of the classroom, and the peer culture, are continually changing as teachers and children conduct their daily lives. Patterns of rules, roles, and rituals do develop over time; however, as seen by examining children's positionings, they are diverse, multiple, and fluid, and occur simultaneously. Teachers' awareness of this complexity will allow them to be flexible with and adaptable to individuals within groups, as well as respond to children's self-positionings in positive, supportive, and accepting ways.

SUMMARY

An ethnographic lens reveals the following: (a) children's individual pathways through school; (b) the multiplicity, integration, and simultaneity of children's construction of themselves as individuals; (c) children actively establishing themselves as individuals through daily interactions; and (d) the co-constructed nature of life in an early childhood classroom. Teachers should use the knowledge gained from this new perspective to (a) develop child-centered, developmentally appropriate curricula that support children's individual pathways through group; (b) incorporate children's individual stances as well as peer culture interests into school culture; (c) balance individual rights and negotiations of self with group rights as they occur in the dynamic world of the classroom; and (d) understand, support, facilitate, and accept individuals as they actively construct themselves as persons in the early childhood classroom.

REFERENCES

Asher, S., & Renshaw, P. (1981). Children without friends: Social knowledge and social skill training. In S. R. Asher & J. M. Gottman (Eds.), *The development of children's friendships* (pp. 207-241). Cambridge: Cambridge University Press.

Bar-Tal, D. (1978). Social outcomes of the schooling process and their taxonomy. In D. Bar-Tal & L. Saxe (Eds.), *Social psychology of education: Theory and research* (pp. 149-164). Washington, DC: Wiley.

Bendixen-Noe, M. K., & Hall, L. D. (1996). The quest for gender equity in America's schools: From preschool and beyond. *Journal of Early Childhood Teacher Education, 17*(2), 50-57.

Birns, B., & Sternglanz, S. H. (1983). Sex-role socialization: Looking back and looking ahead. In M. B. Liss (Ed.), *Social and cognitive skills: Sex roles and children's play* (pp. 235-251). New York: Academic Press.

Bloome, D., Puro, P., & Theodorou, E. (1989). Procedural display and classroom lessons. *Curriculum Inquiry, 19*(3), 265-291.

Blumenfeld, P. C., & Meece, J. L. (1985). Life in classrooms revisited. *Theory Into Practice, 24*(1), 50-56.

Bredekamp, S. (1987). *Developmentally appropriate practice in early childhood programs serving children from birth through age 8.* Washington, DC: NAEYC.

Bredekamp, S., & Copple, C. (1997). *Developmentally appropriate practice in early childhood programs* (rev. ed.). Washington, DC: NAEYC.

Bruner, J. (1982, January). Schooling children in a nasty climate. *Psychology Today,* 57-63.

Bussey, K., & Bandura, A. (1984). Influence of gender constancy and social power on sex linked modeling. *Journal of Personality and Social Psychology, 47*(6), 1292-1302.

Callahan, R. C., & Long, V. O. (1983). Socialization and alienation: Perspectives on schooling. *The Clearing House, 56,* 418-420.

Corsaro, W. A. (1985). *Friendship and peer culture in the early years.* Norwood, NJ: Ablex.

Corsaro, W. A. (1988). Routines in the peer culture of American and Italian nursery school children. *Sociology of Education, 61,* 1-14.

Curry, N., & Bergen, D. (1988). The relationship of play to emotional, social and gender/sex role development. In D. Bergen (Ed.), *Play as a medium for learning and development: A handbook of theory and practice* (pp. 107-132). Portsmouth, NH: Heinemann.

Davies, B. (1989). *Frogs and snails and feminist tales: Preschool children and gender.* Sydney, Australia: Allen & Unwin.

Davies, B. (1993). *Shards of glass: Children reading and writing beyond gendered identities.* Cresskill, NJ: Hampton Press.

Davies, B., & Harre, R. (1990). Positioning: Conversation and the production of selves. *Journal for the Theory of Social Behavior, 20*(1).

Derman-Sparks, L. (1987). "It isn't fair!" Anti-bias curriculum for young children. In B. Neugebauer (Ed.), *Alike and different: Exploring our humanity with young children* (pp. 8-15). Redmond, WA: Exchange Press.

Derman-Sparks, L., & the A.B.C. Task Force. (1989). *Anti-bias curriculum: Tools for empowering young children.* Washington, DC: NAEYC.

Dewey, J. (1966). *Democracy and education.* New York: The Free Press.

Diller, A., Houston, B., Morgan, K. P., & Ayim, M. (1996). *The gender question in education: Theory, pedagogy, and politics.* Boulder, CO: Westview Press.

Dorr-Bremme, D. (1982). *Behaving and making sense: Creating social organization in the classroom.* Unpublished doctoral dissertation, Harvard University, Cambridge, MA.

Dreeben, R. (1967). The contribution of schooling to the learning of norms. *Harvard Educational Review, 37,* 211-237.

Eisenberg, N., Martin, C., & Fabes, R. (1996). Gender development and gender effects. In D. Berliner & R. Calfee (Eds.), *Handbook of educational psychology* (pp. 358-396). New York: MacMillan.

Elgas, M. M. (1988). *The construction of a preschool peer culture: The role of objects and play styles.* Unpublished doctoral dissertation, The Ohio State University, Columbus.

Elgas, P., Klein, E., Kantor, R., & Fernie, D. (1989). Play and the peer culture: Play styles and object use. *Journal Of Research in Childhood Education, 3*(2), 142-153.

Elkin, F., & Handel, G. (1972). *The child and society: The process of socialization.* New York: Random House.

Etaugh, C., & Liss, M. B. (1992). Home, school and playroom: Training grounds for adult gender roles. *Sex Roles, 26*(3/4), 129-147.

Erickson, F. (1982). Classroom discourse as improvisation: Relationships between academic task structure and social participation structure in lessons. In L. Wilkinson (Ed.), *Communicating in the classroom* (pp. 153-181). New York: Academic Press.

Erickson, F., & Mohatt, G. (1982). Cultural organization of participation structures in two classrooms of Indian students. In G. Spindler (Ed.), *Doing the ethnography of schooling: Educational anthropology in action* (pp. 133-174). New York: Holt, Rinehart & Winston.

Fagot, B. I. (1975). *Teacher reinforcement of feminine-preferred behavior revisited.* Paper presented at the Biennial Meeting of the Society for Research in Child Development, Denver, CO.

Fagot, B. I., Leinbach, M. D., & O'Boyle, C. (1992). Gender labeling, gender stereotyping, and parenting behaviors. *Developmental Psychology, 28*(2), 225-230.

Fernie, D. E. (1988). Becoming a student: Messages from first settings. *Theory Into Practice, 27*(1), 3-10.

Fernie, D., Kantor, R., Davies, B., & McMurray, P. (1993). Learning to be a person in the preschool: Creating integrated gender, school culture, and peer culture positionings. *International Journal of Qualitative Studies in Education, 6*(2), 95-110.

Fernie, D. E., Kantor, R., & Klein, E. L. (1988). This issue. *Theory Into Practice, 27*(1), 2.

Fernie, D. E., Kantor, R., Klein, E., Meyer, C., & Elgas, P. (1988). Becoming students and becoming ethnographers in a preschool. *Journal of Research in Childhood Education, 3*(2), 132-141.

Fernie, D. E., Kantor, R., Scott, J. A., McMurray Schwarz, P., Kesner, J., & Klein, E. (1990, April). *The honeymooners: Teachers and children co-construct the school culture of a preschool.* Paper presented at the annual conference of the American Educational Research Association, Boston, MA.

Gardner, H. (1982). *Developmental psychology: An introduction.* Boston: Little, Brown.

Gearing, F., & Epstein, P. (1982). Learning to wait: An ethnographic probe into the operations of an item of hidden curriculum. In G. Spindler (Ed.), *Doing the ethnography of schooling: Educational anthropology in action* (pp. 241-267). New York: Holt, Rinehart & Winston.

Goodenough, W. H. (1970). *Description and comparison in cultural anthropology.* Chicago: Aldine.

Goslin, D. A. (1965). *The school in contemporary society.* Glenview, IL: Scott, Foresman.

Gracey, H. L. (1975). Learning the student role: Kindergarten as academic boot camp. In H. R. Stub (Ed.), *The sociology of education: A sourcebook* (pp. 82-95). Homewood, IL: Dorsey Press.

Green, J., & Harker, J. (1982). Gaining access to learning: Conversational, social, and cognitive demands of group participation. In L. C. Wilkinson (Ed.), *Communicating in the classroom* (pp. 183-222). New York: Academic Press.

Green, J., & Kantor, R. (1988, July). *Exploring the complexity of language and learning in the life of the classroom.* Paper presented at the Language and Learning Symposium, University of Queensland, Brisbane, Australia.

Gumperz, J. J. (1981). Conversational inference and classroom learning. In J. L. Green & C. Wallat (Eds.), *Ethnography and language in educational settings* (pp. 3-23). Norwood, NJ: Ablex.

Gumperz, J. (1986). Interactional sociolinguistics in the study of schooling. In J. Cook-Gumperz (Ed.), *The social construction of literacy* (pp. 45-68). New York: Cambridge University Press.

Hamilton, S. F. (1983). The social side of schooling: Ecological studies of classrooms and schools. *The Elementary School Journal, 83*(4), 313-334.

Havighurst, R. J., & Neugarten, B. L. (1975). *Society and education.* Boston: Allyn & Bacon.

Himmelweit, H. T., & Swift, B. (1969). A model for the understanding of school as a socializing agent. In P. Mussen, J. Langer, & M. Covington (Eds.), *Trends and issues in developmental psychology* (pp. 154-181). New York: Holt, Rinehart & Winston.

Huston, A. C. (1983). Sex-typing. In E. M. Hetherington (Ed.), & P.H. Mussen (Series Ed.), *Handbook of child psychology: Vol. 4. Socialization, personality, and social development* (pp. 387-468). New York: Wiley.

Jackson, P. W. (1968). *Life in classrooms.* New York: Holt, Rinehart & Winston.

Jones, E., & Derman-Sparks, L. (1992). Meeting the challenge of diversity. *Young Children, 47*(2), 12-18.

Kantor, R. (1988). Creating school meaning in preschool curriculum. *Theory Into Practice, 27,* 25-35.

Kantor, R., Elgas, P. M., & Fernie, D. E. (1989). First the look and then the sound: Creating conversations at circle time. *Early Childhood Research Quarterly, 4*(4), 433-448.

Kantor, R., Fernie, D., & Scott, J. (1989). *The honeymooners: Teachers and children co-construct the school culture of a preschool.* Paper presented at the University of Tennessee Continuum on Qualitative Studies in Early Childhood Education, Knoxville.

Katz, L. (1979). The educator's role in socialization. *Journal of Research and Development in Education, 13*(1), 100-104.

Klein, E. L. (1988). How is a teacher different from a mother? Young children's perceptions of the social roles of significant adults. *Theory Into Practice, 27*(1), 36-43.

Kohlberg, L. A. (1966). A cognitive-developmental analysis of children's sex-role concepts and attitudes. In E. E. Maccoby (Ed.), *The development of sex differences* (pp. 82-172). Stanford, CA: Stanford University Press.

Kutnick, P. (1983). *Relating to learning: Toward a developmental social psychology of the primary school.* London: George Allen & Unwin.

LeCompte, M. (1978). Learning to work: The hidden curriculum of the classroom. *Anthropology and Education Quarterly, 9*(1), 22-37.

Leipzig, J. (1987). Helping whole children grow: Non-sexist childrearing for infants and toddlers. In B. Neugebauer (Ed.), *Alike and different: Exploring our humanity with young children* (pp. 36-45). Redmond, WA: Exchange Press.

Liss, M. B. (1986). Play of boys and girls. In G. Fein & M. Rivkin (Eds.), *The young child at play: Reviews of research* (Vol. 4, pp. 127-136). Washington, DC: NAEYC.

Maccoby, E. E., & Jacklin, C. N. (1985). *Gender segregation in nursery school: Predictors and outcomes.* Paper presented at the SRCD Meeting, Toronto.

McCormick, T. M. (1994). *Creating the nonsexist classroom: A multicultural approach.* New York: Teacher's College Press.

McMurray, P. A. (1992). *The construction, negotiation, and integration of gender, school culture, and peer culture, positionings in preschool.* Unpublished doctoral dissertation, The Ohio State University, Columbus.

McMurray, P. A. (1998). Gender behaviors in an early childhood classroom through an ethnographic lens. *Qualitative Studies in Education, 11*(2), 271-290.

Mehan, H. (1980). The competent student. *Anthropology and Education Quarterly, 11*(3), 131-152.

Miller, S. (1991). *Diverse paths to literacy in a preschool classroom: A sociocultural perspective.* Unpublished doctoral dissertation, The Ohio State University, Columbus.

Mischel, W. (1966). A social-learning view of sex differences in behavior. In E. E. Maccoby (Ed.), *The development of sex differences* (pp. 56-81). Stanford, CA: Stanford University Press.

Mischel, W. (1970). Sex typing and socialization. In P. Mussen (Ed.), *Carmichael's manual of child psychology.* New York: Wiley.

NAEYC. (1993). NAEYC position statement on violence in the lives of children. *Young Children, 48*(6), 80-84.

NAEYC, DEC/CEC, & NBPTS. (1996). *Guidelines for preparation of early childhood professionals.* Washington, DC: Author.

NAEYC, & NAECS/SDE. (1991, March). Guidelines for appropriate curriculum content and assessment in programs serving children ages 3 through 8. *Young Children,* 21-38.

Paley, V. G. (1984). *Boys and girls: Superheroes in the doll corner.* Chicago: University of Chicago Press.

Pellegrini, A. D., & Glickman, C. D. (1990, May). Measuring kindergartners' social competence. *Young Children,* 40-44.

Philips, S. (1972). Participant structures and communicative competence: Warm Springs children in community and classrooms. In C. Cazden, V. John, & D. Hymes (Eds.), *Functions of language in the classroom.* New York: Columbia University, Teachers College Press.

Rizzo, T. (1988). *Friendship development among children in school.* Norwood, NJ: Ablex.

Ruble, D. N. (1988). Sex-role development. In M. H. Bornstein & M. E. Lamb (Eds.), *Developmental psychology: An advanced textbook* (pp. 411-460). Hillsdale, NJ: Erlbaum.

Sadker, M., Sadker, D., & Klein, S. S. (1986). Abolishing misconceptions about equity in education. *Theory into Practice, 25,* 219-226.

Saracho, O. N., & Spodek, B. (1983). *Understanding the multicultural experience in early childhood education.* Washington, DC: NAEYC.

Sarason, S. B. (1971). *The culture of the school and the problem of change.* Boston: Allyn & Bacon.

Slaby, R.G., Roedell, W.C., Arezzo, D., & Hendrix, K. (1995). *Early violence prevention: Tools for teachers of young children.* Washington, DC: NAEYC.

Spindler, G., & Spindler, L. (1987). Cultural dialogue and schooling in Schoenhausen and Roseville: A comparative analysis. *Anthropology and Education Quarterly, 18,* 3-16.

Swadener, B. B. (1988). Implementation of education that is multicultural in early childhood settings: A case study of two day-care programs. *The Urban Review, 20*(1), 8-27.

Swadener, B. B. (1989). Race, gender, and exceptionality: Peer interactions in two child care centers. *Educational Policy, 3*(4), 371-387.

Swadener, B. B., Cahill, B., Marsh, M. M., & Arnold, M. S. (in press). Cultural and gender identity in early childhood: Anti-bias, culturally inclusive pedagogy with young learners. In C. A. Grant (Ed.), *In praise of diversity: A resource book for multicultural education.* New York: Scholastic Press.

Thorne, B. (1993). *Gender play: Girls and boys in school.* New Bruswick, NJ: Rutgers University Press.

Walkerdine, V. (1981). Sex, power and pedagogy. *Screen Education, 38,* 14-24.

Weade, R. (1987). Curriculum 'n' instruction: The construction of meaning. *Theory Into Practice, 26*(1), 15-25.

Whaley, K., & Swadener, B. B. (1990, Summer). Multicultural education in infant and toddler settings. *Childhood Education,* 238-240.

Zaharlick, A., & Green, J. L. (1991). Ethnographic research. In J. Flood, J. Jensen, D. Lapp, & J. Squire (Eds.), *Handbook of research in teaching the English language arts.* New York: Macmillan.

6
Diverse Paths to Literacy in a Preschool Classroom

Sandra Marie Miller
Ohio Department of Education

During a small group project in which the children are encouraged to draw anything that they want in their blank books, Nat asks the teacher the following:

Nat: "I need some letters. Put some letters on. Make it say Nat."

At the block corner, the teacher watches what the boys are constructing, enters quietly on the fringe of the play and asks:

Donna: "What do you want your sign to say?"
Jack: "Don't sit in my seat." At the same time Paul joins in:
Paul: "Don't sit in our spaceship."

During the free choice period, paper, paint, glue, and glitter are made available at the art area. In response, the teacher asks Grace if she would like for the teacher to put her name on at the top of her picture. But Grace takes a marker and does her own writing. The teacher compliments Grace on her writing abilities. Leslie, who has just entered the art area, overhears the teacher's favorable comments and announces:

Leslie: "I want to make one of these. You know what I'm going to do? Write my name with the paint and then sparkle on it."

These anecdotes provide a brief look at how these children incorporate print meaningfully into routine events in this preschool. Nat provides information that suggests he understands that letters can mean something, in this case his name. For Jack and Don, the purpose of print during their block building is to communicate to the other children their desire to protect their construction. Leslie uses open-ended art materials as a vehicle to demonstrate her print abilities.

Yet, if one were to define literacy learning within the traditional perspective (i.e., as the mastery of systematic and sequential rules of encoding and decoding print), these anecdotes would not have been considered examples of literacy acquisition. The conventional perspective on literacy learning holds that preschool children are preliterate and therefore incapable of reading and writing (Hall, 1987).

Through the "emergent literacy" perspective, we now recognize that the examples given here reveal children's early literacy development and their understanding of the forms, functions, and complexities of print (Clay, 1975, 1979, 1982; K. Goodman & Goodman, 1979; Smith, 1992). Within this perspective, children are viewed from infancy as "meaning-makers" (Wells, 1986) of the physical and social world. Through their early interactions with adults within and across spoken and written language domains (Y. Goodman 1982, 1983a, 1986), they begin to make meaning of the written word. A summary of early literacy studies suggest the following:

- Literacy emerges before children are formally taught to read.
- Literacy is defined to encompass the whole act of reading, not merely decoding.
- The child's point of view and active involvement with emerging literacy constructs is featured.
- The social setting for literacy is not ignored. (Mason & Sinha, 1993, cited in Campbell, 1998)

With the increasing pressure to have children come to school "ready," early childhood teachers are caught between the traditional readiness-oriented literacy model that focuses on preparing students to read and write and the emergent literacy model, with its much broader interpretation of what counts as literacy and literacy learning for young learners. Questions from many early childhood teachers include "What is an appropriate literacy curriculum?" and "How do I facilitate literacy development that is in keeping with and appropriate for the developmental abilities and understanding of preschool children?"

The examples given here suggest that the children's print abilities and knowledge can be constructed within a variety of play and routine school activities, and that demonstrations of print or use may vary from context to context. A literacy curriculum that is in keeping with children's developmental understanding and production of print considers how children's meaning-making of literacy can be interwoven with the construction of the social and play events of preschool life.

The research reported in this chapter was designed to analyze the routine activities of preschool children to determine where and how literacy was accomplished in the course of daily preschool life. Through the study of children's peer play and teacher-constructed school routines, literacy was traced within two child-controlled events, the art table and the block corner, and within two teacher-initiated small-group circle events. Literacy was neither the main focus nor primary purpose of these contexts, but rather was a way of life within this preschool— embedded within both teacher-initiated and child-initiated activities.

The intention of the study was to determine the meaning of the social action within these events and consequently the literacy yoked to them. The examination of literacy through routine school and peer-constructed events may advance teacher understanding of what a literacy curriculum infused across classroom events might look like for children ages 3 through 5.

EXAMINING OUR BELIEFS: TRADITIONAL AND EMERGENT PERSPECTIVES

The Traditional View

Historically, the traditional learning to read perspective was embedded within the general view of learning that, at the time, evolved as a result of two primary forces within education during the 1920s: the dominance of the maturationist position of G. Stanley Hall and the advancement of standardized testing.

The maturationist model of Hall proposed that development unfolded in a preordained manner. Within this theoretical framework, children need to be neurologically ready, as literacy was thought to be a visuoperceptual skill. The large numbers of children who failed reading instruction during this time period provided justification for a neurological readiness model for reading and writing instruction and supported the development of prereading and prewriting tasks to get children ready to read (Durkin, 1982).

The purpose of standardized testing and measurement was to define norms of development and behavior that could be of use for education. Educational psychologists had as their mission the development of a teaching and learning framework that could be controlled, dependable, and replicable (Smith, 1992). This framework was applied to literacy learning, suggesting that "one can act in a literate way" (Hall, 1987, p. 2) as determined by levels of proficiency within a sequential, preordained literacy curriculum.

Given these early perspectives of learning and literacy, the young child was not considered ready to read but could benefit from "many developmental activities" (Durkin, 1982) as preparation for the reading and writing curriculum. With an increased interest in getting children ready for school, a preliteracy curriculum or readiness program had a place in kindergarten classrooms. The teachers merely down-scaled the traditional formal reading and writing practices to meet the needs of young children (Durkin, 1982). This top–down readiness curriculum for kindergarten was composed of sound–symbol recognition, the identification of the alphabet and selected sight words, the exposure to a limited and controlled vocabulary, and the duplication of simple phrases and sentences. Repetition and drill, inherent within the learning theory framework, were viewed as the methodology for learning these prereading and prewriting skills. For the preschool child, literacy practices were limited to story time, music and finger plays, and the use of a strong oral language program emphasizing vocabulary learning to be learned through experiential activities.

One can see how the conception of learning to read and write, enmeshed within the learning theory framework, dictated how a teacher defined literacy and thus the practices that would help a child to become literate. For the early childhood educator, trained in informal and child-centered methods, such a literacy program was uncomfortable to administer and contradicted the child-centered philosophy typical in the field. Yet there was little in the research to provide guidance and support for a literacy curriculum that could meet the needs of the young learner and fall within the framework of child-centered practice.

THE EMERGENT LITERACY PERSPECTIVE

The shift from the traditional literacy perspective to the emergent perspective has evolved slowly as literacy learning has been reconceptualized. Halliday (1975) argued that learning language is about "learning how to mean," an activity that includes "linguistic, cognitive, and social strategies" (Hall, 1987, p. 5). K. Goodman and Goodman (1979) observe that young children come to know that written language makes sense, and that they can make sense through the use of written language. In this view, learning to read and write are constructive and social activities experienced by children essentially from birth, with their beginnings rooted in the literacy events of daily family life. Children continue to explicate the many functions of print for themselves in contexts such as preschool when they interact in a print-rich environment with people who engage them in literacy events.

Researchers exploring the development of literacy within the emergent literacy perspective have redefined and broadened what counts as literate behavior; for example, recasting scribbling and pretend reading as the earliest forms of reading and writing rather than as merely prereading and prewriting behaviors (Y. Goodman 1983a, 1986). In this regard, longitudinal studies have chronicled children's gradual reconstructions from scribbling and drawing to the inner control over print concepts necessary for conventional and independent reading and writing (Clay, 1991). A line of literacy research with a Piagetian constructivist orientation (Ferriero, 1985, 1986) has revealed the underlying logic evident in children's early print use.

Overall, young children are no longer viewed as passengers in a maturation process that gets them "ready to read"; rather, they are seen as active constructors of their own literacy knowledge in a long process of "becoming literate." This seminal research has primarily focused on and explicated the cognitive/individual "work" accomplished during early childhood, and it builds our understanding of what children learn about written language in the early years and of the cognitive processes involved in such learning.

A more recent approach to literacy and literacy learning, one that moves largely away from cognitive processes, is a sociocultural perspective. This perspective defines literacy in cultural terms and views children as becoming literate within the cultures of their communities (Brice-Heath, 1983; Moll, 1990; Schieffelin & Cochran-Smith, 1984), their families (Taylor, 1983; Taylor & Dorsey-Gaines, 1988), and their schools (Moll, 1990). Within and across these settings, literacy meanings are constructed through the values, practices, routines, and rituals of the members of a sociocultural community.

Researchers with a sociocultural perspective view students within classrooms as constructing a common culture through their everyday interactions, and view language and literacy as defined and given meaning within this culture (Bloome, 1986a, 1986b; Golden, 1990; Green, Kantor, & Rogers, 1991; Weade & Green, 1989). As Green and her colleagues argued, literacy is inextricably tied to the wider events of classroom life:

> From this perspective, in every classroom, teachers and students are constructing particular models of literacy and particular understandings of what is involved in learning how to be literate. That is, as teachers and students construct the norms and expectations and roles and relationships that frame how they will engage in everyday life in classrooms, they are also defining what counts as literacy and literate action in the local events of classroom life. . . . From this perspective, we must talk about literacies and not

literacy, for no one definition can capture the range of occurrence in everyday life in classrooms, the multiplicity of demands, or ways of engaging in literacy within and across groups. (Green, Dixon, Lin, Floriani, & Bradley, in press)

To view literacy and group life together is to take a contextualized or "situated" view of the literacy meanings, purposes, functions, and outcomes that are accomplished and re-accomplished for a group and for individual participants in a group (Green & Meyer, 1991; Green, Kantor, & Rogers, 1991). Thus, literacy from the situated perspective is not examined as something separate from the flow of everyday life. Rather, literacy is viewed as a part of the social history of the group, and as practiced "in the ways" of the group.

Much of the sociocultural research on literacy learning in schools has been conducted at the elementary and secondary school levels. Next, the few early childhood studies with a direct influence on the design of the present study are discussed.

LITERACY LEARNED AT THE WRITING TABLE AND ON THE STORY RUG

Following ethnographic and case study traditions, three early childhood studies used intense observation over time to examine how print and literacy knowledge was constructed as a feature of a particular literacy event. Two studies of interest to this research focused on the writing table as a context for literacy development (Dyson, 1989; Rowe, 1989). Dyson presented evidence that the social worlds of classroom life are fused with the individual interests of children and are often expressed in both children's action and writing. Through related and simultaneous use of the symbols of drawing, talk, and writing, the children in Dyson's study created worlds that encompassed the "social energy of the peer group" (i.e., "the children's desire to link themselves to each other and to distinguish themselves among their friends"; Dyson, 1989, p. 48). This social energy of the children was created through their dramatic play and their art—"their own replayings and graphic organizations of their experienced worlds" (p. 25).

Rowe (1989) provided findings consistent with Dyson's (i.e., that children learn about literacy as they use literacy to reflect on their personal and social lives). Within the supportive environment of the writing and art tables and through dialogue, Rowe revealed how children learned to take the stance of author and audience, confronted new ideas and conflicts about print construction and meaning, and confirmed and expanded their literacy knowledge. The social interaction at the writing table framed the literacy learning and use as the children created text to be appreciated, critiqued, and evaluated by peers as authors and audience.

Cochran-Smith's (1984) ethnographic study focused primarily on a structured literacy event, story time. Unlike Dyson or Rowe, however, Cochran-Smith presented her analysis within what she called "concentric layers of context" (p. 6) that frame the story event. These layers of context include the community's literacy values, orientation, and practices; the material and print environment; time and space organization of the classroom; and the informal social interactions involving print.

Informal literacy events and interactions among children, and between children and adults, were important and occurred everywhere in the classroom. They involved, for example, making a sign for the cage of the sick guinea pig to alert visitors to speak softly, and a sign dictated by block corner superheroes, warning others to "keep out." Through such literacy events, children learn the many purposes and the power of print, in their lives and in the lives of adults. Cochran-Smith argued that both informal literacy and focused literacy events "contribute(s) significantly to understanding (the) children's literacy and literacy socialization" (p. 72). Collectively, the research of Cochran-Smith, Rowe, and Dyson, demonstrate that social dynamics and routine classroom events frame, make purposeful, and support the developing literacies of young children.

A parallel line of studies have focused on curricular and physical environment changes intended to enhance literacy learning within and through symbolic play (Christie, 1990; Morrow & Rand, 1991; Neuman & Roskos, 1991; Schrader, 1990, 1991; Vulkelich, 1991). Common play themes and roles (e.g., storekeeper or doctor) are enhanced by providing literacy props that would be typical within such community settings. The intention is to make writing and reading functional and meaningful to the young learner. Within this approach, the teacher provides appropriate required props and adequate play time, and uses either direct or indirect intervention strategies during the play to highlight or call attention to the children's uses of print.

Neuman and Roskos (1990, 1991) suggested using a variety of classroom contextual changes and teacher interventions to facilitate literacy education. Changes made to the physical setting included better "definition" of the play spaces, labeling throughout all play areas, and the creating four play areas "targeted for literacy enrichment" (Neuman & Roskos, 1990, p. 216). The appropriateness, utility, and authenticity of the materials and props within the play contexts need to be of concern to educators in the creation of classroom contexts for literacy.

These studies reveal that through the adults' restructuring of the classroom environment, children increase their literacy behaviors and the time they spend playing with reading and writing materials (Morrow & Rand, 1991; Neuman & Roskos, 1991; Vulkelich, 1991). Clearly, when teachers choose to highlight and model literacy within activities, children will respond accordingly as the context of the play and the materials serve to "structure" the nature of the activities constructed by the participants.

This body of early childhood literacy research provided important guidance for the study to be reported. The notions that literacy learning is embedded within social events, could be found in the everyday interactions of classroom members, and could be enhanced through teachers' involvements and structuring of the classroom environment, all provided important starting points to guide this study.

Yet the exploration of literacy to be presented also differs from the aforementioned studies in that it was conducted as part of a holistic ethnography, the overall goal of which was to understand the life world of a preschool classroom (Fernie, Kantor, Klein, Meyer, & Elgas, 1988). As a result of prior and subsequent linked analyses described in this volume, much is known about this classroom's culture and how it was constructed, about the distinctive norms for participation, rights, and obligations, roles and relationships constructed within different play and school events. Consequently, this broader knowledge dictated the need for a context-specific look at literacy, and conversely, for an interpretation of literacy contextualized and informed by our evolving understanding of these contexts and of the classroom as a whole.

It is within this framework that literacy was examined: across both the school culture and the play culture events and dynamics constructed by the participants. The study located literacy as part of several contexts or events, as interwoven with the broader purposes, activities, and social dynamics of these contexts. The following specific questions were addressed:

1. What are the different ways in which literacy is constructed by children and teachers of the preschool in the course of their daily life?
2. What kinds of literacy or literacies are constructed within and across both peer culture or school culture events?
3. Within these events, how do children and teachers participate in and use literacy?

RESEARCH METHODS AND PROCEDURES

The general philosophy of the preschool program is based on constructivist and social constructivist theories (Piaget, 1954; Vygotsky, 1978). Children were encouraged to create, problem solve, and question through adult-planned (school culture) and play (peer culture) experiences. The curriculum was emergent, negotiated, and constructed by both teachers and children. "Working from the ideas of children" was an explicit motto of the program.

Consistent with this philosophy, the teachers regarded literacy as "a way of life" within the classroom. Some literacy activity occurred in more formal events such as story time but many instances of literacy were constructed opportunistically, because the teachers were predisposed to use literacy in response to the spontaneous needs and interests children expressed in school events and in play. It was common to see children dictating pretend recipes to teachers in the housekeeping corner, or to see a group of children and a teacher discussing, writing, and posting rules for clean-up as part of a social problem-solving interaction.

The teachers believed that these numerous informal writing experiences formed a pathway to understanding the power and functions of print and to reading itself. For, as Clay (1991) argued, "the first explorations of print in the preschool years may occur in writing rather than reading" (p. 108).

The teachers communicated the early literacy curriculum to the parents through casual teacher–parent communication and parent newsletters (which featured short articles on curricular issues). The parents, in turn, were predisposed to support and prize literacy development within this informal approach.

GENERAL RESEARCH PROCEDURES

The collection of data took place over a three-quarter university schedule. Using ethnographic methods, as detailed in a previous chapter, data was gathered from multiple sources including the following: videorecordings taken of the first 2 weeks of each quarter from six camera locations within the classroom, fieldnotes written daily throughout the academic year by four participant-observers, interviews with the children and their parents, retrospective journals kept by the two teachers, and notes recorded during weekly meetings of the research team.

For the purposes of the study, I adopted Y. Goodman's (1986) definition of *reading* and *writing*: "human interaction with print when the reader and writer believe that they are making sense of and through written language" (p. 6). Thus, literacy was judged to occur whenever a child and/or teacher introduced, or made reference to reading and writing, or constructed print within a classroom event or within peer play.

The examination of literacy was conducted in two phases. The first phase served as the "grand tour" of the data (Hammersley & Atkinson, 1989)—as a way to locate literacy across the preschool day in its many forms and within its many contexts. In the second, an in-depth look was taken at literacy in four curricular formats or events that occurred each day. Spradley's (1980) Developmental Research Sequence provided a means to search systematically for the ways in which literacy was constructed and used by the participants.

FINDINGS

Results from the first phase of analysis demonstrated that literacy occurred in almost all classroom locations and events and suggested that a school culture–peer-culture framework would prove useful in describing the uses and forms of literacy evident across this classroom. On the playground, children were found writing out tickets for speeding bicyclists and creating letters in the sand. Races to open the door leading back to the classroom resulted in a teacher-suggested turn list that was eventually posted at the door. Social conflicts occurring during play were resolved during circle time and the results of the discussion, in the form of "rules" were recorded and made public on large newsprint. Also during circle time, letters were written to friends and the calendar was used as an opportunity to discuss and record upcoming events, birthdays, or impending teacher absences. Small group events, both of which were led by teachers, included literacy incorporated as part of learning experiences.

During free play, the use of paper and pencils was evident in the housekeeping area, the writing/story corner, the woodworking area, and the block area. Children wrote notes to each other, typed often indecipherable messages, and dictated signs to be incorporated into their play themes.

With the exception of story time reading, reading and writing almost always occurred together. For example, during an event or activity, children would dictate their "words" to teachers who would write and then read the text back to the children. Once a sign or list was posted, children would often "read" the text to others, particularly when it was helpful to them in achieving goals or in protecting space ("only two allowed on the climber") or obtaining a privilege ("it says I'm next to feed the guinea pig").

Locating literacy across nearly all preschool events revealed that literacy was purposeful activity and an integral part of life in this classroom—constructed to serve the needs of both children and the teachers. It was determined that literacy was not typically the focus of experience, but rather was interwoven into events in ways similar to Cochran-Smith's (1984) findings. As Cochran-Smith noted, such literacies become part of the material or print culture of the classroom environment and serve a necessary function in socializing children to print.

As a result of the initial look for literacy within classroom life, four daily occurring contexts were selected for in-depth study during a second phase of analysis: two school culture events and two peer culture events. Both the peer and school culture contexts were analyzed to locate all literacy occurrence within the play event or routine school event. Each literacy event was then transcribed and examined in two ways. First, each event was analyzed to determine the structure of the literacy event, that is, who initiated the literacy, who served as author of the message, and who acted as the scribe of the message. Second, each literacy occurrence was analyzed according to two cultural domains (Spradley, 1980) in order to reveal the pattern and range of literacy; the functions of literacy (uses) and the ways to do literacy (formats). Next, the literacy events found in the two school culture contexts are presented, followed by two play contexts. In each case, the reciprocal relationship between the nature of the event and the literacy found there is explicated, drawing both from the literacy analysis and the knowledge of this classroom's everyday life.

Donna's Small Group: Literacy is a Way to Become a Group Member

The goal of Donna's daily small-group event was to develop a sense of "group" and to facilitate child-to-child interactions and communication among this classroom's 10 youngest children (3-year-olds). All of these younger children were new to school and to group experience. Donna provided open-ended art and construction experiences, in which children could learn how to share materials, space, and ideas, and, in so doing, "become a group member" by experiencing group interaction as they explored a variety of hands-on materials. According to the curriculum document for the preschool, a developmental progression is anticipated in the small group process (Kantor & Elgas, 1986):

> Early in the year, we begin the small group curriculum for the younger children with an introduction to new materials. . . . While we each work with our own, but identical materials we talk: we notice each other's work, we describe what we're thinking about, we describe what we're doing. This conversation is made possible by

the teacher's facilitation. . . . During the second half of the year, or whenever the teacher determines that the group is ready, our goal is to work collaboratively on a single project . . . to experience the idea of working in and as a group, of making unique contributions to a group effort through collaboration and cooperation. (pp. 54-57)

An investigation by Williams (1988) revealed that the social construction of this group event was a complex process. Over time, the children and teacher negotiate a participant structure characterized by "social action rules" (Dorr-Bremme, 1982; Wallat & Green, 1979; Williams, 1988) that, whether explicitly stated or implicit in the doing, guide the participants' actions, reactions, and ways of behaving within the event. Williams' moment-by-moment sociolinguistic analysis revealed two kinds of related social action rules: (a) rules that protected the individual's rights within the group (e.g., no one has the right to mark on another's paper), and (b) rules that articulate the group's demands on the individuals and, therefore, the individual's obligations to the group (e.g., you need to wait until everyone is finished before cleaning up).

Williams' investigation made visible that children's early participation in the group focused on the individual, that is, on individuals' attempts to control the events, ideas, materials, and the attention of the teacher in order to meet their needs. Therefore, the challenge for Donna (particularly with these novice school members) was to accommodate the individual needs of each participant while working toward a group goal. From past experience, Donna anticipated that the interactional dynamics of the group would shift to a group focus, with less interest in "self" on the part of the individual children. In Examples 1 and 2 , this individual-within-group tension is revealed.

Example 1

The children are finishing an activity of experimentation with different kinds of glue and paper. One child finishes early and moves toward the musical instruments.

Don: "I want to make some music."

Donna informs him that the group can make music in the next group and asks for his idea. As Don continues to play with the instruments, Donna suggests:

Donna: "Should we put a note. Let's put a note that says next group we'll do our instruments."

Donna takes Don's dictated message. On hearing this, three children jump up and request their names to be included on the note to be posted in the room.

In this example, Donna limited Don's individual interest in the musical instruments at this time in favor of the group's focus on the work with materials. Literacy in this instance served as a "placeholder" to help Don to wait for a future small-group event to try the instruments. Also noteworthy here is that other children's interest was not in the musical instruments but rather in the literacy, and particularly in seeing their own names in print.

In Example 2, Donna similarly tries to limit behavior disruptive to the group, and in doing so, subtly communicates the individual's obligation to group.

Example 2

On this day, one child begins to squeal and soon others have followed her lead. Donna again suggests a note that may serve as a rule to control the behavior. A few days later, during another small-group event, Alice begins to squeal loudly, Donna reminds her of the note posted by the door. Alice runs up to look at the message, followed by Andy. Above the note, Alice spots her name on one of the many lists in the room. Seeing this, she points to her name and remarks that it is her name. She is quickly joined by two other girls who point to their names and comment on their names posted in print. A chant of "my name, my name" takes the place of the squealing. Such a scene was to be repeated during other events.

The children's interest in the print again was individually oriented—in this case, the recognition of their own names in print. Ironically, what they socially constructed was a group chant, "my name, my name," to be heard on many other occasions in this group context.

In these episodes, Donna initiated the use of literacy as a tool to redirect a request and to reaffirm a rule, serving the wider goals of the event. In both cases, literacy was not the primary purpose of the curricular activity, but was constructed in the "doing" of the activity—as a support for the curricular and procedural goals that the teacher was working toward with the group. For their part, the children used these teacher-introduced ideas as opportunities to see their names in print.

As children progressed in their ability to work in the small-group context, projects such as group murals and individual construction ideas displayed collectively were ways in which Donna promoted a sense of group work. Donna initiated the inclusion of child-created text on the murals and in display areas where children's work was grouped together. Initially, these attempts at displaying the group products were rebuffed by the children because they wanted to take their work home. Most importantly, they wanted their names by their "individual" work, even on group-created murals. Following the ideas of the children, Donna would write their names beside their individual contributions. The children would not comment on the creation but rather would say, "Look at my name!" As the year progressed, the children became more interested in writing text to accompany their collective work, and eventually in having their names on this group work to show their contribution to group processes and products.

Table 6.1 displays the entire domain analysis of Donna's small-group context. In keeping with the examples given previously, literacy often was not the primary focus of this daily event, but instead was integrated into the activities and used as a vehicle to create "group." The one exception to this pattern was the planned literacy events, such as making holiday cards, reading recipes, and writing books, which were teacher-introduced formats to accomplish collaborative and group work. In terms of the uses of literacy (i.e., the functional domain analysis), print was used to establish limits and procedures for the group, to claim

Table 6.1. Domain Analyses of Donna's Small-Group Context

A. Ways to do literacy:

    Domain: **Planned literacy**
              Journal writing
              Blank books
              Making holiday cards
              Create Mother's Day cards
              Recipes
    Domain: **Art and Construction**
              Write a label for a mural
              Invite a child to give words about their work
              Painting with a variety of media and tools
              Constructing with legos
    Domain: **Lists and Notes**
              Write a turn list
              Write a note about behavior
              Write a note to serve as a reminder
    Domain: **Names**
              Ask child where name should go on art
              Dictate name to indicate possession
              Request names for note
              Request name on all art/construction projects
              Read names in response to signs/notes posted in room

(continues)

Table 6.1. Continued

B. Literacy is used to:

    Domain: **Establish Limits and Procedures**
                Control squealing during group
                Remind children of rules of behavior for group
                Act as a placeholder for an activity
                Get a turn to open the door
                Get a turn to sit next to the teacher
                Send a note home to extend an activity
                Use a note to redirect behavior
    Domain: **Claim Ownership**
                Indicate possession on art products
                Indicate possession of construction materials
                Identify materials that are for your personal use
                Identify art and construction with labels
    Domain: **Demonstrate Membership**
                Locate your name on a list
                Request your name on a sign
                Get the teacher's/peers attention
                Call attention to one's name in print

ownership of art and construction products, and eventually to demonstrate membership within the group.

The structural analysis revealed that the children initiated 75% of the print in Donna's small-group events. As in the previous examples, the technical control was relegated to Donna (100% of the time). However, it was typical for children to assume authorship, that is, to control the content of the literacy (78% of the time). Thus, the high percentages of initiation and control of literacy suggests that, even for these 3-year-olds, literacy formats introduced by teachers quickly become used by and useful to children in this preschool.

Initially, the use of each child's name was to accommodate individual needs, but as the individual requests infringed on group goals, Donna's use of names in print became a management technique. The children's names in print, in turn, became constructed by the children as a vehicle for the construction of group membership.

Some comments are in order about the salience of children's names in this group event. The importance of children's names in print, noted as early as 1936 by Hildreth (Taylor, 1983), is well articulated by Jerome Bruner: "A special instance of the distinguishing mark is the child's own name. This is in a category of its own, since its immediate usefulness may be less than evident . . . but it has a particular emotive power and often serves as a starting point, a way into the world of written language" (p. 179).

In this small-group event, the desire to see one's name in print became a powerful motive for the children to initiate print, particularly having one's name displayed as part of the teacher-planned events. The printed name was used to protect or assert their individual identity within group—for example, to lay claim of ownership over materials or products, to take a turn, or to express an idea in counterpoint to Donna, when she was using print as a way to establish and regulate group. Eventually, their names in print became a way to experience group affiliation through the chants that the group created. As constructed by the children, it both affirmed membership within group and preserved the identity of the individual within group.

For Donna, the power of names served her goal to facilitate group participation and group development. From past experience, she knew that this would be a challenge and a gradual process because young children come to group with individual agendas, with personal issues, and with a certain amount of self-centeredness. The "immediate usefulness" of writing children's names was a tool to redirect and to remind. In other words, Donna used print to mediate issues within the group, so that individual rights could be respected as group dynamics were established and then maintained. It was the process of individuals becoming a group, with its inherent tensions, that formed one path to literacy for these children.

One implication for practice is that teachers need to understand group membership as a developmental process, which progresses from asserting the individual self to the awareness and valuing of group membership. Furthermore, there is a recognition that literacy can be a tool for facilitation of this emergent group process. Literacy used within this social framework makes a literacy curriculum meaningful, while simultaneously providing children new to school with a way of asserting and maintaining individual needs within group social interaction. Although the literacy lessons within this small group were about names to accompany art and learning the letters within their names on one level, print was also used in subtle but important ways to establish and to enhance children's knowledge of and participation in school life.

Rebecca's Small Group: Literacy is a Way to Learn Collaboration

Whereas Donna's group learned "to do" group over the course of the academic year, Rebecca's small-group events were created for the older preschool children (several of whom were in their second year of this preschool classroom) and presumed to have more advanced group skills. Consequently, the focus in this group was on authentic collaborative work and on the social processes related to collaboration: "Group brainstorming of ideas, using divergent and creative thought, cooperating, group problem solving, sharing and having friendly exchange" (Kantor & Elgas, 1986, p. 60).

There were several basic "formats" used by Rebecca to create collaboration, and they usually included print as one of several forms of representation. For example, in one format called *Lets find out about this and write it down*, Rebecca presented materials to explore (math, science, games, or literacy-related materials). At the conclusion of these experiences, written language was often introduced; for example, a chart to record and classify outcomes of a science exploration. Literacy was used to restate what the children discovered through their experiences.

The curriculum document is very explicit about the importance of the teacher's role:

> The teacher's role during an experience such as this needs to be as co-explorer, co-investigator and facilitator of the children's discoveries and representation. During the group, the teacher works alongside the children. Her conversation is facilitative, supportive, and helps to attach language to physical experience. The work of the teacher is challenging and takes a great deal of thought. Opportunities for meaningful conversation need to be seized and created. (Kantor & Elgas, 1986, pp. 69-70)

In the following example from early in the school year, the children were each given a set of Lego blocks for construction. This format of working side by side with identical materials was reminiscent of the 3-year-old group and, according to Rebecca, is a way to start off slowly and to build a group identity early in the school year. The children were told that when they finished, all of their construction pieces would be displayed. As with the 3-year-olds, print was offered as a way to express feelings or thoughts about what was constructed with the materials. But unlike the 3-year-olds, the 4-year-olds were more interested in capturing their thoughts on paper to go along with their display and were less concerned with the ownership/name issues:

Example 3

Rebecca: "We can write your words and tell about your piece."
Dan: "A fighting thing that goes around."
Paul: "It shoots all the Transformers."
Ken: "Spaceship. Two spaceships and a gas station. Don't touch this."

The words the children chose to describe and label their creations reflected the themes that were emerging in play. These three children (Dan, Paul, and Ken) were becoming members of a "core group" of players described extensively by Elgas (1988) and in chapter 3 here; over time, they came to demonstrate consistent themes, routines, and concerns through play. In Example 3, we see that their emerging interest in superhero and adventure themes were supported and articulated in the school culture format of small group and through its related uses of literacy.

Similarly to Donna's more formal introductions to print, Rebecca's group was introduced to book/story-making experiences. In these formats, children were given blank books to author and illustrate. Later in the year, book/story-making events became more collaborative; the group would construct a single book together with each child contributing a page or two on the same group-constructed topic.

The format of blank books was used within small-group activity during 5 of the 13 literacy occurrences within this context. In early October, the children expressed some telling concerns about the construction of blank books: One child asked disbelievingly, "I can color anywhere?" and another asserted, "I need some letters. Put some letters on. Make it say Nat." For the first child, it is possible that books were conceptualized as finished products with pictures and print already supplied by some adult author, not something that could be created by children. For the second child, letters and perhaps authorship were viewed as salient elements of books. These comments reflect both their surprise about the openness of the format and excitement about the process of becoming an author and an artist of their own books.

The children's early "stories" were merely labels for their "illustrations," but by spring quarter, the use of blank books became a way to foster storybook construction and understanding, as demonstrated in the following episode:

Example 4

Rebecca: "What would you like to say?"
Jack: "This is the street to school."
Rebecca repeats his words as she writes them.

Leslie: "I'm not just staying on the picture. I'm doing the . . . (unintelligible)."
Rebecca: "You're doing the cover. It's called the book cover."
Paul: "Look, look!"
Rebecca: "You wrote letters that you know. An A, and P and a T and a N
             and an M. Good, I've never seen you make those letters, Paul."
Leslie wants to make another book. She has written the word mom on her book and tells Rebecca, "This is for my mommy." Rebecca is interrupted by Jack.

Rebecca: "You want to make a name for your book? Like a title?"
Jack: "The Bat Book by Jack."

The children in this episode explored conventions about books and stories. Their talk and corresponding print described, labeled, and titled their work. The children did not yet have the sophisticated grasp of the conventional language of story formats, but they demonstrated both their emerging skills as authors and artists and a growing facility with "book language."

As this episode continued, Paul wrote more letters as he attempted to write the names of family members, Jack wanted more words written on his pages as he drew pictures encompassing the print in his book, and Leslie created a "rainbow S," offering a creative label for what she had made. Writing some of the text they created in these blank books, the children began to take technical control of the literacy event (although 85% of the actual writing was done by the teacher). Yet compared between Donna's 3-year-old children, Rebecca's 4-year-old group members demonstrated greater relative abilities to conceive of text and to produce conventional text.

Table 6.2 displays the ways to do literacy (means–end domain analysis) in this context, based on 14 small-group events in which 13 literacy occurrences were identified. The analysis revealed how literacy was tied to the accomplishment of specific goals and diverse collaborative projects. Over the year, Rebecca introduced literacy in

Table 6.2. Domain Analyses of Rebecca's Small Group

A. Ways to do literacy:

Domain:	**Planned Events**
	Journal writing
	Blank books
	Letter Bingo
	Offer to take dictation for words
	Display to children the teacher uses for print
	Ask child to spell their name
	Encourage children to take control of their writing
	Invite children to label, identify, talk about their work
	Wait with a book
Domain	**Art and Construction**
	Mural art and writing
	Label Lego constructions

(continues)

Table 6.2. Continued

Domain	**Games and Activities**
	Write rules of safety for tool use at workbench
	To select a name for the guinea pig
	Play a scavenger hunt
	Read clues for a treasure hunt

B. Literacy is used to:

Domain:	**Facilitate Representation Through Talk and Print**
	Describe your art or construction
	Dictate labels or words to describe your art
	Explore the media to construct your name
	Represent a found object
	Facilitate one's literacy knowledge through talk
Domain:	**Demonstrate Technical and Literacy Knowledge**
	Write your name on your work
	Inform a peer about what you can write
	Write "words" about your art
	Read to your friend while your wait for the next activity
	Practice writing your names/words/letters on your work
	Talk about the language of print
Domain:	**Accomplish Goals and Procedures**
	Organize/display ideas and information for school issues
	Provide clues to search for materials in the classroom
	Read while you wait for the next activity

print formats such as games (e.g., as clues in a scavenger hunt), lists that organized activities, in posted rules for the care of a new classroom pet, and for safe tool use (brainstormed by the group), in art and construction projects and in planned literacy events such as journal writing and bookmaking. Literacy, constructed jointly as signs, murals, charts, and books, served as a lasting trace of group effort. Thus, there were a variety of literacy formats introduced and practiced within this curricular context that focused on group collaboration. Interestingly, as in the examples cited, children infused their peer culture interests into this more structured school culture context and often appropriated literacy formats introduced by the teachers to express and incorporate such interests.

The analysis of the uses for literacy (the functional domain analysis) revealed that these literacy occurrences served a variety of different school-related purposes. Within this small-group event, literacy accompanied all that the children did. Collaboration through talk and group projects provided the children with a vehicle to learn how literacy can serve group purposes. It became one more way for children to make meaning, as they discovered that what was expressed in pictures or with speech could also be expressed in print. As Y. Goodman (1983b) suggested, teachers need to ask themselves "How can I turn each activity into a written language experience for the children in my classroom?" We see that this is done easily and naturally by Rebecca and the older preschool children.

Rebecca's small-group time was a context for learning collaboration and where literacy was integral to and fused with this process. Through collaborative dialogue, the children experienced how talk could be transformed into print and can become a permanent reminder of group events. At the same time, the children were learning the stances of author and audience in the construction of text. Within these informal literacy experiences, through the talk about print and story, children learned features of print and text: what a book title is, where letters go to support a picture, how print can inform, detail, and remind. Furthermore, experience with such diverse literacy forms (charts, lists, text) and uses (informational resources, reminders, ways to represent) would be likely to fit well with these children's impending formal school experience.

In this context, the features and functions of print clearly were not "taught" didactically. Rebecca used group time to both support and challenge the children's physical, mathematical, and social knowledge and, at the same time, to reinforce and "nudge" literacy development. Dyson (1990b) wrote that support of this kind "allows children to engage in culturally-valued activities in a more sophisticated way than they could do on their own" (p. 203). Although the children were experimenting and playing with art, construction, math, and science while they were learning how to do group, they were participating in meaningful literacy learning.

In contrast to the two small-group school culture events, the two following events (the activity tables and the block area) took place during a 45-minute free-choice time characterized by children's choices, control, interests, and themes. The children could come and go freely, spending as much or as little time as they desired in these two contexts. Teachers provided a supportive but unobtrusive presence—there for safety purposes and to respond to the children's requests for assistance.

Activity Tables: A Place to Discover Art and Literacy

The activity table area was a context where children were encouraged to try out their ideas through the use of a wide range of art and construction media. A daily free-choice activity, this area was made up of two large tables, placed next to an art easel and within easy reach of paper, markers, scissors, and glue. The open-ended art and construction materials were selected each day by the teacher. These materials for painting, drawing, printing, working with play-dough and clay, constructing collages and sculptures were selected to promote unique, divergent, creative work instead of products that looked "identical" from artist to artist. The main purpose of the activity tables was to introduce children to materials for extensive free exploration. As expressed in the curriculum document:

> This (exploration) establishes a "bank" of ideas; when children have experienced our art curriculum, they will "know" the properties of these materials, how to organize them, what they can and cannot do, how they look when they are combined, taken apart or transformed. They will have used them to symbolically represent hundreds of products of their imagination, most of which will be unrecognizable to anyone but the creator. (Kantor & Elgas, 1985, p. 38)

Although some children were regular visitors to the activity tables, others would join spontaneously on occasions when the materials captured their attention. Children were provided with support in this area by teachers whose role was largely facilitative and nondirective, helping children to articulate, implement, and extend their art and construction ideas and knowledge. Teachers viewed themselves as co-explorers of the media and as co-creators of ideas, although in most cases they followed the lead of the children.

The following narratives illustrate how children spontaneously created and demonstrated print use and knowledge through their exploration of art and construction media. In the first episode, the activity involved painting large sheets of paper with the intention of making superhero capes. Wearing capes (Batman, Superman) was a means by which the core group of boys demonstrated their unity and membership (Elgas, 1988). As a limited resource, the capes were claimed regularly by the core group as a marker for membership and for entry into the play. Controlling the capes, then, became a socially constructed way to dominate the social and material resources of the block area. Aware of the salience of the capes to the non-core group children, the teachers planned an art activity to provide capes for those children who were interested in them but had trouble procuring them.

Example 5

Teacher: "Want your name on it?"

Grace, in response to the teacher's question, takes the marker and writes her own name at the top of the paper. As the teacher comments on Grace's work, Leslie enters the area.

Leslie: "I want to make one of these. You know what I'm gonna do? Write my name with the paint (glue) and then sparkle on it."

Leslie incorporates her name as part of the cape itself.

Mira joins the group while Leslie is finishing her art. Without prompting, Mira writes her name on the top of her cape and announces proudly, "That says Mira" to the teacher seated at the table.

Leslie chose to create her own artistic interpretation of a cape by incorporating her name rather than a superhero logo. Grace and Mira, however, used a more traditional print format for identifying their artwork, that is, placing their names in the top corner of the paper.

Later in this activity, Jack (a member of the core group) joined the art table activity. Although he was asked on two separate occasions by teachers if he wanted his product turned into a cape, he refused both times. Instead, he elected to make a picture and hung it on the wall. Although the research group was puzzled initially by Jack's apparent refusal to affirm his peer-culture interests, further discussion lead us to pose the following interpretation: Jack, as an accepted (rather than a "wannabe") member of the core group, had access to the "real" cloth capes used as entry vehicles for the core group, and thus, may not have felt the need to make a cape with the art materials.

In the next example, the teachers presented a dry mixture of small alphabet noodles and other materials (cornmeal, rice, pasta) as media to explore, weigh, measure, on a balance scale.

Example 6

Rebecca initially questions Lisa about how she can get the scale balanced. In response, Lisa begins to call out letter names she recognizes. Nat comes over and asks Rebecca what she is doing. Instead, the reply comes from Lisa:

Lisa: "We're finding letters."

In response, Nat begins to sing the alphabet song as he joins Lisa in her search for known letters. When Mary enters, Lisa informs her:

Lisa: "I'm scoopin' up some letters."

From this point on, Lisa and Nat, joined by Mary and Jack, searched for letters that belonged in their names. Lisa stayed until she found all of the letters in her name, and then proudly carried them in her hand to show her friend Leslie and her other teacher, Donna.

Lisa: "Do you want to see my name?"

Here, we see the control over the direction of the art activity felt by the children, as they shifted the nature of the activity to initiate a literacy exploration. In doing so, they ignored the teacher's questions and attempts to shift the focus of activity to weight and measurement. The ways to do art and literacy are revealed in Table 6.3. Eleven tapes were transcribed. Of the 11, 6 contained demonstrations of activity related to literacy.

Table 6.3. Domain Analysis of Art and Literacy

A. Ways to do literacy:

Domain: **Planned Events**

Record observations at the water table

Make new nametags

Make holiday cards

Provide a variety of paper and markers for open-ended use

Domain: **To Personalize Activities and/or Experiences With Own Ideas**

Make a sign

Write a note

Create mail

Dictate words to a teacher

Use your name as an art product

Search for alphabet letters that you know

Use art materials to practice literacy

B. Literacy is used to:

Domain: **Make Connections With Others**

Write a sign to indicate behavior at the table

Write a card to your mother

Write a note to your classmate

Share you letter knowledge with a classmate

Share your letter knowledge with your teacher

Create mail with friends

Write a letter to a sick teacher

Write the teacher's name

(continues)

Table 6.3. continued

Domain:	Take Control Over the Activity or Product
	Incorporate your name into the suggested art experience
	Modify a teacher planned activity
	Demonstrate your writing skills
	Demonstrate your letter knowledge
	Dictate words of interest to a teacher
	Write your own name or words on your product
	Write words about your art
	Demonstrate your knowledge about the purposes of print

The ways to do literacy in this context fell into two broad categories: for teachers, literacy was a way to supplement and/or represent a planned activity (e.g., recording outcomes of the media exploration on a chart such as What we found out about mixing cornstarch and water), and; for children, literacy was a way to personalize art and construction products and infuse personal meaning into the experiences at the activity tables (e.g., search for known letters, or incorporate one's name into an art product).

Through the functional analysis or uses for literacy, it was determined that children used print to make connections with others (e.g., classmates, teacher, mother) and to combine it with the other graphic, artistic, and constructive media offered at the activity tables. In this context, the children controlled all of the authorship messages and demonstrated the most technical control (88%) within any of the contexts. Initiation of literacy was divided equally between teachers and children (50%).

It is interesting to note that no child asked a teacher how to write or spell a letter, name, or word at the activity tables. For example, during one letter-writing episode, Winnie instructed a participant-observer sitting next to her to write as she did. Winnie made dots and letter-like forms and announced that it was her name, Winnie, and then proceeded to write the adult's name with dots and dashes, never once asking the adult to spell the letters in her name. Winnie assumed to know how to spell the adult's name (or perhaps that correct spelling was unimportant), and displayed confidence in her writing/spelling ability in this context. When teachers offered to write the children's names and/or words after the children finished their art, the children always quietly refused technical assistance or proclaimed their ability to do their own writing.

Children appeared to use this context, with its implied flexible procedures and open-ended art materials, to create, explore, practice, and take ownership over what they knew or imagined about print. It was with confidence and autonomy that the children displayed their interest in and knowledge of print, as they explored multiple symbolic media and symbolic repertoire. Again, here through the manipulation of art and construction media, the children were learning that meaning could be expressed in a variety of ways, and this included print. Dyson (1990a) reminds us that the art–print connections are interwoven in young children's expression and understanding of symbols.

Through artistic expressions and representations of events or objects often comes the exploration of lines and curves that are assigned print meaning. According to Vygotsky (1978), the evolution from picture to print is transitional—the progression from scribbling to art to print manifests the child's evolving understanding of how speech can be represented by a set of symbols.

Open-ended art media provides children with the occasions to explore how marks on a paper can become pictures that represent and symbols that mean. The open-ended format also gives the children the freedom to explore and to experiment with the technical aspects of print in a safe manner. Whatever the mark, the child assigns and holds the meaning.

For educators of young children, art can be a valuable tool, not only as a vehicle for creative and aesthetic development, but also as a medium for exploring how one can represent speech. What better place to explore and advance one's own conceptual understanding than within a medium that encourages representational and symbolic exploration on one's own terms?

The Block Area: Negotiating Play, Friendship, and Literacy

The block area was bordered by two walls that were filled with an array of small construction blocks, Legos, and bristle blocks, wooden transportation vehicles, traffic signs, dinosaurs, zoo animals, wooden people, and a writing tray with the tools for making signs, letters, messages, and so forth. Stacked against the third wall were large hollow building blocks, wooden ramps and a larger wooden climbing apparatus. This area spilled out into a large floor space that was adjacent to the housekeeping area.

Importantly, the block area was the context with the least amount of teacher involvement. A teacher would often position herself on the periphery of the area so as not to disturb any developing play, and would intervene only to facilitate play themes, to help social negotiations, and to ensure safety.

Through a study detailed in chapter 3 (Elgas 1988), it was determined that this area was dominated by a salient group of boys (the core group) that had constructed and shared "a common set of activities, routines, artifacts, values, concerns, and attitudes" (Corsaro, 1985, p. 171). Their implicit rules of membership, routines of play, and ways of behaving defined them as a cohesive and influential subgroup within this classroom. Their themes were those of superheroes, such as Batman and Superman, and their valued objects were capes, sticks, and "guns," "lasers," and "Transformers" constructed with building materials. The social dynamics played out by this subgroup were those of inclusion and exclusion, hierarchy and leadership, ownership and control of materials and resources.

The following extended narrative demonstrates not only how literacy was offered by teachers and incorporated into the play of the core group, but also how print could provoke new issues among the group of players.

Example 7

Paul invites Jack and Ken to play with him as he constructs a spaceship with large blocks.

Paul: "Gonna make for me and you guys."

Other children, non-members, entered the area.

Paul: "That's my spaceship."

Paul then directs Jack in the placement of a block and tells Don, a non-member, that he's "steppin' on our spaceship."

Teacher: "Is there anything I can do to help? Do you need signs or anything on it?"

Jack and Paul look at each other and with a slight hesitation, Jack responds:

Jack: "Yeh."

The teacher inquires about the color of paper they want for their sign, and when she leaves to get a piece the boys continue to build. As the play continues, Jack introduces a new issue into the play.

Jack: "I'm the boss.
Paul: "Uh-uh," (patting his chest and waving his arms), "All of us, all of us."

As the teacher returns, with paper in hand, she asks:

Teacher: "What do you want the sign to say, guys?"

The boys are deeply involved in their construction and do not respond to her question.

Jack: "Right here, right here."
Paul: "Uh-huh, uh-huh, that's where we sit."
Teacher: "What do you want it to say?"

The teacher repeats the question again, as the boys begin to negotiate where the signs should be placed, where the smoke will come out of the spaceship, the number and location of the seats, etc.

Jack: "Don't sit in my seat."

At the same time, Paul states:

Paul: "Don't sit in our spaceship."

When the teacher asks if there is anything else the boys want to put on their sign, Paul and Jack turn to discuss who the leaders are.

Paul: "All of us. Yeh, and I'm the leader."

Again Jack brings up a new issue.

Jack: "I gotta take all these signs home."

As the teacher writes the message for the boys, Jack requests another sign.

Jack: "Transformers."

He says this to the teacher and informs Ken about what she is writing.

Ken: "And make a face too."

Ken, Jack, and Paul describe for the teacher what a Transformer looks like and how she should draw it.

In this example, the teacher introduced literacy opportunistically, as a way to supplement and represent the experiences and interests important to the players. This was a regular offer made to children playing in the block area. In turn, the children seized the teacher's offer to serve as scribe to address their social concerns. They used literacy in this event to serve the peer dynamics of their core group in several ways: It permitted them to articulate their theme; it helped them to protect their "interactive space" (Corsaro, 1985) from the intrusion of others; and it allowed them to define and to affirm their membership as a group. The power of print may even have provoked them to consider what it was important to make public about their group, for example, who was the "boss."

Play and print were negotiated and interwoven for the boys within this event. In other episodes recorded at the block area, the players constructed signs to control the climber ("It says for Andy and Alice"), to indicate rules of behavior in play ("Don can't get in unless he don't steal money"), and to differentiate "good guy" from "bad guy" ways of playing ("If you're good you can come in, not if you're bad").

Table 6.4. Domain Analysis of the Block Area

A. Ways to do literacy:

Domain:	**Signs**
	Read signs to peers
	Teacher takes dictation for signs
	Requests a sign to be used in play
	Write your name on a sign
	Write a sign about materials used for play
	Write a sign for behavior in the block area
Domain:	**Lists and Notes**
	Write a note for clean-up procedures
	Write a contract for clean-up
	Create a turn list for the climber
	Write a note to give to a peer or teacher
Domain:	**Journal Writing**
	Write a story about your play
	Write a story to accompany the photograph taken of your products of play

B. Literacy is used to:

Domain:	**Control and/or Direct the Play**
	Get a turn on the climber
	Indicate ownership of a sign used for the play
	Read the climber rules to a peer
	Identify a play theme
	Identify a play structure
	Control the climber for self and friends
	Indicate possession of a play structure
	Indicate the leaders of play and membership
	Report a child's behavior
	Indicate possession of objects created in the play
Domain:	**Play With Others**
	To play with a friend
	To gain play entry by writing a note
	To get the teacher to play by writing a note or message

The structural analysis for the block area events revealed that teachers initiated the majority of literacy events (83%) by "seizing the moment" to offer print as a way to clarify, articulate, settle, and advance their play. Teachers also served as the technicians of print (88% of the events).

The messages of play in this context clearly belonged to the players, as children dictated the text (89%). Prominent ways to do literacy (means–end domain analysis) included signs (e.g., "Don't sit in our spaceship"), lists or notes (e.g., to get a turn on the climber), and journal writing (e.g., teacher offered children the opportunity to write about their play). The uses of literacy (functional domain analysis) were to control or direct the play (e.g., signs and lists), to initiate play (e.g., writing notes to give each other), and to enhance children's play themes (e.g., giving pretend labels to equipment and areas). Thus, the messages constructed by the children clearly reflected both their play themes and the social issues they played out during play.

Print served the needs of the players in the block area by providing a way of expressing and mediating often conflict ridden issues of ownership, membership, and turn-taking. A problem of ownership (such as who owned the spaceship) was mediated through literacy. Importantly, this solution itself became an issue of conflict as discussion was created over who owned the signs. Thus, literacy provided both a means to negotiate and a reason to negotiate during play.

For the core group members, as well as for the other children, print was a way to communicate publicly what was important about their play. In so doing, children were learning that language in print held power in the mediation of social issues.

The block area, typically a place where children control the events and construction, is a context filled with opportunities to learn about the social world of peers. Through their play, the boys were learning skills of negotiation, resolution of conflict, and maintenance of ongoing play. These social issues were carried out, not only in play, but also simultaneously through print. Such purposeful learning provided the children with ways to construct and control their social lives and also to learn how print can represent the messages of play.

Dyson (1989) said that "children benefit from learning situations that allow them to explore and to experience in their own ways the symbolic and social medium they are learning, and they benefit as well from 'authentic' experiences that highlight, rather than obscure, the nature of that medium" (p. 271). The boys' play activities were authentic experiences for social development and vehicles to literacy learning as well. In turn, literacy was a path to express their understanding of their social worlds.

It is fair to speculate, that without the social needs of the players and the accommodating involvement of sensitive teachers, there would have been little literacy in the block corner. On one hand, the teachers used print as a way to extend and deepen children's play; on the other hand, the teachers capitalized on the play of children as a vehicle to help children construct diverse functions and purposes of print, stances as both author and audience, and the notion of story as written text. This requires careful intervention so as not to disrupt or diminish the play. Teachers need to understand how the peer dynamics of a particular playgroup serves to facilitate social development. When wedded to the children's construction play rituals and routines, literacy serves the needs of the players.

DISCUSSION

By taking a sociocultural perspective in this study, one can begin to see the dynamic relationship between the distinctive contexts of this preschool classroom and the literacies constructed across them. This study began with the general expectation that literacy would be a way of life in this classroom, but without the knowledge of how literacy would specifically relate to the group's ways of living. Through the multiple and linked analyses of this classroom, how literacy was embedded within the wider classroom events was revealed. One can see that there was a mutually enhancing and reciprocal relationship between the literate actions of the participants and their school culture and peer-culture activities.

Through this analysis, literacy came to be viewed not only as a topic to be learned in school, but also as a vehicle to learn about both the school culture and peer culture of this classroom. In this classroom, each context's activities, materials, purposes, and participation structure framed literacy use in distinctive ways. In the school culture contexts of the two small group activities, the goals of collaboration and community generated certain kinds of literate action. To cite a few examples, teachers planned literacy events (bookmaking) and used literacy opportunistically (a promissory note) in service of these curricular goals; children used literacy to maintain their individual identity (their names) and to create community (socially constructed text to accompany a group display).

In the peer-culture contexts of the activity tables and the block area, the relative openness fostered by the teachers is reflected in the many examples of literate action found there. Children integrated print with other graphic media at the art tables (embellishing one's name in print with glitter); they used print there to signal autonomy (writing one's own name on art products); in the block area, children used print to signal friendship ("this is for you and me") and to establish and communicate issues of hierarchy ("tell who the boss is") and inclusion or exclusion ("keep out"); finally, teachers offered print as one representational medium to label and describe another (block structures), and to support children's negotiation of peer culture dynamics.

Although most teachers of young children have philosophical beliefs about how young children develop and learn, and plan their curriculum accordingly, this study demonstrates the need to go beyond this framework to illuminate the contexts for teacher-planned events and play. If a teacher embraces the philosophy of emergent literacy practices for young children, then it is important to study how natural reading and writing is presented to the children. Does the context as structured by the participants, the materials, and the activities either limit or expand the boundaries for literacy development? Bloome and Twymon (1985) suggested that it is "important to look at the multiple layers of classroom interaction" (p. 153) to determine the difference between what is being taught and what is being learned. Here, too, we see how the social worlds of children impact upon school, and reciprocally how school can make use of the knowledge of children. Teale (1982) stated that "in order to formulate a theory which accounts for the process of children's natural literacy development in the preschool years, we need to keep in mind that literacy is, above all, a social process" (p. 563).

In focusing on "the doing" across contexts, the ethnographic perspective revealed the dynamic way in which the formats and content of print arose; often, print formats were appropriated by both teachers and children across school culture and peer-culture realms. A sign first introduced by a teacher to mediate a turn-taking conflict among peers would be used subsequently by peers to claim ownership of a valued resource. The text created during a bookmaking activity during small group would be used by peers as an opportunity to talk about "Transformers," and the behavior of an oppositional, squealing group of peers would be modulated by a teacher's written reminder of the rule. Just as children participated in literacy events motivated by teachers, teachers sensitively integrated literacy within peer-controlled free play. In fact, much of the literacy introduced here could be described as opportunistic, with teachers helping to meet individual, social, and academic needs as they arose in the course of everyday life.

As children became members of a school culture through the routine construction of daily life, literacy became interwoven into the social history of the classroom as an integral part of doing school; as children became friends in the peer culture, literacy became an important way to deal with the issues at the forefront of their social worlds. The reciprocal relationships found across this classroom suggest that just as school was a way to learn literacy, so was literacy a way to learn school. Thus, in this classroom, there was no one path to becoming literate, but multiple paths.

The close tie between the particular culture of this classroom and the literacy patterns would suggest that similar relationships could be constructed in other classrooms. One can imagine, for example, that a classroom with a more teacher-controlled participation structure would define and delimit literacy very differently from what was found here. From the perspective presented in this chapter and by others (Green & Meyer 1991; Green et al., in press), the dynamic nature of literacy in the classroom is captured:

> Literacy is not monolithic; rather, it depends on the community for its definition . . . within a community the nature of literacy is not static . . . people are continuously building and rebuilding literacy. On the one hand, the nature of literacy has continuity across a community, while one the other hand, it is continuously evolving and situation specific. (Bloome, 1986a, p. 72)

Ironically, the specific description of multiple literacies in this classroom does not imply a specific literacy curriculum for other preschool programs. The broader implication is that a literacy curriculum must respect and reflect the nature of daily life within a particular setting. Such guidance requires that teachers be aware of the possibilities and power of print to support the social and educational needs of young learners. In their description of a classroom context for reading and writing, Teale and Martinez (1989) emphasized that formal literacy activities themselves do not make for a literacy curriculum; rather, it is the many ways in which teachers help children make connections between what is being done in the classroom and reading and writing.

It is my contention, and that of the teachers in this classroom, that the connections constructed between experience and literacy are best made as print is woven in and through the fabric of classroom life, its school culture and peer-culture activities. Literacy then takes on shape, pattern, and texture as it is constructed to meet individual and group needs, and is meaningful for the young learner.

The understanding and construction of conventional forms of print is a complex process for young children (Taylor, 1989). It is a long journey, and the literacy within early childhood curricula is an important stop in this journey. In classrooms such as this one, the paths to literacy are not taught directly, but rather evolve in the course of, and in support of, the particular purposes and themes of a school experience. As Hall (2000) suggested of the findings of a study of play and literacy for 5- and 6-year-old children, "The children were not particularly conscious that they were engaged in a literacy learning experience. This was living rather than learning" (p. 203). These children too were learning ways to become literate within and through a variety of school and peer culture experiences, not often associated with formal literacy-teaching events.

Thus, there was no one path to becoming literate in this classroom, but rather multiple paths linking literate action with wider social action. Literacy was multifaceted and transformative, in keeping with the larger developmental and cultural concerns of the classroom community. As a skill, literacy was something to learn about, but, in the doing, it was a disposition that enabled participants to "empower action, feeling, and thinking in the context of purposeful social activity" (Wells, 1990, p. 14). These were the ways of this classroom and thus, the ways that children would progress toward becoming literate in this preschool.

REFERENCES

Bloome, D. (1986a). Building literacy and the classroom community. *Theory Into Practice, 15*(2), 71-76.

Bloome, D. (1986b). *Literacy and schooling.* Norwood, NJ: Ablex.

Bloome, D., & Twymon, S. (1985, Summer). Exploring classroom interaction. *Educational Horizons,* pp. 150-153.

Brice-Heath, S. B. (1983). *Ways with words.* Cambridge, MA: Cambridge University Press.

Campbell, R. (1998). *Facilitating preschool literacy.* Newark, DE: International Reading Association.

Christie, J. (1990). Dramatic play: A context for meaningful engagements. *The Reading Teacher, 43,* 542-545.

Clay, M. M. (1975). *What did I write?* Auckland: Heinemann Educational Books.

Clay, M. M. (1979). *Reading: The patterning of complex behavior.* Auckland, NZ: Heinemann.

Clay, M.M. (1982). *Observing young readers.* Portsmouth, NH: Heinemann Educational Books.

Clay, M. M. (1991). *Becoming literate.* Portsmouth, NH: Heinemann.

Cochran-Smith, M. (1984). *The making of a reader.* Norwood, NJ: Ablex.

Corsaro, W. (1985). *Friendship and peer culture in the early years.* Norwood, NJ: Ablex.

Dorr-Bremme, D. (1982). *Behaving and making sense: Creating social organization in the classroom.* Unpublished doctoral dissertation, Harvard University, Cambridge, MA.

Durkin, D. (1982). *Getting reading started.* Boston: Allyn & Bacon.

Dyson, A. H. (1989). *Multiple worlds of child writers: Friends learning to write.* New York: Teachers College Press.

Dyson, A. (1990a). Symbol makers, symbol weavers: How children link play, pictures, and print. *Young Children, 45*(2), 50-57.

Dyson, A. (1990b). Weaving possibilities: Rethinking metaphors for early literacy development. *The Reading Teacher, 44*(3), 202-213.

Elgas, P. (1988). *The construction of a preschool peer culture: The role of objects and play styles.* Unpublished doctoral dissertation, The Ohio State University, Columbus.

Fernie, D. E., Kantor, R., Klein, E., Meyer, C., & Elgas, P. (1988). Becoming students and becoming ethnographers in a preschool. *Journal of Research in Childhood Education, 3*(2), 132-141.

Ferriero, E. (1985). Literacy development: A psychogenetic perspective. In D. Olson, N. Torrance, & A. Hildegard (Eds.), *Literacy, language and learning: The nature and consequences of reading and writing.* Cambridge: Cambridge University Press.

Ferreiro, E. (1986). The interplay between information and assimilation in beginning literacy. In W. Teale & E. Sulzby (Eds.), *Emergent literacy* (pp. 15-49). Norwood, NJ: Ablex.

Golden, J. (1990). *The narrative symbol in childhood literature.* New York: Mouton de Gruyter.

Goodman, K. S., & Goodman, Y. M. (1979). Learning to read is natural. In L. B. Resnick & P. A. Weaver (Eds.), *Theory and practice of early reading* (Vol. 2). Hillsdale, NJ: Erlbaum.

Goodman, Y. (1982). The development of initial literacy. In H. Goelman, A. Oberz, & F. Smith (Eds.), *Awakening to literacy* (pp. 102-109). Portsmouth, NH: Heinemann.

Goodman, Y. (1983a). The development of initial literacy. In H. Goelman, A. Oberz, & F. Smith (Eds.), *Awakening to literacy* (pp. 102-109). Portsmouth, NH: Heinemann.

Goodman, Y. (1983b). Reading and writing relationships: Pragmatic function. *Language Arts, 60*(5), 590-599.

Goodman, Y. (1986). Children coming to know literacy. In W. Teale & E. Sulzby (Eds.), *Emergent literacy.* Norwood, NJ: Ablex.

Green, J., Dixon, C., Lin, L., Floriani, A., & Bradley, M. (in press). *Constructing literacy in classrooms: Literate action a social accomplishment.* Santa Barbara, CA: Santa Barbara Classroom Discourse Group.

Green, J., Kantor, R., & Rogers, T. (1991). Exploring the complexity of language and learning in the classroom. In B. Jones & L. Idol (Eds.), *Educational values and cognitive instruction: Implications for reform* (Vol. 2, pp. 333-364). Hillsdale, NJ: Erlbaum.

Green, J., & Meyer, L. (1991). The embeddedness of reading in classroom life: Reading as a situated process. In C. Baker & A. Luke (Eds.), *The critical sociology of reading pedagogy* (pp. 141-160). The Netherlands: John Benjamins.

Hall, N. (1987). *The emergence of literacy.* Portsmouth, NH: Heinemann.

Hall, N. (2000). Literacy, play and authentic experience. In. K. A. Roskos & J. F. Christie (Eds.), *Play and literacy in early childhood*. Mahwah, NJ: Erlbaum.

Halliday, M. A. K. (1975). *Learning how to mean: Exploration in the development of language*. London: Edward Arnold.

Hammersley, M., & Atkinson, P. (1989). *Ethnography: Principles in practice*. New York: Routledge.

Kantor, R., & Elgas, P. (1985). *Unpublished curriculum document*. Columbus: The A. Sophie Rogers Laboratory School at the Ohio State University.

Kantor, R., & Elgas, P., (1986). *Curriculum document*. Columbus: The A. Sophie Rogers Laboratory for Child and Family Studies, The Ohio State University.

Moll, R. (1990, April). *Literacy research in community and classrooms: A sociocultural approach*. Paper presented at the National Conference on Research in English, Chicago, IL.

Morrow, L., & Rand, M. (1991). Preparing the classroom environment to promote literacy during play. In J. F. Christie (Ed.), *Play and early literacy development* (pp. 141-167). Albany: State University of New York Press.

Neuman, S. B., & Roskos, K. (1990). Play, print and purpose: Enriching play environments for literacy development. *The Reading Teacher, 44*(3), 214-221.

Neuman, S. B., & Roskos, K. (1991). The influence of literacy-enriched play centers on preschoolers' conceptions of the functions of print. In J. F. Christie (Ed.), *Play and early literacy development* (pp. 167-189). Albany: State University of New York Press.

Piaget, J. (1954). *The construction of reality in the child*. New York: Basic Books.

Rowe, D. W. (1989). Author/audience interaction in the preschool: The role of social interaction in literacy lessons. *Journal of Reading Behavior, 21*(4), 311-349.

Scheiffelin, B., & Cochran-Smith, M. (1984). Learning to read culturally: Literacy before schooling. In H. Goelman, A. Oberg, & F. Smith (Eds.), *Awakening to literacy* (pp. 3-23). Portsmouth, NH: Heinemann.

Schrader, C. (1990). Symbolic play as a curricular tool for early literacy development. *Early Childhood Research Quarterly, 5*, 79-103.

Schrader, C. (1991). Symbolic play: A source of meaningful engagements with writing and reading. In J. F. Christie (Ed.), *Play and early literacy development* (pp. 215-233). Albany: State University of New York Press.

Smith, F. (1992). Learning to read: The never-ending debate. *Phi Delta Kappan, 73*(6), 432-441.

Spradley, J. P. (1980). *Participant observation.* New York: Holt, Rinehart & Winston.

Taylor, D. (1983). *Family literacy: Young children learning to read and write.* Exeter, NH: Heinemann.

Taylor, D. (1989). Toward a unified theory of literacy learning and instructional practices. *Phi Delta Kappan, 71*(3), 184-193.

Taylor, D., & Dorsey-Gaines, C. (1988). *Growing up literate.* Portsmouth, NH: Heinemann.

Teale, W. H. (1982). Toward a theory of how children learn to read and write naturally. *Language Arts, 59,* 555-570.

Teale, W. H., & Sulzby, E. (1987). Introduction: Emergent literacy as a perspective for examining how young children become writers and readers. In W. H. Teale & E. Sulzby (Eds.), *Emergent literacy.* Norwood, NJ: Ablex.

Teale, W. H., & Martinez, M. G. (1989). Fostering emergent literacy in kindergarten children. In J. Mason (Ed.), *Reading and writing connections* (pp. 177-198). Boston: Allyn & Bacon.

Vulkelich, C. (1991). Materials and modeling: Promoting literacy during play. In J. Christie (Ed.), *Play and early literacy development* (pp. 215-223). Albany: State University of New York Press.

Vygotsky, L. S. (1978). *Mind in society.* Cambridge, MA: Harvard University Press.

Wallat, J., & Green, J. (1979). Social rules and communicative contexts in kindergarten. *Theory into Practice, 18,* 275-284.

Weade, J., & Green, J., (1989). Reading in the instructional context: An interactional sociolinguistic/ethnographic perspective. In C. Emihovich (Ed.), *Locating learning across the curriculum: Ethnographic perspectives on classroom research* (pp. 17-56). Norwood, NJ: Ablex.

Wells, G. (1986). *The meaning makers.* Portsmouth, NH: Heinemann.

Wells, G. (1990). Creating the conditions to encourage literate thinking. *Educational Leadership, 47,* 13-17.

Williams, D. (1988). *The complexities of small group process for beginning preschoolers.* Unpublished master thesis, The Ohio State University, Columbus, OH.

7

Deaf Children
in Inclusive Early Childhood
Classrooms

Cheri Williams
University of Cincinnati

Until the late 1970s, most children with disabilities were either excluded entirely from public school education or were educated in "special," segregated classrooms specifically designed for handicapped children. Then, in 1975, Congress enacted Public Law 94-142, The Education for All Handicapped Children Act. This law guarantees a free, appropriate education for all children, regardless of their disability or perceived educability, and stipulates that children who have disabilities must be educated "in the least restrictive environment" appropriate to an individual child's needs (J. Harvey & Siantz, 1979). Since that landmark legislation, the trend has been to *mainstream* or integrate school-aged children who have disabilities into regular educational programs with typically developing children as much as is appropriate for the children with disabilities. Although mainstreaming has proven successful for many children, in more recent days, many special educators and regular educators alike are calling for fuller *inclusion,* in which students with disabilities receive all their educational services in the general education classroom and are provided "special" support within that class as needed (see NASBE final report, 1992).

In 1986, after gathering evidence about the effectiveness of early intervention with young children who have disabilities, Congress passed Public Law 99-457, The Education of the Handicapped Act Amendments Law. A primary provision of this law is that all states provide appropriate educational services to children between the ages of 3 and 5 who have disabilities. Implementation of this legislation, and the call for fuller inclusion, have resulted in the gradual emergence of integrated or inclusive preschools in which young children who have disabilities attend preschool with typically developing children (e.g., Diamond, 1994; Radonovich & Houck, 1990; Solit, 1990).

Integrated preschool programs offer a number of benefits both to children who have disabilities and to typically developing children. These inclusive programs are thought to (a) increase all children's understanding of and sensitivity to individual diversity, (b) increase opportunities for children who have disabilities to learn from observing and interacting with their typically developing peers, (c) provide opportunities for typically developing children to learn altruistic behaviors or skills, and (d) increase the number of "real-life" experiences for children who have disabilities (Burstein, 1986; Guralnick, 1976; Peck & Cooke, 1983). Given these benefits, many parents of young children with and without disabilities favor integrated or inclusive settings (Bailey & Winton, 1987; Luetke-Stahlman, 1991; L. Miller et al., 1992).

The movement toward fuller inclusion of children who have disabilities with typically developing children at both the school-age and preschool levels has prompted researchers and educators to examine instructional approaches that are responsive to the educational needs of all children. For example, many educators have found that whole-language instruction and/or an integrated literacy curriculum are particularly appropriate for children with special needs. Whole language instruction has been successful with children who have limited proficiency in English (Edelsky, Altwerger, & Flores, 1991), children who have learning disabilities (Scala, 1993), children who have language impairments (Zucker, 1993), children who require speech therapy (Hoffman, Norris, & Monjure, 1990), and children who are deaf or hearing impaired (Livingston, 1997; Schirmer, 2000). An integrated literacy curriculum, the basis for literacy instruction in many regular kindergartens, has also been found to benefit young children who have visual impairments and are learning to read Braille (Swenson, 1988).

As we explore instructional approaches that blur the lines between the "abled" and the "disabled," we also seek to identify the similarities between children who have disabilities and those who do not. This chapter describes a qualitative study that documents several similarities between preschool deaf children and preschool hearing children in their literacy knowledge, participation, and use. The investigation suggests that instructional approaches used with young hearing children may be appropriate for many young deaf children. The study also supports inclusion of children who have disabilities in early childhood programs with typically developing children. We begin with a review of the traditional literature that has guided classroom practice with respect to deaf children's literacy learning.

TRADITIONAL LITERATURE

Research on the literacy achievements of deaf students has typically painted a bleak picture. The research consistently demonstrates that the reading achievement of high school deaf students is significantly lower than that of hearing students (Babbini & Quigley, 1970; Gentile & DiFrancesca, 1969; Quigley & Kretschmer, 1982; Trybus & Karchmer, 1977). Deaf children born to deaf parents tend to achieve higher levels of literacy than do deaf children of hearing parents (Vernon & Koh, 1970), but, for the most part, their overall achievements do not match those of hearing children. In fact, the literature in deaf education generally suggests that deaf students' average reading ability has traditionally been at about a fourth-grade level (see Paul & Quigley, 1990; Wolk & Allen, 1984).

Educators typically assumed that deaf students' lower reading achievement was primarily due to their lack of meaningful experiences with spoken or signed language in their early childhood years (Brasel & Quigley, 1975; Hart, 1978). This assumption was based on the reading readiness perspective, the prevailing educational thought at that time. Regular educators believed that proficiency with oral language was a prerequisite to young children's reading and writing development. This readiness perspective, with its focus on oral language as the prior accomplishment to literacy development, posed quite a challenge for educators of young deaf students whose language development was often severely delayed.

In line with this prevailing perspective, teachers of young deaf children generally focused their instruction on the children's acquisition and development of face-to-face language (i.e., both oral and/or signed language) as a prerequisite to literacy instruction. It was largely assumed that in early childhood, deaf children were acquiring the face-to-face language that would provide a base for later literacy learning in the elementary school years. One preschool teacher (a participant in the present study) summed up this position:

Sue's teacher, Elizabeth, Interview, 2/15

Writing is important, but language skills—speech skills for the oral child and signing skills for the total communication child—are what's going to carry them through. You can't teach if they don't have these basic needs.

With this emphasis on face-to-face language acquisition in the early childhood program, few researchers investigated the emergent literacy development of young deaf children.

Reading readiness is an educational viewpoint that still dominates classroom practice in many early childhood and elementary school settings (Freeman & Hatch, 1989; Shannon, 1989; Taylor, 1989). The readiness perspective asserts that oral language must develop before young children will be successful in learning to read and write: That is, proficiency in oral language is a prerequisite to young children's literacy learning. Following this line of thinking, preschool teachers typically engaged young children in oral language instructional activities of all kinds throughout the early childhood program (Harste, Woodward, & Burke, 1984). The assumption was that because oral language is a basic skill, special emphasis should be placed on it in preschool and kindergarten programs. The readiness perspective also holds that young children must learn a set of highly sequenced skills to learn to read and write (see McGee & Richgels, 1990; Morrow, 1989; Teale & Sulzby, 1986). Based on this assumption, preschool teachers have generally taught young children the skills believed to be prerequisite to literacy development (e.g., visual and auditory discrimination, letter recognition, sound–symbol correspondence).

The reading readiness perspective posed a difficult challenge for educators of young deaf children. If literacy learning was dependent on face-to-face language acquisition, how would young deaf children learn to read and write, because they typically demonstrated little proficiency with face-to-face language? Furthermore, given the fact that many deaf children's experiences with face-to-face language were multiple, varying, and diverse, how could these teachers support the children's language acquisition? To appreciate the challenge these teachers faced, it is important to understand the complex nature of many young deaf children's experiences with face-to-face language. The following section describes the language experiences of many deaf children.

FACE-TO-FACE LANGUAGE WORLDS

Many profoundly deaf children's experiences with face-to-face language are dramatically different from hearing children's experiences with spoken language. Whereas hearing children learn language with seemingly little effort, many hearing-impaired children acquire language with great difficulty, depending on the severity of their hearing loss and their ability to use residual hearing (Luetke-Stahlman & Luckner, 1991). The communication barriers imposed by a profound hearing loss often isolate the young deaf child from meaningful experiences with people, particularly in the earliest years (Meadow-Orlans, 1990). This is perhaps the most significant difference between the face-to-face language experiences of many profoundly deaf children and the spoken language experiences of hearing children.

To complicate matters, there is often a great deal of diversity in a deaf child's face-to-face language world. The young deaf child may be exposed to two distinct languages, American Sign Language (ASL) and/or English, and two distinct communication modes, oral and/or manual (Quigley & Kretschmer, 1982). The only exception to this scenario is the case of deaf children born to deaf parents, who acquire language naturally and in ways that are very similar to hearing children, either through the use of ASL, oral English, or both (Bellugi, 1988; Bellugi & Klima, 1972; Hoffmeister, 1982; Kantor, 1982; Meier, 1991; Siple & Akamatsu, 1991). Approximately 90% of deaf children, however, are born to hearing parents who do not know ASL. Consequently, meaningful interaction may be very limited until the parents and child develop a shared face-to-face language and communication system (M. Harvey, 1984; Lederberg & Mobley, 1990). This system is occasionally ASL, sometimes cued speech, frequently oral English, or, quite often, a signed system of English.

ASL is the only manual language that is not based on spoken language. It is a visual-gestural, spatially based language with a grammar and modality different from that of standard English, and, consequently, it does not have a one-to-one correspondence to English (Liddell, 1980). In contrast to ASL, several "signed systems" have been developed by educators of deaf children to reflect English. These manual systems are not languages; they did not naturally evolve over time within a human community of users. Instead, they are communication forms or "codes" based on spoken English that attempt to follow English morphology and syntax but do so with varying degrees of accuracy (Wilbur, 1987). Oral English is a mode of communication designed to maintain a one-to-one correspondence with spoken English. Hearing-impaired children are taught to use their residual hearing and to speechread spoken English. Unfortunately, speechreading is extremely difficult for many hearing-impaired children. Approximately 50% of the sounds of English are indiscriminate from other sounds (e.g., pan, ban, and man look identical on the lips), and it takes the skill of an experienced speechreader to understand every word in an utterance (see Luetke-Stahlman & Luckner, 1991). In cued speech, spoken English is supplemented by hand cues which signal various phonemes that cannot be differentiated solely by speechreading (Cornett, 1967).

This presents, then, a second major difference between the face-to-face language experiences of many profoundly deaf children and the spoken language experiences of hearing children. Due to the limitations of both the oral and manual communication modalities, the linguistic corpus many profoundly deaf children experience often only approximates English (Kluwin, 1981; Marmor & Pettito, 1979; Reich & Bick, 1977; Strong & Charlson, 1987; see also Luetke-Stahlman, 1988).

A third difference between the language experiences of hearing children and profoundly deaf children is the amount and kinds of language interactions hearing children experience as a part of everyday life. Parents often have extended conversations with their young children as they go about daily activities (Nelson, 1985). Because it takes time to develop a shared face-to-face language and communication modality, many profoundly deaf children do not have extensive interaction with their hearing parents during the early childhood years (Lederberg & Mobley, 1990; Meadow-Orlans, 1990). Although recent research suggests that the signing skills of hearing parents of deaf children are improving, parents' proficiency with sign language is still low (Meyers & Bartee, 1992). As well, it takes time for oral children to perfect their speechreading skills and learn to maximize their use of residual hearing.

A profoundly deaf child's experiences with face-to-face language also varies depending on extended family and community members' abilities to communicate using the young child's mode of communication. Hearing individuals may not understand the deaf child's spoken English, or they may not be able to understand the child's signs. Moreover, even profoundly deaf children from the same neighborhood may not be able to interact with one another in meaningful ways if their mode of communication is very different. For example, a profoundly deaf child who communicates through ASL may have great difficulty understanding his young deaf friend who converses with oral English.

To complicate matters further, when young hearing-impaired children attend school, they often increase the multiplicity of their face-to-face language worlds. The mode of communication used at home may be different from the modality used within the classroom. The mode of communication used in the classroom may differ from the modality that dominates peer group play. An individual child might experience any and all of these face-to-face language worlds, going back and forth between them, within the course of daily interaction. Furthermore, profoundly deaf children may experience both ASL and English as they navigate among home, school, and community contexts. This is especially true for deaf children of deaf parents. Consequently, it is not uncommon for the profoundly deaf child to navigate among multiple, diverse, and varying face-to-face language worlds (see Rodda, Cumming, & Fewer, 1993).

There are, then, dramatic differences between the face-to-face language worlds of many profoundly deaf children and the spoken language worlds of hearing children. In particular, profoundly deaf children lack access to a fully elaborated, shared face-to-face language system through which they can mediate early childhood activities and experiences. This situation has consequences for the children's language development. Although most 5-year-olds can be considered linguistically proficient, many profoundly deaf children of this age are delayed in their language acquisition (Kampfe & Turecheck, 1987; Meadow-Orlans, 1990; Moores, 1987; Quigley & King, 1985).

From these descriptions, we can see how young deaf children's early experiences with face-to-face language complicated the "oral language first" perspective on emergent literacy learning for teachers of young deaf children. How were these children to acquire face-to-face language given their complex experiences? And if they did not acquire face-to-face language, how would they acquire literacy skills? The oral language first perspective, then, served as a catalyst for the emphasis special education teachers placed on face-to-face language acquisition in early childhood classrooms for young deaf children.

A SHIFTING VIEW OF EMERGENT LITERACY

Although the reading readiness perspective has dominated educational theory and classroom practice for decades, many teachers and researchers have moved away from this line of thinking. In recent years, researchers have investigated the emergent literacy development of preschool children. Scholars have explored very young children's knowledge and understandings of literacy, the purposes for which they use written language, and the contexts in which emergent literacy learning occurs. This research has produced a large body of influential literature that describes the nature and importance of young children's emergent literacy development (Clay, 1967; Ferreiro, 1986; Snow & Ninio, 1986; Wells, 1986).

Many emergent literacy researchers have examined children's literacy learning as it takes place within purposeful activity and social interaction. These researchers have embraced a "social construction of literacy" perspective (Cook-Gumperz, 1986) as they examine the patterns of social interaction through which young children become literate (e.g., Dyson, 1981, 1989; Heath, 1983) and/or the purposes for which young children use written language (e.g., Taylor, 1983). Socially oriented researchers view literacy learning as sociologically rooted and "understandable only when viewed within its social contexts" (Harste et al., 1984, p. 49).

Some emergent literacy researchers have embraced a more cognitive orientation (see, e.g., Clay, 1967, 1991; Ferreiro, 1984, 1985).

These researchers view literacy as a body of cognitive knowledge about written language and a set of processes for using that knowledge that gradually develop over time. These researchers seek to identify the individual literacy constructions young children accomplish during early childhood.

The social and cognitive orientations to emergent literacy learning are not totally distinct. A number of researchers merge these perspectives and seek to understand the interaction of social and cognitive factors in emergent literacy learning. The research strongly suggests that literacy learning is a continuous, evolving process, and that, as active constructors of meaning, young children learn much about written language long before they pass through the doorway of a first-grade classroom (Harste et al., 1984). In turn, findings challenge the appropriateness of common early educational practices (Teale & Sulzby, 1986).

Research on young children's emergent literacy development has challenged both the oral language first assumption and traditional notions of literacy. The findings of emergent literacy research suggest that young children's language acquisition and emergent literacy learning are simultaneous and interrelated processes (Goodman & Altwerger, 1981; Harste et al., 1984). Spoken language and written language learning mutually reinforce one another in development.

This new perspective also challenges traditional notions of literacy. Rather than defining literacy as simply decoding and encoding print, literacy is viewed as a complex phenomenon that involves constructing and communicating meaning. The perspective suggests that young children are becoming literate, virtually from birth, as they begin to make sense of the written language in their worlds. They see print in their homes and in their communities. As they encounter written language, they try to "figure out how it works" (Teale & Sulzby, 1989, p. 4), and, thus, they come to know and use literacy in authentic and meaningful ways.

The findings of this emergent literacy research, with its challenges to the reading readiness perspective and its oral language first assumption, have prompted researchers and special educators to rethink their positions on deaf children's emergent literacy learning and related educational practice. If language acquisition and literacy development occur simultaneously among hearing children, the same could be true for young deaf children.

Several researchers have begun to explore young deaf children's emergent literacy learning. Pioneering research investigated young deaf children's environmental print awareness (Ewoldt, 1990), early reading development (Maxwell, 1984), and development of writing (Conway, 1985; Ewoldt, 1985). Recent studies examined young deaf children's understanding of how the alphabet system works (Andrews & Gonzales, 1991), their use of drawing and writing as primary forms of communication (Rottenberg & Searfoss, 1992), their hypotheses about writing (Ruiz, 1995), and the ways in which they use face-to-face language to support their writing endeavors (Williams, 1999). These studies suggest that young deaf children are learning a great deal about written language prior to formal literacy instruction despite their limited proficiency with face-to-face language. Furthermore, they suggest that young deaf children's literacy learning is similar to young hearing children's literacy learning. This finding is particularly significant given the trend toward fuller inclusion of children who have disabilities into regular educational settings.

The purpose of the study reported here was to investigate, in detail, three profoundly deaf preschool children's experiences with face-to-face language and their emergent literacy learning. Due to their profound deafness, the two youngest children's face-to-face language development was severely delayed. The oldest child had acquired a relatively strong internalized knowledge of spoken English through the use of English-based signing in his home, but all three children's receptive language development was delayed in comparison to that of hearing children of similar ages. The children's delayed language acquisition provided an opportunity to explore further the relationship between face-to-face language development and emergent literacy learning. The study also provided opportunities to examine similarities between the emergent literacy learning of young deaf children and young hearing children. This information would be particularly useful given the current trend toward fuller inclusion. As well, findings of the study would inform current practice in early childhood programs.

RESEARCH APPROACH AND METHODS

To investigate the children's experiences with face-to-face language and their developing literacy, it was necessary to observe the children as they experienced and participated in language and literacy events as a part of everyday life. To do so, an ethnographic approach to data collection and analysis was essential. An ethnographic approach permitted an examination of the ways in which the children, their parents, and their teachers engaged in language and literacy events in routine ways throughout the day. An ethnographic perspective is based on the belief that the meaning of all human behavior, including language and literacy behavior, is embedded within social and cultural contexts (Cochran-Smith, 1984). Thus, it was necessary to observe the children within these contexts.

In the present study, the social and cognitive orientations were interfaced in a multiple perspective approach. In keeping with a social perspective, an ethnographic orientation to data collection provided a naturalistic means for the researcher to examine the children's experiences and learnings as they occurred within everyday activities of the home and preschool classroom. In keeping with a cognitive perspective, two informal literacy measures were used to examine the children's individual knowledge and understandings about written language. This multiple perspective approach, with its ethnographic orientation and a new conceptualization of young children's literacy learning, permitted an in-depth investigation into the language and literacy learning of young deaf children. The following specific questions were addressed:

1. How do the children experience and participate in face-to-face language at home and within the preschool classroom?
2. How do the children experience literacy and how is literacy used at home and within the preschool classroom?
3. What knowledge and understandings about written language do the children demonstrate at home, in their preschool class, and on informal literacy measures?

Using primarily ethnographic methods, the children's language and literacy worlds were investigated through observations and interviews in the children's homes and in their preschool classrooms. Additionally, the researcher examined each child's understandings about print through two informal literacy assessment tools, Clay's (1979) *Diagnostic Survey* and the *Literacy Tasks* of Harste, Woodward, and Burke (1981). In all, the data collected included fieldnotes, audio- and videotape recordings, photographs of the children participating in language and literacy events, audiotaped interviews, samples of the children's writing/drawing, and results from the informal assessments. These data were collected weekly over a 6-month period. The research strategy was to examine the language and literacy connections across these settings for the three young deaf children who attended the same preschool.

Using the procedures and techniques related to grounded theory analysis (Strauss & Corbin, 1990), the data were analyzed inductively in order to explore two major strands, the children's face-to-face language worlds and their written language worlds. An initial systematic review of the data provided a thorough description of the children's experiences with face-to-face language both at home and in their preschool classrooms. A second review of the data provided descriptions and explanations for the children's experiences with, participation in, uses for, and understandings of written language across both home and school contexts.

The children's written language worlds are emphasized in this chapter because they provide insight into early childhood classroom processes, highlight similarities to the literacy learning of young hearing children, and hold implications for developmental theory. Descriptions and explanations of the children's face-to-face language worlds have been detailed elsewhere (Williams, 1994) and are reviewed here only as they are important to the interpretation of the children's written language development.

THE CASE STUDY CHILDREN: SUE, ANDREW, AND JOHN[1]

Sue, Andrew, and John were each profoundly deaf and they attended an urban, early childhood intervention preschool that served hearing-impaired children 3 to 7 years of age (see Table 7.1). The primary purpose of the program was to support the children's acquisition and development of face-to-face language. The preschool was divided into three levels, Preschool I, Preschool II, and kindergarten. Two instructional options, oral English[2] or total communication[3] were available at each level. In the total communication option, teachers and children simultaneously spoke as they signed. Teachers labeled their sign language as Pidgin Sign English (PSE). PSE is not an invented signed system. It is the use of ASL as much as possible in an English word order without the use of English-based grammatical markers. PSE may be referred to as English-based or "English-like" signing (Paul & Quigley, 1990, p. 161).

Sue's, Andrew's, and John's experiences with face-to-face language reflected the multiple, diverse, and varying language worlds described earlier. Although all three children had hearing parents, their experiences with face-to-face language were dramatically different from one another and were true to the experiences of many profoundly deaf children.

---

[1]The participants chose their own pseudonyms or asked the researcher to do so.

[2]In the oral instructional approach, children receive language input through speechreading (lipreading) and amplification of sound. Teachers and children express themselves through speech. Most often, gestures and signs are prohibited (Moores, 1987). Children are taught to speechread and to rely on their residual hearing (use of audition) to understand the communication of others.

[3]In 1976, the Conference of Executives of American Schools for the Deaf posited the following definition of *total communication:* "Total communication is a philosophy requiring the incorporation of appropriate aural, manual, and oral modes of communication in order to ensure effective communication with and among hearing-impaired persons" (cited in Gustason, Pfetzing, & Zawolkow, 1980).

Table 7.1. Demographic Information for the Three Case-Study Children

	Child		
Characteristics	Sue	Andrew	John
Age beginning/ending	3.11/4.5	5.0/5.6	5.10/6.4
Hearing loss (PTA unaided)	R = 98, L = 99	R = 112, L = 111	R = 99, L = 95
SAT, aided, in sound field	60	45	50
Level in preschool	Preschool I	Preschool II	Kindergarten
Number of years in school	First	Third (retained)	Third
Classroom modality	Auditory/oral	Total communication	Auditory/oral
Primary/secondary modality at home	Oral/Total communication	Oral/Total communication	Total Communication/oral
Child's use of signs	Limited	Proficient PSE	Proficient PSE (some ASL)
Parents' use of signs	Extremely limited	Very limited	Proficient PSE
Siblings	—	Younger hearing	Older profoundly deaf
Siblings' use of signs	—	Extremely limited	Proficient PSE (some ASL)
Additional schooling	—	—	Mainstreamed with hearing children in regular kindergarten class 2 afternoons a week
Community	Rural	Urban	Affluent suburb

DIVERSITY IN THE CHILDREN'S FACE-TO-FACE LANGUAGE WORLDS AT HOME AND AT SCHOOL

Analysis of the data on face-to-face language indicated that the three children's experiences with face-to-face language were not only dramatically different from one another's, they were also very different from hearing children's experiences with spoken language. The sections that follow describe each child's experiences with face-to-face language both at home and in the preschool classroom. These descriptions demonstrate the complex nature of face-to-face language acquisition for many profoundly deaf children.

Sue's Face-to-Face Language Worlds

Sue was almost 4 years old when the study began. She was in Preschool I, and it was her first year in the program. Her parents, Alan and Jordan, chose the oral English instructional option at the preschool, and they used spoken English as their primary mode of communication at home. However, Sue experienced face-to-face language in at least four different forms within her home. Her interactions with her mother, her father, her babysitter, and her grandparents were each very different.

Sue's mother had learned several signs that she frequently used as she interacted with Sue. Sue's father, on the other hand, rarely signed or gestured when he spoke. He was determined that Sue would be an oral child. Both parents often spoke to Sue in two- and three-word utterances, to make the task of speechreading easier. For example, once when Sue put a small toy in her mouth her mother quickly responded, "Play. No eat!" and her father said, "Take out now!" Sue's babysitter, in contrast, interacted with Sue as if she were a hearing child. Taking yet another approach, both sets of Sue's grandparents primarily gestured when they interacted with Sue and rarely used their voices.

Sue's face-to-face language experiences at the preschool were just as diverse. Although she was in an oral class, her Preschool I teacher, Elizabeth, was a proficient signer who often inadvertently signed and frequently gestured as she spoke. Joan, Sue's speech therapist, however, rarely signed or gestured as she spoke. At recess, Sue played with the total communication children and, consequently, learned many signs throughout the course of the investigation. She used these signs with her parents, teachers, and peers which, in turn, influenced the ways in which they communicated with her. Consequently, Sue's experiences with face-to-face language were constantly changing.

Andrew's Face-to-Face Language Worlds

Andrew was 5 years old at the beginning of the study. He was in Preschool II, in the total communication instructional option. When Andrew entered Preschool I, his mother, Cathy, chose the oral instructional option, and Andrew continued in this instructional option into Preschool II. Andrew did not acquire spoken language satisfactorily, however, and he was retained in Preschool II and moved to a total communication class. As a result, Andrew was in Preschool II but in his third year in the program.

Andrew had two very distinct face-to-face language worlds. At home, he was in an oral English environment, but at school he was in a total communication environment. There was a sharp division in his experiences. Andrew's mother, Cathy, knew very little sign language. In fact, she had just begun her first sign language course when the study began (PSE). Learning to sign fluently takes considerable time and effort, and although Cathy learned many new signs throughout the investigation, communication in the home was predominantly spoken English supported by the signs that she knew.

Cathy knew that Andrew needed a total communication environment, so at times she tried to sign every word she spoke. When she did, her speech was very slow and unnatural, and she often used incomplete sentences. Sometimes Cathy used the wrong signs. During one home visit, for example, she praised Andrew and said "You're so smart" but she signed "You don't know." On several occasions, she misunderstood Andrew's signed and/or spoken communication. For example, on one occasion he signed and voiced "wrong" and she thought he had asked "why." Because Cathy did not know all the signs Andrew used, she had to rely heavily on the context and his spoken English. Bradley, Andrew's younger brother, most often gestured without speaking when he interacted with Andrew. In fact, the boys' primary modality was a gestural system, which Cathy suggested was "their own form of communication."

Andrew's experiences with face-to-face language at the preschool were very different from his experiences at home. Andrew's Preschool II teacher, Anna, was an adept signer. Her sign language vocabulary was very large, and she was amazingly proficient; in fact, Anna was often able to sign the majority of words she spoke. As well, Anna understood Andrew's signed communication, and they interacted with one another in personally meaningful ways throughout the preschool day.

Anna required that the children use simultaneous communication with one another and with her during all teacher-directed activities. When Andrew and his classmates interacted on their own, however, they only signed. They rarely used their voices with one another.

John's Face-to-Face Language Worlds

John was almost 6 years old when the study began, and he was in an oral English kindergarten class. It was his third year at the preschool and in the oral instructional option. John was a proficient signer, however, because his parents, Henry and Mary, and his older, profoundly deaf sister, Whitney, signed to him from birth. When Whitney was identified as profoundly deaf at 8 months of age, Mary and Henry decided to use PSE as their mode of communication. By the time John was born, they were proficient signers, and, in a very real sense, John experienced and learned face-to-face language naturally, much like the language learning of a hearing child or a deaf child of deaf parents.

John's face-to-face language worlds were, perhaps, the most diverse. He experienced face-to-face language in a multiplicity of forms across home and school contexts. At home, John's parents, Mary and Henry, used simultaneous communication when interacting with John and his sister, Whitney, and, for the most part, they required the children to speak and sign simultaneously. When John and Whitney interacted with one another, however, they often signed without speaking.

Because John had learned face-to-face language in very natural ways, he demonstrated considerable linguistic and communicative competence and performance. Consequently, his parents enrolled him in oral classes at the preschool in hopes that he would develop intelligible spoken language. At the preschool, John experienced face-to-face language in a variety of forms. His oral peers and teachers communicated with him through spoken English. This spoken English varied along a continuum, from oral language free of any form of manual communication to speech that was heavily supported by gestures, pantomime, and/or sign. And because John was a fluent signer, the total communication children and teachers interacted with him through ASL, PSE, and/or simultaneous communication. John navigated in these multiple and diverse face-to-face language worlds using whatever modalities were appropriate.

Two afternoons a week, John was mainstreamed into a regular kindergarten classroom near his home. John's experiences with face-to-face language in this regular kindergarten classroom were dramatically different from his experiences at home or at the preschool. Because the children knew that John was deaf, they primarily gestured and moved their lips without using their voices when interacting with him. One child knew a few signs and used them to interact with John, but she rarely used her voice when signing. Janice, John's teacher, often gestured when she spoke to John, and, on occasion, she used a sign she had learned. Although John could speechread, for the most part his interpreter had to interpret both Janice's and the children's spoken language and she always interpreted whole-group activities.

Clearly, John's experiences with language were more diverse than Sue's or Andrew's. Between his home and his two kindergarten classes, it was not uncommon for John to navigate within several face-to-face language worlds on a given day.

The experiences that Sue, Andrew, and John had with face-to-face language appeared to be less than conducive to language acquisition and development. Yet these children were making sense of these inconsistent experiences, and each child was developing face-to-face language. The children's language development was clearly delayed, however, compared to the language proficiency of hearing children of similar ages, particularly in Sue's and Andrew's cases.

SIMILARITIES IN THE CHILDREN'S WRITTEN LANGUAGE WORLDS AT HOME AND AT SCHOOL

Although these children's experiences with face-to-face language were dramatically different from one another's and from hearing children's experiences with spoken language, their experiences with written language were strikingly similar to one another's. Data analysis revealed remarkable similarities among the children's written language worlds both at home and (especially) in their preschool classrooms, as well as a high degree of convergence in their family and preschool literacy. Furthermore, as described here, the children's written language worlds were very much like those of hearing children, as documented in the current literature on emergent literacy development.

Family Literacy

Although the children's experiences with face-to-face language at home were dramatically different, family literacy for Sue, Andrew, and John was strikingly similar. Table 7.2 illustrates the similarities (and some of the differences) that existed in the children's experiences with, participation in, and uses for written language at home. As the table demonstrates, there were many common literacy patterns across the children's written language worlds.

All of the parents engaged their children in reading events on a regular basis. They read to their children, with their children, and/or provided opportunities for their children to independently explore books. Sue and her parents spent considerable time interacting around children's picture books. Sue's parents, Jordan and Alan, did not read to

Sue in the traditional sense; they used children's picture books to "teach language." They had a keen desire for Sue to develop intelligible spoken language and spent hours practicing the correct pronunciation and

Table 7.2. Similarities and Differences in Family Literacy

	Similarities
Parents	Used written language to extend their children's vocabulary
	Engaged the children in reading events on a regular basis
	Provided numerous books and writing materials for the children's exploration of written language
	Asked their children questions about items and events in books
	Drew attention to the text during book-reading events
	Wrote words or gave the correct spelling of words at their children's request
	Interpreted print in the environment for their children
	Tried to extend the children's literacy knowledge
	Demonstrated a myriad of uses for print in their daily lives
Children	Read books by using the illustrations, the text, and/or the sign print to make sense of the text
	Sue often looked at the illustrations, the text, and/or the sign print.
	Andrew often signed and/or voiced printed words he recognized.
	John read words he knew and used illustrations to identify unknown words.
	Asked questions about items/events in books
	Asked parents about written words and/or asked parents to write specific words
	Answered their parents' questions about items/events in books
	Sometimes refused to participate in literacy events their parents initiated
	Drew pictures and wrote:
	Sue drew faces and various items that she labeled with letterlike shapes.
	Andrew drew faces and various items that he labeled with letterlike shapes, and he wrote some conventional letters.
	John drew detailed, elaborate pictures and labeled them with words.
	Used face-to-face language as a self-monitoring strategy as they wrote

(continues)

Table 7.2. Continued

Differences

Sue's parents and Andrew's mother:
Used picture books, particularly alphabet books, to support their children's speech development
Used written language to communicate specific concepts to their children

John's parents and Andrew's mother:
Read in front of their children, modeling their interest and the value they placed on reading

Sue and John:
Used written language to correspond with family members and friends
Played literacy and literacy-related games with their family
Tried to make sense of environmental print

Sue and Andrew
Made life-to-text connections with print
Reenacted book-reading events
Intently studied the illustrations, text, and/or sign print in books

articulation of words. They used the illustrations and/or the text in children's picture books, particularly alphabet books, to extend Sue's vocabulary and to teach her to pronounce new words. Thus, written language often served as a vehicle for Sue's speech and language development.

Andrew's mother, Cathy, also used children's books to promote intelligible speech and to extend Andrew's vocabulary. As well, Cathy was concerned with Andrew's literacy development, and she placed great emphasis on reading. Due to her limited sign language vocabulary, reading to Andrew was very difficult, so Cathy required Andrew and his brother to "read" books independently each evening before they went to bed. As the boys read, so did she, demonstrating her interest in and the value she placed on reading.

Excerpt from Home Visit 2, 11/7

Cathy: We do books almost 5 out of 7 nights. I don't read to them. I read my book, and they read their own books. We'll sit there for an hour. They've figured out that as long as they read their books, they don't have to go to bed—which is fine with me. But sometimes they stay up too late. If there's anything that we do, it's all of us looking at our books.

John's parents also read in their children's presence, and because communication was not a problem, they frequently read with and to their children as well. Three or 4 nights a week, Mary or Henry would read to the children at bedtime. On occasion, John's older sister, Whitney, also read to him, and she frequently read children's chapter books in his presence as she completed her homework.

As the families interacted around books, the parents often asked their children about items and events in the stories, eliciting speech and/or monitoring their children's literacy understandings. In turn, the children frequently asked their parents questions about the illustrations or text in books they read. Sue and Andrew often reenacted story book events. For example, after reading the story, *Little Red Riding Hood*, with his mother and brother, Andrew pretended to be the wolf and proceeded to lock his mother in an imaginary closet. The children also made "life-to-text" connections (Cochran-Smith, 1984, p. 169) with the stories they read (i.e., they related events and/or items in the stories to similar events and/or items in their own lives).

Excerpt from Home Visit (SVT 6), 2/9

Sue, Alan, and Jordan are looking at an alphabet book. Sue sees a picture of a jungle gym and tells Jordan that she plays on a jungle gym at school.

Sue: Play, school.
Jordan: Let Mommy see. (Jordan looks at the picture). Jungle gym (labeling it for Sue). That's right, you play at school.

Although reading was the most frequent type of literacy event in each of the children's homes, Sue, Andrew, and John also participated in writing events. All of the parents provided materials and opportunities for their children to explore written language. The children colored in coloring books, scribbled and drew pictures, and wrote their names. Sue and John wrote letters to family and friends. All of the children used written language for their own purposes. Once when John invited a few of his friends over to play, he asked his mother how to spell, "Don't never touch," so he could tape this warning on the television.

The children's parents demonstrated a myriad of uses for written language in their daily lives. All three mothers frequently used written language to communicate with their child's preschool teacher. Each family used written language to extend their child's vocabulary and to explain complex or abstract concepts. Each of the parents shared retrospective accounts about interpreting print in the environment for their children, and all three families displayed their children's written work in their homes. Family literacy was more alike than it was different, despite the high degree of diversity among the children's face-to-face language worlds.

Not only were the children's written language worlds remarkably similar to one another's, the types and uses of literacy evident in Sue's, Andrew's, and John's homes strongly resembled the types and uses of literacy of hearing children and their families documented in the current research literature (cf. Heath, 1983; Taylor, 1983; Taylor & Dorsey-Gaines, 1988).

In *Growing up Literate*, Taylor and Dorsey-Gaines (1988) built a theoretical frame in which they compared the literate practices of several diverse groups; the White and Black working-class communities (Roadville and Trackton) and the mainstream community (Townspeople) of Heath's (1983) investigation of literacy in the Carolina Piedmont, the White middle-class families in Taylor's (1983) investigation of family literacy, and the inner-city families of their own investigation of literacy in urban settings (Taylor & Dorsey-Gaines, 1988). This comparison revealed similar types and uses of literacy across all families, despite their differences in socioeconomic and educational status. A comparison of Sue's, Andrew's, and John's family literacy practices to those same groups revealed many common patterns, with each family demonstrating various instrumental, social-interactional, reinforcement/substitute for oral messages, memory-aid, and educational types and uses of literacy (see Tables 7.3 and 7.4).

Thus, family literacy has important similarities, not only across boundaries of socioeconomic and educational status, but also across differences in face-to-face language practice and use. Sue's, Andrew's, and John's complex experiences with face-to-face language and their delayed language development did not prevent them from experiencing, participating in, and using written language in their homes in ways that are similar to the ways hearing children experience, participate in, and use written language at home.

Preschool Literacy

As mentioned earlier, the primary purpose of the preschool program was to support the children's acquisition and development of face-to-face language; so, teachers and support staff focused their attention on language acquisition in the form of intelligible oral language and/or sign language and activities designed to support it. Interestingly, however, these activities almost always involved the use of written language in some form, despite the fact that literacy development was not an instructional goal in the two prekindergarten classes.

Sue's teacher, Elizabeth, and John's teacher, Denise, each embraced the reading readiness perspective to some degree. In particular, they believed that the children would learn to read and write most efficiently only after they had acquired a strong face-to-face

Table 7.3. Family Literacy in a Comparative Frame: Types and Uses of Reading

Types and Uses of Reading	Group Studied	Examples
Instrumental types and uses of reading for gaining information, for scheduling events of daily life, meeting practical needs, dealing with agencies	Shay Avenue neighborhood (*Growing Up Literate*, Taylor & Dorsey-Gaines, 1988)	Notes left on refrigerator of items to buy at the store; applications for food stamps; phone numbers and addresses in address books; recipes; job applications; food coupons
	Roadville (*Ways with Words*, Heath, 1983)	Patterns for dressmaking; telephone dials; school message; notes; labels on products; bills and checks
	Suburban families (*Family Literacy*, Taylor, 1983)	Food coupons in papers and magazines; address books; bills and checks; knitting and dressmaking patterns; notes to oneself and others; lists; recipes; price tags
	Case study families (present study)	Notes to oneself and to children; lists of chores; phone numbers and addresses in address books; appointment books; calendar with reminder notes; food coupons
Social-interactional types and uses of reading to gain information pertinent to building and maintaining social relationships	Shay Avenue neighborhood	Letters from friends; greeting cards; storybooks shared with children; notices of local events; births; letters from prisoners
	Trackton (*Ways with Words*, Heath, 1983)	Greeting cards; political flyers; letters; newspaper features; announcements of community meetings; cartoons

(continues)

Table 7.3. continued

Types and Uses of Reading	Group Studied	Examples
	Suburban families	Letters from family and friends; greeting cards; notices of school/church events; phone messages; storybooks shared with children; newspaper features
	Case study families	Greeting cards; letters from family and friends; notices of preschool events; storybooks shared with children; nonfiction books
Educational types and uses of reading to fulfill requirements of school courses; to build and maintain career; to discuss educational, political, and social issues	Townspeople (*Ways with Words*, Heath, 1983)	News magazines; the Bible; popular novels and nonfiction books; reviews of Broadway plays and ballet/symphony
	Roadville	Advertisements for home shows, movies or musical programs; ball game schedules; funny papers or comics; bedtime stories
	Case study families	Books/journal articles on the education of the deaf; textbooks; nonfiction books; computer visual and printouts; magazines; office paperwork; sign language books

Table 7.4. Family Literacy in a Comparative Frame: Types and Uses of Writing

Types and Uses of Writing	Group Studied	Examples
Reinforcement/substitute for oral messages	Roadville	Messages left by adults for children coming home before parent; notes for absence from school; assignments following class discussions
	Townspeople	Notes for tardiness to school; notes left by family members for one another
	Shay Avenue neighborhood	Letters written to teachers regarding homework; messages written to children and other family members
	Case study families	Daily/weekly correspondence with preschool teacher; print used when speech was unintelligible; messages left by one family member to another
Social-interactional	Suburban families	Letters to and from children; greeting cards; writing and drawing with young children
	Shay Avenue neighborhood	Letters to family members and friends; cards sent at Christmas, Valentine's Day, and birthdays; writing and drawing with young children
	Case study families	Letters to family and friends; greeting cards of all kinds; notes to parents and children; children's writing and drawing
Memory aids	Roadville	Grocery lists; frequently called numbers written in front of phone book; labels in baby books
	Shay Avenue neighborhood	Bathroom schedule for potty-training youngsters
	Case study families	Notes on refrigerator; notes written on calendar; lists; telephone numbers and addresses

187

language base. An example from Elizabeth's interview was given earlier. Following is a statement taken from Denise's interview.

John's teacher, Denise, Interview, 2/5

Deaf children need a language to help them learn. A hearing child has a language for teaching them reading; they associate the language to print. Deaf children need to understand that what we say is written down.

Although Anna did not personally embrace the oral language first perspective, she, too, emphasized face-to-face language acquisition and development activities throughout the preschool day, in line with the focus of the preschool.

The teachers felt their responsibility was to "build up" the children's face-to-face language base by directly "teaching language" and/or by "immersing the children" in face-to-face language activities. Elizabeth (Sue's teacher) believed that language acquisition for profoundly deaf children was "three-fourths a teaching process," in which teachers needed to teach individual words to the children. Anna believed that profoundly deaf children learn language naturally (i.e., without being directly taught) when they are immersed in or "bombarded with language." Denise both immersed her children in language activities and directly taught individual words.

Based on these beliefs, throughout the preschool day the teachers engaged the children in activities designed to support the children's acquisition of face-to-face language. One of the most common language activities in all three classrooms was the reading of children's picture books. Elizabeth, Anna, and Denise often read aloud books that included vocabulary items they wanted the children to learn. As they read, they pointed to the illustrations and emphasized the words they were teaching. This was especially true of Elizabeth, who emphasized specific words in the flow of speech by saying them louder, and often slower, than the rest of the text.

Elizabeth, Videotape (SVT 4), 1/30

Elizabeth is reading The Winter Picnic (Welber) to the children.

Elizabeth: This is Adam. He's a boy. A boy. (pointing to the picture) He has a hat (pointing to it), a coat (pointing), and a scarf (pointing).

Elizabeth: (reading) He wore his mittens. (emphasizing) Mittens. (pointing) These are mittens.

Anna read to her students three or four times each day. She believed the stories in children's picture books provided an ideal opportunity for her students to experience language in meaningful ways. The books Anna chose were often related to thematic units and included specific vocabulary items she wanted the children to learn. Anna did not, however, directly teach the words as Elizabeth did; Anna believed that by experiencing the words repeatedly in natural contexts, the children would come to understand them.

Anna, Interview, 2/4

Anna: I think reading to children is a natural way to teach language. The vocabulary that I want is in those stories. I don't "teach" the words; they come up in the story. They come up in the activity we do afterwards. They come up throughout the day, hopefully, and in other situations that we set up.

Denise frequently read children's picture books to "build vocabulary," and, like Elizabeth, she emphasized specific lexical items in the flow of speech. After Denise read, she often "quizzed" the students on the vocabulary items.

Denise, Videotape (JVT 1), 11/27

Denise has just finished reading a children's book about Indians.

Denise: I'm going to show you the pictures that have to do with Indians. We've talked about them before. I want to see if you know what they all are. I'm going to show you the picture, but don't say it. Look first, until I ask you, so that everybody can look first.

Denise puts her finger on her mouth as she passes a picture of a teepee in front of each child. She takes her finger down and says, "Okay," signaling the children to respond. All the children call out "teepee." She continues for the words, canoe, bow, arrow, feather, etc.

Throughout the investigation, the teachers used children's picture books as a vehicle for speech and language development. Additionally, they wrote individual words on cards, charts, and the chalkboard, and taught the children to say and/or sign the words. During these activities, literacy learning was rarely the primary instructional focus. Rather, the teachers were clearly emphasizing speech articulation and language acquisition. By their actions, Elizabeth and Denise demonstrated their beliefs that face-to-face language acquisition preceded literacy development. Ironically, their behaviors also demonstrated that language and literacy learning are simultaneous, interrelated, and overlapping rather than sequential or linear processes. Elizabeth and Denise were operating on a traditional model of literacy, a "first language, then literacy" orientation. They taught the children face-to-face language to prepare them for later literacy learning, but, actually, they were teaching literacy as well.

The use of children's picture books to "teach" face-to-face language was not the only use of print in the preschool classrooms. All four teachers, Elizabeth, Anna, Denise, and Janice (the regular kindergarten teacher) routinely used written language in functional ways throughout the preschool day. Each teacher used print to show ownership, placing the children's names on their desks, crayon buckets, coat hooks, and so on. All of the teachers wrote notes to the children's parents. They used written language to gain information, to organize the children's classroom responsibilities, and to plan preschool activities. Everyday, the teachers demonstrated to their students the many ways in which reading and writing can be used for personal and social purposes. Although Sue was in an oral class, Andrew was in a total communication class, and John was in both an oral class and a regular kindergarten, the ways in which their teachers presented and used written language and the ways in which the three children participated in literacy events was very much the same. Table 7.5 illustrates the common patterns of literacy experience and use across the children's preschool classrooms.

All four teachers established a print-reliant approach to learning (i.e., they used written language to present new information, concepts, and skills). For example, when Denise explained the landing of the Pilgrims, she pointed to the words "England" and "America" on a globe and moved her finger from one point to the other to demonstrate the voyage. Janice introduced Ground Hog Day by reading a local newspaper clipping about ground hogs. The teachers frequently documented in print the children's learnings and/or experiences.

As the teachers used written language in functional ways throughout the day, they inadvertently or, in some cases, intentionally taught the children various concepts about print. All four teachers modeled book-reading behaviors, such as left to right direction and one-to-one correspondence. Sometimes they focused the children's attention on individual letters and/or words. They linked the children's current literacy knowledge to new literacy concepts and modeled a variety of sense-making strategies. For example, they drew the children's attention to the illustrations in books to help the children make sense of the text (e.g., "What's happening? See, the pictures show what is happening in the story." "The pictures go with the words." "The pictures give you a lot of clues."). As they used written language, they also demonstrated the mechanical competencies involved in reading and writing.

Table 7.5. Similarities and Differences in Preschool Literacy

	Similarities	Differences
Teachers	*The children's teachers used written language:*	*Denise and Janice*
	To organize children's responsibilities	Taught the names of and
	To teach language/extend vocabulary	how to print alphabet letters
	To communicate with parents	Taught letter–sound
	To document what was learned/ experienced	correspondences
	To assist in learning new information/concepts/skills	*Elizabeth and Denise:*
	To organize the day's/week's/month's activities	Used written language to support the development of intelligible speech,
	To gain information	speechreading, and
	To convey information	listening skills
	To show ownership	Used written language to
	As a model or guide for the children's writing	terminate an activity
	As an authority	
	As a label	

During literacy events, the teachers:
Made clarifying remarks about the text
Required specific storyreading behaviors
Made life-to-text, text-to-life, and/or text-to-text connections with stories
Focused the children's attention on individual words and/or letters
Drew the children's attention to the illustrations in books to help children make sense of the stories that were read
Emphasized left-to-right directionality
Modeled one-to-one correspondence
Taught concepts about print
Linked the children's literacy knowledge to new concepts they were presently learning
Directed the children to use written models for the children's writing
Drew the children's attention to environmental print
Encouraged social interaction around print

(continues)

Table 7.5. continued

Children	*All three children used print:*

As an authority
To show ownership
To convey information
As a substitute for, or in addition to, their face-to-face
  language communications

All three children participated in literacy events by:

Actively attending and/or contributing (unless
  speech reading became too difficult for Sue or John)
Frequently demonstrating engagement with print
"Reading" texts silently or aloud
Revisiting their favorite children's books
Making life-to-text connections with print
Using illustrations, text, and/or sign print to make
  sense of text
Asking literacy-related questions
Interacting with peers and/or adults
Drawing pictures and writing various texts
Using face-to-face language as a self-monitoring strategy
  when writing

When they read aloud, all four teachers required similar "readiness for reading"[4] behaviors. That is, they required the children to sit on their bottoms with their legs crossed, attend to the teacher, refrain from individual conversations with peers, and visually attend to the book being read. While Anna and Janice permitted more social interaction during storyreading events than did Elizabeth and Denise, all four teachers made comments that helped to establish and maintain the norms for storyreading behavior (e.g., "You need to sit on your bottom", "Cross your legs.") As they read, the teachers made clarifying remarks about the text, and they frequently made "life-to-text," text-to-

[4]Cochran-Smith (1984, pp. 120-121) defined *readiness for reading* interactions as those interaction sequences teachers used to help establish and maintain the norms for storyreading behavior. These norms included sitting on the rug facing the storyreader, visually attending to the book being read, and attending closely to relationships between words and pictures.

life," and/or "text-to-text" connections[5] with stories (Cochran-Smith, 1984). "Life-to-text" interactions helped the children make sense of the books by relating the characters, items, and/or events to people, items, and/or similar events in the children's lives.

Excerpt from Videotape Analysis (SVT 4), 1/30

Elizabeth is reading <u>The Winter Picnic</u> (Welber). In the story, the little boy makes sandwiches for the picnic.

Elizabeth: (reading) He went to the kitchen and took out the bread. He made peanut butter and jelly sandwiches. (commenting) Do you remember last week we made peanut butter and jelly sandwiches? Remember? Well, he's doing that.

"Text-to-life" interactions assisted the children in using the information, themes, or messages in books that were shared. In these interactions, the teachers most often used the information in books to help children make sense of or prepare for events in their lives (e.g., "This book is called *Dear Zoo*, and it's about the animals we'll see at the zoo on Thursday."). In "text-to-text" interactions, teachers made connections between texts they were reading and texts they had previously read (e.g., "See this bird? He's the same as Round Robin. Do you remember the story about Round Robin? This bird is the same. He eats seeds like Round Robin did.") In these interactional sequences, the teachers were helping the children learn to become "readers" and were instructing them "in behaviors that accompanied and supported the activity of reading" (Cochran-Smith, 1984, p. 106).

Despite their different communication modes for face-to-face interaction, Elizabeth, Anna, Denise, and Janice presented and used literacy in very similar ways. Furthermore, the children's participation in preschool literacy events and their personal uses of literacy were also similar. All three children used written language to show ownership and to convey information. They respected print as an authority in their classrooms. All three children used written language to communicate messages that their face-to-face language failed to communicate, as in the following example.

---

[5]Cochran-Smith (1984, p. 169) defined *text-to-life* interactions as those interaction sequences that assist children in using the information, themes, or messages in books that are shared. I have used the term *text-to-text* to describe the connections teachers made between two or more books that were read.

Excerpt from Videotape Analysis (SVT 4), 1/17

[Free play in the High Scope Room.] Sue wants to fingerpaint, but Aaron is using the only fingerpainting tray. Sue begins to interact with Aaron, trying to get his tray.

Sue: Finish you. Finish you. Finish you. (signing clearly, but voicing only softly).

Aaron ignores Sue and continues to paint. Sue moves closer and touches him on the shoulder.

Sue: Finish you. Finish you. Finish you. (signing only)

Aaron still ignores her, and Sue starts to take the tray from him. Aaron grabs the sides of the tray. At this point, Sue walks over to the shelf, grabs a stamp, and rushes back to the table. She stamps Aaron's hand and again signs and voices "Finish you." When she does this, Aaron begins to scream, and a teacher rushes over to settle the dispute.

In this interaction, face-to-face language was not effective for Sue. She interacted with Aaron in sign and voice, but to no avail. Knowing that, in this preschool, stamps on the hand terminate an activity, Sue used print in this manner to communicate what she wanted.

All three children actively participated during preschool literacy events, except in instances where speech-reading became too difficult for Sue or John. They frequently demonstrated engagement with print and they often made "life-to-text" connections with the stories their teachers read. All of the children asked literacy-related questions about written language. When their teachers provided opportunities for independent and/or buddy reading, all three children frequently revisited favorite storybooks, often choosing books their teachers had read aloud. As they read, the children used the illustrations, the print, and/or the sign print to make sense of the text. They frequently voiced and/or signed the words they had learned through teacher read-alouds of these storybooks. The teachers' use of the storybooks had clearly enhanced the children's language learning, demonstrating again the simultaneous nature of language and literacy development.

Sue and Andrew had daily opportunities to write their own messages, and, as at home, they used letters and letter-like shapes to write. They drew pictures, which they labeled with letters and letter-like shapes, and they frequently wrote names. When the children wrote, all three used face-to-face language as a self-monitoring strategy. That is, they spoke and/or signed to themselves to direct what they would write next, to confirm their work, or to evaluate what they had written.

Excerpt from Videotape Analysis (AVT 1), 11/13

Andrew is writing letters from left to right across the page. He makes a letter, pauses, then, without looking up from his paper, he signs "Wrong, forgot." He corrects the letter, then signs, "Fine, know."

Excerpt from informal assessment (JVT 6), 2/7

John is writing the story of the three little pigs. As he writes, he signs or says each word before he writes it. (He asks for the spelling of most words.) After he writes each word, he rereads what he has written, then he signs and/or says what he will write next. As he works, his eyes do not leave his paper. He is clearly talking to himself.

The children also used face-to-face language to interact with peers and/or adults at the writing table. As they wrote, they frequently shifted from author to audience roles. Sue primarily talked with adults as she worked at the writing table. As author, she made comments about her own work, and, as audience, she asked adults about theirs. Andrew interacted with both peers and adults. He often solicited their assistance for his endeavors, and he frequently evaluated his peers' writing. John had little opportunity to write in Denise's class, and in Janice's class he could not effectively communicate with his hearing peers. Consequently, he primarily interacted with his interpreter during free-choice writing times. As audience, he asked questions about both the form and function of print (in his work, in his peers' work, and in books he read), and, as author, he frequently asked for the correct spelling of words he was writing.

Like their family literacy, Sue's, Andrew's, and John's preschool literacy was notably similar. Furthermore, their experiences with, participation in, and uses of literacy in the preschool strongly resembled that of hearing children in the preschool literacy studies of Cochran-Smith (1984), Dyson (1981, 1989), and Rowe (1989). Table 7.6 compares some of the preschool literacy practices documented in those studies to Sue's, Andrew's, and John's preschool literacy.

As the comparative frame makes evident, there were many similarities in the ways literacy was experienced and used by the three children in this investigation and the hearing children in Cochran-Smith's (1984), Dyson's (1981, 1989), and Rowe's (1989) investigations. Despite the dramatic differences between their spoken and face-to-face language worlds, the children's preschool literacy worlds, like their family literacy worlds, were remarkably similar. This point is significant in terms of the current move toward full inclusion. It suggests that young deaf children who are included in regular education classrooms can participate in literacy events with their hearing peers.

Table 7.6. Preschool Literacy in a Comparative Frame

Experiences with, Participation in, and Uses for Written Language	Group Studied	Examples
Teachers' uses for written language	Preschool children's teachers (Cochran-Smith, 1984)	To communicate with parents; to gain information; to organize and present information efficiently; to clarify the status of material items
	Case study children's teachers	To communicate with parents; to gain information; to assist in learning new information/concepts/skills; to indicate ownership; to teach language/extend vocabulary; to organize activities and responsibilities
Teachers' storybook readings	Preschool children's teachers (Cochran-Smith, 1984)	Teachers engaged the children in "readiness for reading" interactions, "life-to-text" interactions, and "text-to-life" interactions. Teachers annotated the storybook text.
	Case study children's teachers	Teachers engaged the children in "readiness for reading," "life-to-text," "text-to-life," and "text-to-text" interactions. Teachers either revised the text or read the text almost verbatim and added clarifying remarks.
Children's uses of oral or face-to-face language	Kindergarten children (Dyson, 1981, 1989)	To give information about events or situations (representational language); to monitor, plan, encode (directive language); to maintain social relationships (interactional language)

(continues)

Table 7.6 continued

Experiences with, Participation in, and Uses for Written Language	Group Studied	Examples
	Case study children	To label drawings and writing (representational); as a self-monitoring strategy to direct their writing; to control or direct text construction (directive); to interact with adults and peers around print; to establish, maintain, discontinue relationships (interactional)
Children's participation as authors/ during the writing process	Preschool children (Rowe, 1989)	As authors, children asked for assistance; as audience they challenged others' literacy knowledge
	Case study children	As authors, the children requested assistance from adults and/or peers; as audience, they evaluated their own as well as peers' and/or adults' writing; they shifted from author to audience stances

Sue's, Andrew's, and John's teachers presented and used literacy in the same ways teachers of hearing children presented and used literacy. Most notable were the similarities in the teachers' functional uses of literacy and in storyreading events. The comparative frame also shows that Sue, Andrew, and John participated in literacy events and used written language in ways that were similar to the hearing children in Dyson's (1981, 1989) and Rowe's (1989) investigations. Most notable were the similarities in the children's participation in writing events. This comparison suggests that Sue's, Andrew's, and John's diverse experiences with face-to-face language and their delayed language development did not prevent them from participating in and using written language in their preschool classrooms in ways similar to the ways hearing children experience and use written language at school.

Throughout the investigation and during the administration of the informal assessments, Sue, Andrew, and John demonstrated considerable knowledge and understanding about written language. They understood that written language has meaning, is used for specific purposes, and can be translated into speech and/or sign. Because of the differences in their ages and experiences with print, their knowledge about written language was different. John was a conventional reader and writer; Sue and Andrew were learning to read and write.

Sue and Andrew demonstrated left-to-right direction and return sweep in their book-reading behaviors and in their writing. They distinguished between the top and bottom of a page, and they understood that the print carries the message. Both children were able to read their names, their family's names, their classmates' and teachers' names, and various words (i.e., cat, dog, mom, dad, etc.) in print, words that they had learned through their interactions at home and at school. With increasing conventionality, they also wrote these names and words. Andrew could read the days of the week and many color words, and he knew the names of several alphabet letters.

When John read, he read for meaning. That is, he expected the print to make sense, and he attempted to make sense of it, often predicting the story line based upon his own experiences and/or the book's illustrations. He identified patterns in repetitive texts, he reread text that seemed incongruous with his own knowledge of the story, and when faced with an unknown word, he looked for information in the illustrations. When John wrote, he always asked for the spelling of unfamiliar words, demonstrating his understanding of the relationship between alphabet letters and words.

Despite their delayed language acquisition, Sue, Andrew, and John demonstrated knowledge and understandings of written language and uses for literacy that were remarkably similar to those of hearing children of comparable ages. This finding corroborates that of other researchers (Conway, 1985; Ewoldt, 1985; Rottenberg & Searfoss, 1992; Ruiz, 1995) who have found that hearing-impaired children make gains in literacy knowledge comparable to those made by hearing children.

DISCUSSION

The descriptions of language and literacy events and the excerpts from interviews presented in this study demonstrate the values the children's parents and teachers placed on face-to-face language acquisition and development. The parents wanted their children to acquire intelligible spoken language; the teachers (especially Elizabeth and Denise) believed that a strong language base was a prerequisite to later literacy development. This emphasis on language acquisition came as no surprise. The literature on young deaf children's language and literacy development suggests that educators have generally embraced the "language first" assumption of the reading readiness perspective. Findings of this study indicate, however, that for John, and especially for Sue and Andrew, face-to-face language acquisition and written language development were occurring simultaneously and were mutually reinforcing the other in development. Despite their lack of proficiency with face-to-face language, all three children demonstrated knowledge and understandings of written language and participation in and uses for literacy that were age appropriate. The children were learning a great deal about written language as they were acquiring face-to-face language and vice versa. It appears that face-to-face language and written language are parallel forms of the same meaning-based language, and development in one mutually supports development in the other.

This finding has important implications for educational practice. Face-to-face language activities should not precede literacy activities in the early childhood program for either deaf or hearing children. Rather, face-to-face language and literacy activities should be fully integrated throughout the curriculum. For example, reading and writing activities in which children interact with one another and with the teacher weave together face-to-face language and written language in natural, informal ways.

Although an emphasis on language acquisition came as no surprise, what was unexpected at the outset of this investigation was the role of written language in the children's face-to-face language acquisition and development. For the three children in this study, knowledge of written language became one pathway to language development. That is, as the children's teachers and parents used written language to "teach" spoken and/or signed language, Sue,

Andrew, and John often appeared to relate meaning to print as well as to signs and/or speech. This was especially true for Sue whose preschool teacher frequently introduced new words by printing them on small cards.

In these instances, written language not only supported but, in some sense, became an avenue to face-to-face language development. Several researchers have suggested that written language may support the development of other forms of communication for deaf children (Brannon & Livingston, 1986; Maxwell, 1985; Rottenberg & Searfoss, 1992; Soderbergh, 1976, 1985). In fact, Blackwell Engen, Fischgrund, and Zarcadoolas (1978) argued that written language development may be "an aid in lessening the language problem" (p. 63). In the current study, written language development clearly supported the children's face-to-face language acquisition. Could this phenomenon be true for other children as well? Is it possible that knowledge of written language may be a pathway to spoken language acquisition for some hearing children? For children with other disabilities? These questions present an important agenda for future research.

This study also points to a distinctiveness between face-to-face language and written language development. Face-to-face language and written language are not only parallel forms of the same meaning-based language, they are also alternative forms. Although the children's written language development was related to their experiences with face-to-face language, in many ways it was different and separate from the children's face-to-face language worlds. Written language was accessible to the children, and it was consistent in their experience. It was, in fact, the only form of English that was consistent across all contexts. Although their face-to-face language worlds were characterized by multiplicity, diversity, and variability, written language remained constant across home and school contexts and within contexts at school. Written language was a system with its own integrity, a world in and of itself, its own world to be explored. This finding, too, holds important implications for classroom practice in the early childhood program. All children will not come to literacy along the same avenue. In fact, there is now evidence to suggest that children take diverse pathways to literacy development (see S. Miller, 1990). Early childhood educators must create learning environments and engage in the kind of opportunistic teaching that encourages and supports children in their construction of literacy along varied and, perhaps, diverse pathways.

A final point to consider is the similarity found here across the literacy learning of young deaf children and the literacy learning of young hearing children. This study suggests that young deaf children can participate in literacy events and use written language in ways that hearing children participate in and use literacy. As we move toward fuller inclusion, there is an obvious need to identify and find similarities in how we teach different children. Relatedly, both the reconceptualization of literacy and an ethnographic orientation made it possible to see this similarity. A broadened conception of what literacy is will permit us to look for these similarities, and an ethnographic lens will allow us to see them "in the doing."

REFERENCES

Andrews, J., & Gonzales, K. (1991). Free writing of deaf children in kindergarten. *Sign Language Studies, 73*, 63-78.

Babbini, B. E., & Quigley, S. P. (1970). *A study of the growth patterns in language, communication, and educational achievement in six residential schools for deaf students.* Urbana-Champaign: University of Illinois, Institute for Research on Exceptional Children.

Bailey, D. B., & Winton, P. J. (1987). Stability and change in parents' expectations about mainstreaming. *Topics in Early Childhood Special Education, 7*(1), 73-88.

Bellugi, U. (1988). The acquisition of a spatial language. In F. Kessel (Ed.), *The development of language and language researchers: Essays in honor of Roger Brown* (pp. 153-185). Hillsdale, NJ: Erlbaum.

Bellugi, U., & Klima, E. S. (1972). The roots of language in the sign talk of the deaf. *Psychology Today, 76*, 61-64.

Blackwell, P. M., Engen, E., Fischgrund, J. E., & Zarcadoolas, C. (1978). *Sentences and other systems.* Washington, DC: A. G. Bell Association for the Deaf.

Brannon, L., & Livingston, S. (1986). An alternative view of education for deaf children: Part II. *American Annals of the Deaf, 131*, 229-231.

Brasel, K., & Quigley, S. (1975). *The influence of early language and communication environments on the development of language in deaf children.* Urbana-Champaign: University of Illinois, Institute for Research on Exceptional Children.

Burstein, N. D. (1986). The effects of classroom organization on mainstreamed preschool children. *Exceptional Children, 52*, 425-434.

Clay, M. M. (1967). The reading behavior of five-year-old children: A research report. *New Zealand Journal of Educational Studies, 2*, 11-31.

Clay, M. M. (1979). *The early detection of reading difficulties.* Auckland, New Zealand: Heinemann.

Clay, M. M. (1991). *Becoming literate: The construction of inner control.* Portsmouth, NH: Heinemann.

Cochran-Smith, M. (1984). *The making of a reader*. Norwood, NJ: Ablex.

Conway, D. (1985). Children (re)creating writing: A preliminary look at the purposes of free-choice writing of hearing-impaired kindergarteners. *The Volta Review, 87*(5), 91-107.

Cook-Gumperz, J. (1986). Introduction: The social construction of literacy. In J. Cook-Gumperz (Ed.), *The social construction of literacy* (pp. 1-15). Cambridge, MA: Cambridge University Press.

Cornett, R. O. (1967). Cued speech. *American Annals of the Deaf, 112*, 3-13.

Diamond, K. K. (1994). Inclusion. Counterpoint. *National Association of State Directors of Special Education, 14*(3), 11.

Dyson, A. H. (1981). *A case study examination of the role of oral language in the writing process of kindergarteners*. Unpublished doctoral dissertation, The University of Texas, Austin.

Dyson, A. H. (1989). *Multiple worlds of child writers: Friends learning to write*. New York: Teachers College Press.

Edelsky, C., Altwerger, B., & Flores, B. (1991). *Whole language: What's the difference?* Portsmouth, NH: Heinemann.

Ewoldt, C. (1985). A descriptive study of the developing literacy of young hearing-impaired children. *The Volta Review, 87*(5), 109-126.

Ewoldt, C. (1990). The early literacy development of young deaf children. In D. Moores & K. Meadow-Orlans (Eds.), *Research in educational and developmental aspects of deafness* (pp. 85-114). Washington, DC: The Gallaudet Press.

Ferreiro, E. (1984). The underlying logic of literacy development. In H. Goelman, A. Oberg, & F. Smith (Eds.), *Awakening to literacy* (pp. 154-173). Portsmouth, NH: Heinemann.

Ferreiro, E. (1985). Literacy development: A psychogenetic perspective. In D. Olson, N. Torrence, & A. Hildyard (Eds.), *Literacy, language, and learning*. Portsmouth, NH: Heinemann.

Ferreiro, E. (1986). The interplay between information assimilation in beginning literacy. In W. Teale & E. Sulzby (Eds.), *Emergent literacy* (pp. 15-49). Norwood, NJ: Ablex.

Freeman, E., & Hatch, A. (1989). Emergent literacy: Reconceptualizing kindergarten practice. *Childhood Education, 66*(1), 21-24.

Gentile, A., & DiFrancesca, S. (1969). *American achievement test performance of hearing-impaired students* (Rep. No. 1, Series D). Washington, DC: Gallaudet College, Office of Demographic Studies.

Goodman, Y., & Altwerger, B. (1981). *Print awareness in preschool children: A working paper. The development of literacy in preschool children* (Program in Language and Literacy, Occasional Paper No. 4). Tucson: Arizona University, College of Education.

Green, J., & Wallat, C. (1981). *Ethnography and language in educational settings*. Norwood, NJ: Ablex.

Guralnick, M. J. (1976). The value of integrating handicapped and non-handicapped preschool children. *American Journal of Ortho-psychiatry, 42*, 136-245.

Gustason, G., Pfetzing, D., & Zawolkow, E. (1980). *Signing exact English.* Los Alamitos, CA: Modern Signs Press.

Harste, J., Burke, C., & Woodward, V. (1981). *Children, their language and world: Initial encounters with print.* ERIC document: ED213041, U.S. Department of Education.

Harste, J., Woodward, V., & Burke, C. (1984). *Language stories and literacy lessons.* Portsmouth, NH: Heinemann.

Hart, B. (1978). *Teaching reading to deaf children.* Washington, DC: A. G. Bell Association for the Deaf.

Harvey, J., & Siantz, J. (1979). Public education and the handicapped. *Journal of Research and Development in Education, 12*(1), 19.

Harvey, M. (1984). Family therapy with deaf persons: The systematic utilization of an interpreter. *Family Process, 23*, 205-221.

Heath, S. B. (1983). *Ways with words: Language, life, and work in communities and classrooms.* Cambridge, MA: Cambridge University Press.

Hoffman, P., Norris, J., & Monjure, J. (1990). Comparison of process targeting and whole language treatments for phonologically delayed preschool children. *Language, Speech, and Hearing in Schools, 21*, 102-109.

Hoffmeister, R. (1982). The acquisition of sign language by deaf children: A review. In H. Hoeman & R. Wilbur (Eds.), *Communication in two societies* (Monographs and Social Aspects of Deafness). Washington DC: Gallaudet College.

Kampfe, C. M., & Turecheck, A. G. (1987). Reading achievement of prelingually deaf students and its relationship to parental method of communication: A review of the literature. *American Annals of the Deaf, 132*(1), 11-15.

Kantor, R. (1982). Communicative interaction: Mother modification and child acquisition of American Sign Language. *Sign Language Studies, 36*, 233-282.

Kluwin, T. (1981). The grammaticality of manual representation of English in classroom settings. *American Annals of the Deaf, 126*, 417-421.

Lederberg, A. R., & Mobley, C. E. (1990). The effect of hearing impairment on the quality of attachment and mother–toddler interaction. *Child Development, 61*, 1596-1604.

Liddell, S. (1980). *American sign language syntax.* The Hague: Mouton.

Livingston, S. (1997). *Rethinking the education of deaf students: Theory and practice from a teacher's perspective.* Portsmouth, NH: Heinemann

Luetke-Stahlman, B. (1988). The benefit of using CAI to a six-year-old hearing-impaired boy learning previously unknown vocabulary and spelling words. *Early Childhood Development and Care, 32*, 14.

Luetke-Stahlman, B. (1991). Hearing-impaired preschoolers in integrated child care. *Perspectives in Education and Deafness, 9*(4), 8-11.

Luetke-Stahlman, B., & Luckner, J. (1991). *Effectively educating students with hearing impairments.* New York: Longman.

Marmor, G., & Pettito, L. (1979). Simultaneous communication in the classroom: How well is English grammar represented? *Sign Language Studies, 23,* 99-136.

Maxwell, M. M. (1984). A deaf child's natural development of literacy. *Sign Language Studies, 44,* 191-224.

Maxwell, M. M. (1985). Some functions and uses of literacy in the deaf community. *Language in Society, 14,* 205-221.

McGee, L., & Richgels, D. (1990). *Literacy's beginnings: Supporting young readers and writers.* Boston: Allyn & Bacon.

Meadow-Orlans, K. (1990). Research on developmental aspects of deafness. In D. Moores & K. Meadow-Orlans (Eds.), *Educational and developmental aspects of deafness* (pp. 283-298). Washington, DC: Gallaudet University Press.

Meier, R. P. (1991). Language acquisition by deaf children. *American Scientist, 79,* 60-70.

Meyers, J., & Bartee, J. (1992). Improvements in the signing skills of hearing parents of deaf children. *American Annals of the Deaf, 137*(2), 257-260.

Miller, L. J., Strain, P. S., Boyd, K., Hunsicker, S., McKinley, J., & Wu, A. (1992). Parental attitudes toward integration. *Topics in Early Childhood Special Education, 12,* 230-246.

Miller, S. (1990). *Diverse paths to literacy in a preschool classroom: A sociocultural perspective.* Unpublished doctoral dissertation, The Ohio State University, Columbus.

Moores, D. F. (1987). *Educating the deaf: Psychology, principles, and practices* (3rd ed.). Boston: Houghton Mifflin.

Morrow, L. M. (1989). *Literacy development in the early years.* Englewood Cliffs, NJ: Prentice-Hall.

NASBE Study Group on Special Education. (1992). *Winners all: A call for inclusive schools.* Alexandria, VA: NASBE.

Nelson, K. (1985). *Making sense: The acquisition of shared meaning.* New York: Academic Press.

Paul, P., & Quigley, S. (1990). *Education and deafness.* White Plains, NY: Longman.

Peck, C. A., & Cooke, T. (1983). Benefits of mainstreaming at the early childhood level: How much can we expect? *Analysis and Intervention in Developmental Disabilities, 3,* 122.

Quigley, S., & King, C. (1985). *Reading and deafness.* San Diego, CA: College-Hill Press.

Quigley, S., & Kretschmer, R. (1982). *The education of deaf children.* Baltimore, MD: University Park Press.

Radonovich, S., & Houck, C. (1990). An integrated preschool: Developing a program for children with developmental handicaps. *Teaching Exceptional Children, 23,* 22-26.

Reich, P., & Bick, M. (1977). How visible is visible English? *Sign Language Studies, 14,* 59-72.

Rodda, M., Cumming, C., & Fewer, D. (1993). Memory, learning, and language: Implications for deaf education. In M. Marschark & M. D. Clark (Eds.), *Psychological perspectives on deafness.* Hillsdale, NJ: Erlbaum.

Rottenberg, C., & Searfoss, L. (1992). Becoming literate in a preschool class: Literacy development of hearing-impaired children. *Journal of Reading Behavior, 24*(4), 463-479.

Rowe, D. W. (1989). Author/audience interaction in the preschool: The role of social interaction in literacy lessons. *Journal of Reading Behavior, 21*(4), 311-349.

Ruiz, N. T. (1995). A young deaf child learns to write: Implications for literacy development. *The Reading Teacher, 49*(3), 206-217.

Scala, M. M. (1993). What whole language in the mainstream means for children with learning disabilities. *The Reading Teacher, 47*(3), 222-229.

Schirmer, B. R. (2000). *Language and literacy development in children who are deaf* (2nd ed.). New York: Merrill.

Shannon, P. (1989). *The struggle for control of literacy lessons. Language Arts, 66*(6), 625-634.

Siple, P., & Akamatsu, C. T. (1991). Emergence of American Sign Language in a set of fraternal twins. In P. Siple & S. D. Fischer (Eds.), *Theoretical issues in sign language research* (Vol. 2, pp. 25-40). Chicago: University of Chicago Press.

Snow, C., & Ninio, A. (1986). The contracts of literacy: What children learn from learning to read books. In W. Teale & E. Sulzby (Eds.), *Emergent literacy* (pp. 116-138). Norwood, NJ: Ablex.

Soderbergh, R. (1976). Learning to read between two and five: Some observations on normal hearing and deaf children. In C. Rameh (Ed.), *Semantics: Theory and application* (pp. 257-279). Washington, DC: Georgetown University Press.

Soderbergh, R. (1985). Early reading with deaf children. *Prospects, 15*(1), 77-85.

Solit, G. (1990). Deaf and hearing children together: A cooperative approach to child care. *Perspectives in Education and Deafness, 8*(3), 26.

Strauss, A., & Corbin, J. (1990). *Basics of qualitative research: Grounded theory procedures and techniques.* Newbury Park, CA: Sage.

Strong, M., & Charlson, E. (1987). Simultaneous communication: Are teachers attempting an impossible task? *American Annals of the Deaf, 132,* 376-382.

Swenson, A. M. (1988). Using an integrated literacy curriculum with beginning Braille readers. *Journal of Visual Impairment and Blindness, 82,* 336-338.

Taylor, D. (1983). *Family literacy: Young children learning to read and write.* Portsmouth, NH: Heinemann.

Taylor, D. (1989, November). Toward a unified theory of literacy learning and instructional practices. *Phi Delta Kappan,* pp. 184-193.

Taylor, D., & Dorsey-Gaines, C. (1988). *Growing up literate: Learning from inner-city families.* Portsmouth, NH: Heinemann.

Teale, W. H., & Sulzby, E. (1986). Introduction: Emergent literacy as a perspective for examining how young children become writers and readers. In W. H. Teale & E. Sulzby (Eds.), *Emergent literacy* (pp. vii-xxv). Norwood, NJ: Ablex.

Teale, W. H., & Sulzby, E. (1989). Emergent literacy: New perspectives. In D. Strickland & L. Morrow (Eds.), *Emerging literacy: Young children learn to read and write* (pp. 1-15). Newark, DE: International Reading Association.

Trybus, R., & Karchmer, M. (1977). School achievement scores of hearing impaired children: National data on achievement status and growth patterns. *American Annals of the Deaf, 122,* 62-69.

Vernon, M., & Koh, S. (1970). Early manual communication and deaf children's achievement. *American Annals of the Deaf, 115,* 527-536.

Wells, G. (1986). *The meaning makers: Children learning language and using language to learn.* Portsmouth, NH: Heinemann.

Wilbur, R. (1987). *American Sign Language: Linguistic and applied dimensions.* Boston, MA: Little, Brown.

Williams, C. L. (1994). The language and literacy worlds of three profoundly deaf preschool children. *Reading Research Quarterly, 29*(2), 125-155.

Williams, C. L. (1999). Preschool deaf children's use of signed language during writing events. *Journal of Literacy Research, 31*(2), 183-212.

Wolk, S., & Allen, T. E. (1984). A 5-year follow-up of reading-comprehension achievement of hearing-impaired students in special education programs. *Journal of Special Education, 18,* 161-176.

Zucker, C. (1993). Using whole language with students who have language and learning disabilities. *The Reading Teacher, 46*(8), 660-670.

8
What We Have Learned
Through an Ethnographic Lens

Rebecca Kantor
David Fernie
The Ohio State University

In this final chapter we relate the separate analyses to a set of cross-cutting cultural themes that emerged during the study, reflect on the broader implications for theory and practice, and articulate lessons learned during the course of doing this ethnography. Although each analysis has independent meaning as an exploration of a topic, collectively they tell a more comprehensive and integrated story of this classroom and its participants, this research project, and its participants.

Here we address questions that emerge when the analyses are considered together. The chapter is organized to explore what we have learned about classrooms, children and their development, research, and teacher education within higher education. As we explore these topics, we also reflect on how educational opportunities were accomplished by children and teachers and what we gain as teachers and researchers by taking this ethnographic, sociocultural approach.

WHAT HAVE WE LEARNED ABOUT CLASSROOMS?

A central and guiding idea within this study has been that the life teachers and children create together in the early childhood classroom can be viewed productively as a group culture. According to Noble (1990) "Culture is to humans as water is to fish. It is our total environment. As such, education as well as curriculum development are cultural phenomena" (p. 6). In other words, the complex stream of classroom action, socially constructed by the group of participants, becomes more understandable when thought of in terms of its cultural elements—activities and events, routines and rituals, norms and expectations, roles and relationships, and so forth. From a research standpoint, the goal of this collaborative ethnography was to understand and describe daily life within this classroom in terms of these cultural elements, separately, collectively, and in relationship to one another. In a process aptly described by Gumperz (1986), ethnography tends to progress back and forth between separate analyses that, in turn, inform the whole. At the same time, as early childhood educators, we were interested in the potential of this cultural lens to inform topics relevant to early childhood practice and to the first school experience for many children; early literacy development, children's play and friendship, and the initial learning of first school culture formats such as circle time and small-group work.

What have we learned about classrooms by doing this ethnography? At a broad level, we have become convinced that every aspect of classroom life is a matter of social construction, that is, each aspect is co-constructed by teachers and children, over time, in face-to-face interactions. Sometimes, the lead role in this co-construction belongs to the teacher. So, for example, in school culture events such as the small-group time analyzed by Williams, the teacher has the more obvious and pivotal role: She decides when to schedule the event, where to locate it, and what basic procedures and norms will guide the participants as they conduct these events. This makes sense given that these are school culture formats and thus, are new to children in their first school experience and familiar to experienced teachers. However, when the face-to-face interaction of small group is analyzed ethnographically, we see that the shape of the event has a great deal to do with the interests and contributions of the children—the norms they introduce, the peer culture interests they infuse, and their growing ability to participate in the event. In the construction of other aspects of classroom life, the children seem to have the lead role. In Elgas' study of the peer life of the core group, for example, we saw that the children had the major influence on the norms, routines, and activities that defined them as a group; still, the teachers had some influence over how children's social lives were conducted, as did other, less socially prominent children. We saw the teachers validating the meanings children had created (e.g., calling them by their superhero names as they left circle) and helping to negotiate acceptable parameters around children's play interests (e.g., using the smooth, red rhythm sticks instead of the jagged real sticks). At times, the relatively private, child-controlled nature of peer play limited the teachers' awareness of and influence on the nature and the course of children's peer-culture life. We saw this inaccessibility in the case of Don, where teachers were unaware of the extent to which Don was being scapegoated by the core group's rituals. The researchers, too, were unaware of this phenomenon until long after the fact. (We became aware of this interpretation only when we analyzed videotapes focused on their play.)

What can others gain from our insights into the culture of this classroom? Certainly, the particular cultural patterns we found were specific to this classroom, but the broad cultural elements we looked for should be relevant to other classrooms. For example, one would not expect that red rhythm sticks would necessarily be significant artifacts in another setting, but should anticipate that significant meanings would be constructed locally for some objects/artifacts, and attempt to identify them and their meanings. In early childhood classrooms emphasizing play and child-initiated activity, the peer-culture life should be robust, relatively easy to locate, and is important for teachers to understand. And for every new event, procedure, and format introduced into schooling, from circle time, to hand-washing, to reading groups, consensual ways of accomplishing them will be co-constructed by all participants, not just transmitted by adults and passively received by children. Another implication of a cultural perspective is that these elements are related to one another, and must at times be considered together. For instance, "trying on" a curricular event (e.g., project work) that requires new roles and relationships, norms and expectations, without considering changes in these related elements, probably will fail. Teachers will be more successful if they provoke and lead explicit discussion and negotiation of what the new event might require. To cite another example, children who want access to particular peer groups may be coached about entry strategies, but will be more successful if they are encouraged to see the valued routines and objects that define particular peer groups. In our study, an informed understanding of the core group involved not just the objects they used, but also their shared knowledge of play and language routines, their attitudes, and the nature of their relationships. In our view, innovations and "interventions" often fail because the related cultural surround is not considered or well understood.

More broadly, for any teacher, an understanding of these socially constructed and related elements provides a way to interpret the "doing" of daily life as a dynamic face-to-face process, to become aware of how procedures become established and evolve over time in continuing negotiation, and to understand how complex interactional events can to be accomplished relatively smoothly. For example, the orderly transition in this classroom from circle time to the next event depends on everyone's shared understanding of how that procedure will go; the expectations for both the constant elements (like "you wait for a dismissal routine," as opposed to getting up all at once and leaving en masse) and the more negotiated elements (like how the routine gets played out, e.g., the children requesting to be dismissed by the teacher by their favorite superhero's name—such as "call me She-Ra"). With shared norms and procedures revealed, we can better understand what causes events to be disrupted (e.g., the outsiders refusal to conform to the norms during circle time and other school events).

Another useful way to think about classroom group culture is to relate it to the idea of *classroom structure*. Traditionally, classroom structure is described in terms of schedule, rules, and teacher control or direction. So, classrooms with more teacher control, a more strict adherence to schedule, and more teacher-directed curriculum are described as *highly structured*, whereas more child-centered and informal classrooms, with more input from children, more flexible schedules, and more open activities, are described as *unstructured*. In our view, a shared understanding of the classroom culture provides the structure of classroom life. In light of this way of thinking about structure, classrooms characterized as unstructured are not unstructured at all, but rather are structured differently. For example, the term *free play* suggests "openness" or a lack of structure, yet we believe that it is still structured in several ways: by the possibilities and limits of the physical environment, by the socially constructed peer culture of this event (a patterned history of who plays with whom, around what themes, where, with what materials), by the wider school culture (norms and expectations for materials use, appropriate and inappropriate behavior, etc.), and by participants explicit and implicit understandings of this way of doing everyday life in their setting.

This culture, this structure, guides and gives meaning to the actions of participants. As part of our study, we toured the room with individual children while class was not in session midway through the school year and asked them about different locations in the room: What goes on here? Who plays here? With whom? What do they like to play? What things do they like to play with? We were struck by the amount of information the children could articulate and how consistent their observations were with ours. In a sense, we found that the children were natural ethnographers, aware of the culture and how its stable patterns defined their participation and that of others.

Complementing the notion that certain aspects of patterns are stable is the equally powerful notion that the culture is dynamic and evolving. This is especially important in charting the growth and development of the classroom culture over time. In other words, the culture is both patterned and dynamic, shifting over time. In chapter 2, D. Williams revealed that the complex event structure of small group has both stable and dynamic elements. For example, learning where to sit, how to share time, space, and materials are structures that are established early on and remain evident throughout the school year. Other procedures for participation, such as those related to collaborative processes and products, were established later in response to the children's progress in learning how to collaborate.

Thinking of classrooms as dynamic and patterned cultures provides a new and useful framework for looking at and understanding what is going on in a particular classroom—the "feel" or personality of the group, why things are either going well or not going well for a teacher or particular children. In our terms, specific issues reflect the group culture that is being constructed there, and understanding that culture should be prerequisite to teacher's attempts to change the patterns of classroom life. Locating these elements gives teachers the ability to be self-conscious about the establishment or redirection of these group dynamics. Potentially, this reframes "classroom management" from a perspective that positions teachers as controlling and largely responsible for shaping the "behavior" of the group, to one that sees classroom life as co-constructed with teachers in the position to help negotiate shifts in the culture and to hold all members accountable to each other. The power of the sociocultural perspective lies in its ability to inform teachers' understanding of classroom life at any and all levels of education, because all groups of students and teachers who spend time together in face-to-face interaction will construct a culture that can be revealed, made explicit, and socially constructed to support the educational aims of the group.

This broad conception of the classroom as culture proved to be highly productive for us, in terms of generating meanings and insights. However, a further differentiation of culture into domains of school culture and peer culture proved an even more powerful heuristic and guide in helping us to understand life in this classroom, as we describe next.

SCHOOL CULTURE AND PEER CULTURE

As the ethnography progressed, we further developed our view of classroom culture, conceiving of it as a differentiated social world composed of two intersecting and overlapping realms of group culture (Fernie, Kantor, Klein, Meyer, & Elgas, 1988). We followed Corsaro's (1985) definition of *peer culture* as including "a set of common activities or routines, artifacts, values, concerns, and attitudes" (p. 171) constructed and shared by a group of children. Paralleling Corsaro's peer-culture definition, we defined the *school culture* as including a common set of activities, routines, events, values, concerns and attitudes related to the broad educational mission and demands for group living inherent within classroom life (Fernie et al., 1988). We also became interested in how these realms related to one another—a notion we called *intersections*. Over the course of the ethnography, thinking in terms of these domains and their interrelationship helped us to interpret various instances of classroom behavior and interaction, to guide discussions within our research group, to frame topics for analysis, to organize insights and their implications in useful ways, and to share our work with others in courses and presentations.

The notion of intersections was one of our earliest interpretations of peer-culture life in this classroom and was provoked by the activity captured in Fernie et al. (1988):

> During the first week of preschool, Bob brought to school his interest in sticks. . . . As he became involved with other children, stick collecting became a common and expected activity for a peer group of five or six other children. . . . Soon the sticks became props for a variety of shared sociodramatic activities. (p. 138)

The sticks evoked in us Corsaro's images of an emergent peer culture. Faced with the somewhat overwhelming complexity of classroom life and the research task of making sense of it, the research team was encouraged (and even relieved) as we recognized the sticks as a salient cultural artifact and stick collecting as a socially constructed routine. With heightened awareness, we continued to observe the use of the sticks by children and the teachers' responses to this use:

> Due to potential safety hazards, the teachers asked the children to store the sticks in their cubbies but they supported the children's interest in stick play in other ways. For example, they allowed the children to use the smooth red, wooden rhythm sticks from the music area with limits on where and when these sticks could be used. Sensing the importance of sociodramatic play with sticks, teachers also helped children to make capes and other appropriate props. (p. 138)

It was the teachers' response to the use of sticks that led us to the further insight that in this classroom the school culture and peer culture spheres of the classroom were not separate domains of activity but were "configured so that they frequently met and intersected in meaningful ways" (p. 138). Put differently, we came to the awareness that teachers and children co-construct the whole of everyday life, whether peer-culture play or quintessential school events, through these kinds of ongoing negotiations. This image of intersecting realms of activity became an important heuristic in our teaching and research—a way to make visible the idea that teachers and children can negotiate mutually satisfying ways of living together in the classroom; in this case satisfying the children's peer culture interest in sticks while respecting the school culture concern for safety expressed by the teachers.

This conceptualization of two realms of life that both co-exist and overlap became even more powerful for us over time, as it proved meaningful in making sense of many moments and aspects of daily life in this setting. Furthermore, it served to structure and guide investigations of diverse phenomena within the research group. As discussed in chapter 3, Elgas went on to detail the peer-culture meanings children had constructed for the sticks. By systematically looking at many instances of stick use over time, we were able to see the evolution of stick use, from a coveted play object for a popular small group to a marker of affiliation among the larger group of peers. Just as the stick use had multiple and shifting meanings within the classroom peer life, its meanings evolved, too, in the social and interpretive processes among the researchers. This use of the sticks to mark affiliation complements our prior understanding of the sticks as an example of the intersection of school culture and peer culture.

Scott's work (chap. 4), too, was critically informed by this heuristic. His goal was to examine the social difficulties experienced by two children in this setting. Typically, problems of rejected children are assumed to occur in peer culture play and are researched largely within play (or laboratory) contexts. But, guided by the awareness our research group had constructed, Scott looked across both peer-culture and school culture contexts. In so doing, he was able to see the fullness of the socially constructed "outsider" status of the children, played out in related yet distinctive ways across both domains. This heuristic proved fruitful throughout the entire research project, in guiding subsequent investigations of literacy (Miller, 1991), gender (McMurray, 1992), and social competence (Kantor, Elgas, & Fernie, 1993) across both school culture and peer-culture domains.

For the teachers with whom we have worked and talked, thinking of the classroom in terms of both peer culture and school culture is a constant reminder that children's first school experiences involve the creation of both of these parallel worlds—one of group play, first friendships, and a nascent life with peers, the other of new group formats, academic learnings, and concerns focused toward new learnings and their future school competence. With this balance in mind, it becomes easier to envision the creation of exemplary and supportive practices for preschool education—what we have called *educational possibilities* (Fernie & Kantor, 1994).

WHAT HAVE WE LEARNED ABOUT CHILDREN AND DEVELOPMENT?

Perhaps the most influential guidance of the past decade to early childhood teachers comes from the National Association for the Education of Young Children's position on Developmentally Appropriate Practice (DAP). In its original (Bredekamp, 1987) and more recent versions (Bredekamp & Copple, 1997), DAP heavily relies (as the name implies) on child development knowledge as the base for child-centered practice and as a major determinant of program quality. The concept of developmental appropriateness was conceptualized originally as having two dimensions: age appropriateness and individual appropriateness. In its original form, the latter dimension was emphasized, such that the extent to which a program was considered "developmentally appropriate" was related to "the extent to which knowledge of child development is applied in program practices" (Bredekamp, 1987, p. 1).

In its next version (Bredekamp & Copple, 1997), the authors expanded the DAP discussion to include some aspects that critics of DAP (e.g., Kessler, 1991; Lubeck, 1998) articulated as missing or underemphasized, such as other legitimate sources for the content and development of the curriculum and issues of diversity and multiculturalism, and to emphasize the importance of the teacher as a decision maker. Putting aside the question of whether these modifications were successful, they certainly were attempts to flesh out and differentiate the individual appropriateness dimension of DAP by addressing issues of culture, social class, family, abilities, and learning styles.

In articulating what we have learned about children from our study, it is important not to minimize the value that child development knowledge holds for teachers. For example, teachers' knowledge of stage theories (such as Piaget's) helps them to know what to expect (generally) from children, to interpret children's thoughts, actions and behaviors in light of particular theoretical frameworks, and to respond to children "at their level." Furthermore, knowledge of the more dynamic aspects of development (e.g., Kamii & DeVries, 1978), focusing on how the child actively constructs and reconstructs knowledge, seems especially useful in planning curriculum and environments supportive of children's explorations. And such salient examples of developmental knowledge as Piaget's (1952, 1964) descriptions of cognition, Kohlberg's (1984) descriptions of sociomoral development, and Selman's (1980) descriptions of interpersonal relations all provoke consideration and interpretation of children's thinking, actions, and ways of interacting. The citing of such stage theories, related research, and derived principles throughout all versions and revisions of DAP demonstrate the essentially "constructivist" flavor of this guidance to practitioners.

With respect to culture, the newer documents better recognize culture at the macro-level: "We define culture as the customary beliefs and patterns of and for behavior, both explicit and implicit, that are passed on by future generations by the society they live in and/or by a social, religious, or ethnic group within it" (Bredekamp & Copple, 1997, p. 12). In our view, however, this traditional view of macro-culture as transmitted generationally fails to help teachers to understand how classrooms are and can be socially constructed as distinct, local micro-cultures. Through our research, we have become convinced that the individual focus of child development research needs to be broadened and brought together with a sociocultural perspective in order to more fully grasp the inherently social nature of both classroom life and children's growth and progress. Next, we demonstrate that much social growth in classroom life is left unexplained in traditional developmental research, and argue that a new conception of growth, one more germane to educational experience, is needed in order to provide fuller guidance to teachers.

To justify the need for such a modification in perspective, it is important to recognize the limits of child development knowledge. The mainstream of the field of child development, as a subspecialty within developmental or individual psychology, has been guided by purposes, assumptions and models quite distinctive from those guiding educational endeavors. Its central purpose, according to Feldman (1981), is the identification within the individual of broad universals in and/or across several domains (i.e., "the achievements that all human beings in all human societies will experience"; p. 22). Given the level of generality of such accomplishments (e.g., logical and abstract thought), such research leads us away from looking at those aspects of growth that may or may not occur, depending on the kinds of supports provided within particular educational settings (Feldman, 1981).

A related assumption is that such developmental growth can be well described as a series of qualitatively distinct, hierarchical, and sequential stages, with the mature adult as the proposed endpoint. However, the dominance of a linear stage model in the interpretation of children's growth and change has obscured the often recursive nature of children's developmental issues. Consider, for example, children's continuing search for friendship, belonging, and participation as children move each year to new classrooms. From year to year, they must learn what counts as friendship, how to gain access to a reconfigured group of peers, how to participate in the creation and recognition of a new classroom culture, how to create intimacy with friends, and community with classmates and teachers. These everyday, true-to-life examples of children's growth in classrooms (and beyond) do not count as development, because formal stage criteria (e.g., Kohlberg, 1984) are not met or because these more contextualized accomplishments are not easily linked to global stage theories. Thus, the field's definitions divert our attention away from growth that doesn't fit with the label development. Perhaps more importantly, this exclusion implicitly diminishes the importance of children's social worlds that children create, their perspectives, and especially their childhood concerns and ways of being.

As mentioned previously, another major assumption is that development occurs within and is the purview of the individual—thus the term *individual psychology* to describe the field. So, despite acknowledging genetic and environmental/social influences, development (whether in cognitive, emotional, physical, and even moral, social moral, and language domains) is seen ultimately as residing within the individual. Accordingly, the individual is the focus and "unit of description" in capturing the accomplishment of development. Because of these purposes and assumptions framing the concept of development, stage theory models can be seen as narrow in defining what counts as development, as conservative in their reinforcement of the typical over the possible, and as "adultomorphic" (Corsaro, 1985) in their tendency to cast children's growth in our adult terms.

In order to understand growth in educational settings more fully, individual and group growth needs to be considered together rather than separately. It is clear to us that classrooms are inherently social places—with group life, rather than individual life, at their center. Circle time, snack time, and clean-up times are school culture formats experienced typically as a whole-group participation; progress over time in how they get accomplished can be thought of as *whole-group* development and can be described in terms of language and social processes and its educational outcomes. Elsewhere, for example, we described the gradual and guided accomplishment of whole-group conversation abilities during a classroom's circle time (Kantor, Elgas, & Fernie, 1989). Art and construction activities, collaborative work, and peer-culture activities, although they may have whole group aspects to them, typically are experienced in small groups with either stable or changing membership. The development of cohesive and stable friendship groups within the classroom's peer culture (Elgas, chap. 3, this volume; Elgas, Klein, Kantor, & Fernie, 1988) as well as the development of collaborative processes in the planned, school culture event called small-group time (C. Williams, chap. 2, this volume; Williams, 1988) are two examples of change and/or growth best described as small-group development. Finally, even the experience of individuals within the classroom can be understood as connected to the group. In *individual-within-group* development, we can describe how different children position themselves in both successful and unsuccessful attempts to participate in school culture formats such as small group, as well as in peer-culture friendship groups (Fernie, Davies, Kantor, & McMurray, 1993; Scott, 1992).

When classroom phenomena are seen in these ways, the classroom is not viewed merely as the sum of separate individuals, each proceeding within his or her own sphere of development as he or she interacts with a material and social environment: Rather, the classroom is viewed as a milieu in which a classroom culture is socially constructed over time by the group, as individual children and teachers become a community of learners. Consequently, all levels of progress in a classroom, whole group, small group and individual within group, are inextricably bound to and contribute to the overall, particular classroom culture. And given their importance for success in school and beyond, if such accomplishments are not viewed as legitimate growth and progress then perhaps the concept of development as it is currently socially constructed that is in need of modification.

In this chapter so far, we have described several concepts/perspectives on the classroom that emerged as meaningful in the course of our research, perspectives we feel may be useful to others in interpreting their early childhood settings: classroom life as a social construction, the more specific framework of peer culture and school culture, and social/group processes as a necessity for understanding important aspects of children's classroom-based growth. These ways of interpreting the classroom have given us insight into the "educational possibilities" of this classroom and into ways of understanding them. To illustrate how these perspectives together give meanings to teachers and researchers, we reintroduce the example of small group described by Williams in chapter 2. Next, we return to Williams' empirical example of a "small-group time" created by her and 10 three-year-olds to demonstrate how these three interrelated concepts helped us to understand the educational possibility of this daily curricular event.

Interpreting the Small-Group Event

For this piece of daily curriculum in the lab school, the preschool class is divided (roughly by age) into two stable ongoing groups, each one consistently led by one of the two teachers. For the younger group, all of whom are typically new to school and group experience, the teacher's goals for the year can be described in terms of group development: First, she guides them in becoming a group, and then she supports the group as they engage in collaborative projects.

From the very beginning, these goals are approached as a process of social construction. In the early part of the year, the teacher and undergraduate student teachers help the group to become a group. They present diverse, open-ended materials to provide a vehicle for each child to explore his or her own ideas within a group context. For example, teachers offer colored markers and individually sized paper to the children, who proceed to draw pictures. Children's ideas are elicited and acknowledged as they explore diverse materials and learn to represent their experiences across different media and symbol systems. As children work, explore materials, and offer ideas, the teacher makes comments about each student's participation and asks students to describe what they are doing. Additionally, she works alongside the children helping them to experience being together as a group and to learn how to share space, materials, and ideas for using materials.

Over time, the teacher facilitates the children's development as a small group: She helps them choose a name for their group through a democratic group process; she suggests and creates a group display of their individual art products; and she uses conversation to help children become aware of each other, of their responsibilities to the emerging group, and of their individual rights within it. The teacher's talk shifts from a focus on individuals' responsibility to the group (e.g., "William, we need you to be careful of your neighbor's work when you reach for the paint") toward a focus on the social interactions of the group (e.g., "We will all have to work hard today to clean up the messy materials"). Children's talk shifts from an initial focus on themselves, their concerns, and their rights (e.g., "Where's my glue") toward a greater awareness of and interest in other group members (e.g., "What's William doing?") and in the group itself (e.g., "I know what we can do!").

Eventually, the children's guided progress enables them to engage in collaborative inquiry and, in turn, in new and more socially involved curricular formats. For example, the previous focus on individually constructed art with open-ended materials is extended to collaborative activities such as group murals and wood constructions. By the end of the year, such group-oriented projects (Katz & Chard, 1989; Kilpatrick, 1918) are the small group's primary focus and the result of its collaborative inquiry.

To connect our themes, we see that this development of inquiry within small group is a *social construction* to which teachers and children make distinctive contributions. As shown previously, the teacher uses talk and social action to help children first to become a group and then to act as one. Yet, although the lead and student teachers in this setting have starting points in mind for reaching their school culture goals for the small group, they primarily follow the lead of the children, which often takes the group in new and unanticipated directions. The children author words to describe their group murals, and generally infuse their peer-culture (Corsaro, 1985) interests into the group's artwork and literacy activities (Kantor, Miller, & Fernie, 1992). For example, the lead teacher once brought in a variety of construction materials (e.g., toilet paper rolls, cardboard, wood, industrial junk), with the idea in mind that the small group might want to create a city. But, after her deliberately neutral introduction of the materials ("I thought we could use these to build something today"), the children worked together to build a teenage mutant ninja turtle sewer, following their intense interest at that time in these popular media characters.

Peer-culture concerns were evident in other ways during small group as well; for example, choosing to sit by friends, engaging in group resistance to school culture authority and routines, and constructing "side routines" within peer groups (e.g., piling up the pillows until they collapsed) that were at odds with the teacher's agenda for the group.

Over time, the group development is reflected in the changing nature of social action, in both teacher's and children's talk, and in the socially constructed products of the group. In similar fashion, we could show individual-within-group development by tracing the contributions of particular individuals over time to the socially constructed progress of the group. Through such an analysis, it would be possible to see distinctive positions taken up by individuals but meaningful only in relation to the group—some of them productive to the group ("facilitating," "innovating"), others a force for teachers to reckon with ("detracting," "obstructing").

If teachers are interested in creating and interpreting the educational possibility of small group, the constructs of social construction, school culture and peer culture, and group-defined development are useful; conversely, such an example of group development in education is not guided by a relevant child development literature. Indeed, such a phenomenon is not a good child development topic, in light of that field's purposes, assumptions, and models as previously described. Although both individual-within-group progress in small group and development of the subgroup are meaningful to talk about, it is not helpful in our view to discuss this progress in the individual terms typical of child development topics.

Given the child development emphasis on broad and inevitable universal accomplishments, the accomplishing of effective small-group membership and collaboration is something neither universally accomplished nor necessarily even universally desired across educational settings: It is not inevitable but an optional accomplishment, the result of sustained and sensitive educational interventions; the progress is not well described in stages, for it may not endure across contexts or continue without further nurturance; finally, such growth is not easily explicable in individual terms, for it is growth of, by, and within the group. In summary, then, it is not surprising that despite whatever value the development of small-group collaboration may hold as a curricular format and goal, there is scant child development theory and research available to guide its practice.

D. Williams' thesis work within the broader ethnography both revealed to us the nature of group developmental process and confirmed for us that indeed young children and their teachers can create meaningful and productive small-group experience. It provided a description of the social construction of the small group that informed both our research and practical understanding of this daily event. More recently, we have also found validation in the writings of Katz (Katz & Chard, 1989) and in the work at the Reggio Emilia preschools in Italy (Edwards, Gandini, & Forman, 1998; Edwards & Gandini, 1989; New, 1990). Although we provided only this one example of an educational possibility here, in order to highlight the relevance of major themes, these same ideas are central to understanding other educational possibilities supported in this classroom, such as collaborative conversation in large-group circle time (see Kantor et al., 1989), and the social construction of beginning literacy across peer-culture and school culture contexts.

WHAT HAVE WE LEARNED ABOUT RESEARCH?

We have learned many significant things about conducting research, but most of all we have discovered our preferences for the ways we work with others (collaborative inquiry) and the kind of research work we like to do (situated inquiry). The first of these learnings has to do with establishing new roles within a collective research project. This kind of in-depth study of a single setting, benefits greatly from the efforts of a group. Over time, our collaborative research group has included a dynamic mix of classroom teachers, honors undergraduate students, masters and doctoral students and professors, with new contributors joining or completing analyses within the project and then moving on to other aspects of their careers. Undoubtedly, this project has benefited from the multiple perspectives and diverse insights which various colleagues have contributed.

As a part of this approach to learning about the classroom, we disrupted the usual dichotomy between the "insider" and the "outsider," the "researcher" and the "researched" by having colleagues who were both members of the research team and participants in the classroom (Kantor and Williams). Although this was an important part of the richness of the project, it was also awkward initially because we had to deconstruct, both for ourselves and for the academic audience, the traditional notions of the objective, outside researchers who study classroom "subjects." For ourselves, the teachers' closeness to the dual contexts of the classroom and the research process made access to the teachers' role so automatic (a real advantage for the most part) that we sometimes forgot to make it explicit for others. In our early experiences sharing our work at research meetings, we were often questioned about the teachers and alerted to our tendency to leave them out of our descriptions because we were too close to the action to make it explicit. We are reminded of the idea that the "fish is often the last to see the water." Over the course of the project, and since then, it has been validating to see the varieties of inquiry conducted by teachers and teachers and researchers together that have become prominent in the reconceptualizing of educational research (and teacher education) (Cochran-Smith & Lytle, 1993; Johnston, 1997; Kemmis & McTaggart, 1988; Kessler & Swadener, 1992).

The ways in which the research group proceeded reduced the traditional hierarchies between professors and students as we attempted to establish a more co-equal and collegial environment. Students were invited into the project and to locate and negotiate appropriate (contextualized) topics of interest within the classroom. So the ways in which the social group proceeded were socially created and emergent over time.

> The research group met each week to work on various aspects of the research—conceptualizing topics, analyzing data, and critiquing and contributing written text to manuscripts and presentations. Although individuals often took the lead in pursuing individual topics, we worked extensively with students and students worked collaboratively with each other and with teachers in the lab to develop research strategies inductively, to code and triangulate data, and to develop and articulate interpretations of data. (Fernie & Kantor, 1998, p. 87)

Beyond learning about the social structure needed to accomplish such a multiple topic, or comprehensive ethnography (Zaharlick & Green, 1991), we have also learned about the value of conducting an in-depth, ethnographic case study of a single setting. Part of the study's depth comes from the interrelationship among topics and linked analyses. For example, Elgas' study of the core group's play and Miller's literacy analysis helped us to understand how children's peer culture play is both a context for children's natural exploration of literacy as well as an opportunity for teachers to extend literacy learning. Furthermore, Miller knew to look for literacy in children's peer-culture activity because of the analysis Elgas had conducted. Elgas' analysis similarly framed Scott's "outsiders" analysis because we knew by then that the core group consistently opposed their entry into play. These are two examples of the many ways in which knowledge from one linked analysis framed and guided subsequent analyses. This spread of new knowledge within the team is made possible because the potentially separate constituencies (professors, undergraduate and graduate students, lab school teachers, and children) have been brought together through the lab school and the ethnography to create both a social network of mentorship and collaboration, and a synergy of ideas and experimentation.

Another part of the study's depth comes from prolonged engagement with the setting. As researchers and as teachers, we were continually focused on the meanings of social action within the classroom, a process that has been described as "recursive" and "reflexive" by various qualitative researchers. Our experience of this process is that in order to make sense of complex lives, we had to step back at times to reflect on sets of events, to make emergent interpretations, then return to the classroom to look again with more informed eyes, then reflect again in light of new observations and new insights. Here, our easy access to the classroom and its participants, and the dual roles of the two teacher-researchers allowed us to engage in this process on a daily basis and without some of the usual obstacles and access issues often faced by researchers. In this classroom, there also was an easy praxis, a combination of research and related action in the classroom, as teachers applied the insights gained in this research to their planning, responding to, and understanding of happenings in the classroom.

This in-depth case study provides specific descriptions of this particular setting and, of course, the specifics of other settings will differ. But, there are lessons that others may take from this study. One lesson is that in every classroom social constructions of both peer-culture and school culture elements will occur, and that taking on a sociocultural perspective will allow one to see and to interpret these social constructions. It is our hope that in sharing our view of our setting, the example may provide others with the foresight of how to approach such an interpretive inquiry process in their own setting (just as our understanding of the work of Corsaro, Green and others provided theory and example for us).

WHAT HAVE WE LEARNED ABOUT TEACHER EDUCATION AND HIGHER EDUCATION?

Before the ethnography, we envisioned the theme of educational possibilities only as it related to young children and to the early childhood curriculum. This fit with the original intention in hiring Rebecca Kantor to teach in the lab school (i.e., to move the program in more constructivist-oriented directions as outlined in such work as Kamii & DeVries, 1978, and Forman & Kushner, 1977). Over time, however, the idea of educational possibilities, even within the classroom, moved in new and more social constructionist directions consistent with the wider enterprise described in this book.

Part of what we learned about teacher education is that knowledge derived from ethnographic study broadens the knowledge base of early childhood education. In attempting to understand the nature of daily life in this classroom, we were led to topics (e.g., small-group development, group conversation, peer culture dynamics) that are beyond the typical purview of constructivist research and other prominent early childhood research literatures, and to envision traditional topics (e.g., literacy, rejected children) through a different (ethnographic) lens. As our research topics and findings have been examined and discussed across research meetings, college classrooms, and in the lab school itself, the theoretical language and dynamics of social constructionism has become shared knowledge—knowledge socially constructed among teachers, students, and researchers. Our students, from undergraduate to doctoral levels, speak the language and share the lens of the classroom as a social world, a complement to the traditional child development knowledge base.

Collaborative inquiry as a mode has grown over time among the lab school teachers and in the training of undergraduates during and after the study. The lab school teachers now often present local, state, and national workshops and presentations based on their socially constructed understanding of the classroom.

Grouped as a cohort for their practicum and seminar experience, undergraduate student teachers collaborated in seminar with the lead teachers and with one another, engaged in collaborative inquiry with children, and learned to develop a transformational or emergent curriculum. Ultimately, the goal is that they come away with the commitment to collaborative inquiry and to "action research" as a continuing feature of their work with peers and with children. For all of us, integrating the research process with teaching and program development has been transformative—that is, it has forever changed what we see, think about, and can describe in the classroom. Since the completion of the ethnography, Rebecca Kantor has taken a new role as a faculty member in the School of Teaching and Learning in the College of Education. As we look toward an involvement in a newly designed early childhood licensure, we hope to incorporate many of these lessons learned into the new program.

The ethnography we conducted in the lab school has contributed more broadly to each of the activities within our early childhood enterprise than we originally anticipated. In terms of our faculty research agenda, it gave us a coherent program of research centered on the in depth understanding of a single classroom.

Within our teaching at all levels, we have used the conceptualization of peer culture and school culture and our systematic data analyses as heuristic tools. Within university undergraduate and graduate courses, as well as within workshops and presentations to community educators, the ethnographic perspective helps teachers to see this setting and their own classrooms as complex, yet patterned social worlds. The ethnography gives us convincing real-life examples (and video illustrations of them) for purposes of demonstration and discussion.

At another level, the educational possibilities of the laboratory school itself have been redefined—both in terms of the kinds of preschool curriculum being developed there and in terms of the kinds of research being conducted within it. As we began our collaboration, planned "themes" or curricular "units" were (and continue to be) a very prominent curricular strategy within early childhood education. The lab school's emphasis on the social construction of emergent curriculum (as illustrated in the passages from the curriculum document) was "progressive."

Over time, and as a result of all of the experiences described in this chapter, a main function of the lab school has become to envision and explore educational possibilities. Lab schools are often criticized for being "ivory tower," "ideal," or even irrelevant. We would agree that they are ideal, for lab schools generally do not have the chronic problems of other child-care settings (e.g., staffs with high levels of turnover and low levels of training). But, we disagree that they are irrelevant; without these "real-world" pressures and with optimal conditions, lab schools are in a unique position to take a lead in exploring educational possibilities for children, curricu-lum, and programs.

In terms of the educational possibilities for research within the laboratory, we set a precedent which has been continued by other researchers here who are now using the laboratory to conduct observational and/or interpretive programs of research (e.g., Whaley & Rubenstein, 1994). Classroom-focused research, we contend, is a very relevant and useful kind of research for a lab school: Simultaneously, it creates new knowledge for the field as it informs and enhances practice within its own local classroom. Within this perspective, lab schools are defined as places of experimentation, inquiry, and research that do not conflict with, and indeed, do enhance the program agenda. Such an approach bridges the schism between laboratory schools as research sites, and as programs serving young children and their families.

The most summative and unanticipated educational possibility that has emerged in the doing of our collaborative agenda, is the one for ourselves as higher educators. In the collaboration described here, we have experienced new ways of working with each other, with students within and across two colleges, and with colleagues in research and teaching activities. At the same time, it has greatly influenced our teaching of both undergraduate and graduate audiences, giving us the sociocultural lens we had been searching for to explicate and to communicate our ideas about social life and educational possibilities in the preschool classroom.

FINAL COMMENTS

The essential impetus for the project described in this book was to find a better match between the nature of our "burning" questions and the lens to explore them. Child development theory did not provide us with a way to understand the social construction of everyday life, and how the early childhood educational and social processes of interest to us— play, friendship, peer culture, language and literacy, participation in school culture—are situated within this group life. In a long-term, ethnographic study within a single preschool classroom, we explored many of these topics with our colleagues through a series of linked and mutually informing sociocultural analyses. What emerged during this over-time experience was the satisfaction of working collaboratively with graduate students, and a strong professional partnership with each other that has survived the tensions of tenure and promotion review at a large research university with the individualistic and positivistic traditions of the "Academy."

So within our research during this time period, we reconceptualized the theoretical perspective guiding our work, the social structure formed to conduct that research, and our faculty roles across two colleges, at a time when we had to be concerned with conservative traditions of university cultures. As we moved forward with this newly constructed approach, we nevertheless discovered the value in deconstructing this experience as well. Our work in the preschool ethnography was grounded in the discipline of cognitive anthropology (Goodenough, 1970) and strongly influenced by the work of our mentors Corsaro (1985) and Green (Green & Harker, 1982; Zaharlick & Green,

1991). And as we encountered the community of early childhood "reconceptualists" (as represented in diverse works including books by Kessler & Swadener, 1992; Cannella, 1997; Graue & Walsh, 1998; Tobin, 1997; Dahlberg, Moss, & Pence, 1999) and interacted with its members, we have benefited from the ongoing dialogue and critique that situates our theoretical perspective among diverse and current critical and postmodern perspectives. This has allowed us to better understand both the benefits and limitations of any single theoretical approach, and provides a push toward reflection and circumspection.

As a final thought, we hope that reading this book will provide such a push for our audience to reflect on and think about their practice and life in classrooms in new ways. By taking a sociocultural look at life within this single preschool setting, we hope you agree that the accomplishments of these young children with their responsive teachers are impressive. The ability of children as young as three and four, in their first school experience, to participate in and contribute to the creation of such a complex "life in a crowded place" (Peterson, 1992) has to be admired. Here we saw children ably becoming students and becoming friends—creating rich domains of peer culture life and first school experiences.

Our overriding goal in this project was to see the "whole" of the early childhood classroom through an ethnographic lens. The approach we have taken here, and the understandings it generated for us, are of great value to us, but are by no means the only way to understand what goes on in early childhood classrooms (or for that matter, in any other classroom). Still, we see it as an important resource for gaining a fuller understanding of life in a preschool and hope you agree.

REFERENCES

Bredekamp, S. (1987). *Developmentally appropriate practice in early childhood programs serving children from birth through age 8.* Washington, DC: NAEYC.

Bredekamp, S., & Copple, C. (1997). *Developmentally appropriate practice in early childhood programs* (rev. ed.). Washington, DC: NAEYC.

Cannella, G. S. (1997). *Deconstructing early childhood education: Social justice and revolution.* New York: Peter Lang.

Cochran-Smith, M., & Lytle, S. L. (1993). *Inside/outside: Teacher research and knowledge.* New York: Teachers College Press.

Corsaro, W. (1985). *Friendship and peer culture in the early years.* Norwood, NJ: Ablex.

Dahlberg, G., Moss, P., & Pence, A. (1999). *Beyond quality in early childhood education and care.* London: Falmer Press.

Edwards, C. P., & Gandini, L. (1989). Teachers' expectations about the timing of developmental skills: A cross-cultural story. *Young Children, 44*(4), 15-19.

Edwards, C., Gandini, L., & Forman, G. (1998). *The hundred languages of children* (2nd ed.). Greenwich, CT: Ablex.

Elgas, P. M., Klein, E., Kantor, R., & Fernie, D. E. (1988). Play and peer culture: Play styles and object use. *Journal of Research in Childhood Education, 3*(2), 142-153.

Feldman, D. H. (1981). Beyond universals: Toward a developmental psychology of education. *Educational Researcher, 11,* 21-31.

Fernie, D., Davies, B., Kantor, R., & McMurray, P. (1993). Learning to be a person in the preschool: Creating integrated gender, school culture, and peer culture positionings. *International Journal of Qualitative Studies in Education, 6*(2), 95-110.

Fernie, D., & Kantor, R. (1994). Viewed through a prism: The enterprise of early childhood in higher education. In S. Goffin & D. Day (Eds.), *New perspectives on early childhood teacher education* (pp. 156-166). New York: Teachers College Press.

Fernie, D. E., & Kantor, R. (1998). Our reflection on a collaborative research experience. In M. E. Graue & D. J. Walsh (Eds.), *Studying children in context* (pp. 83-90). Thousand Oaks, CA: Sage.

Fernie, D., Kantor, R., Klein, E., Meyer, C., & Elgas, P. (1988). Becoming students and becoming ethnographers in a preschool. *Journal of Research in Childhood Education, 3*(2), 132-141.

Forman, G.E., & Kushner, D.S. (1977). *The child's construction of knowledge: Piaget for teaching children.* Monterey, CA: Brooks/Cole.

Goodenough, W. H. (1970). *Description and comparison in cultural anthropology.* Chicago: Aldine.

Graue, M. E., & Walsh, D. J. (1998). *Studying children in context.* Thousand Oaks, CA: Sage.

Green, J., & Harker, J. (1982). Gaining access to learning: Conversational, social, and cognitive demands of group participation. In L. C. Wilkinson (Ed.), *Communities in the classroom* (pp. 183-222). New York: Academic Press.

Gumperz, J. (1986). Interactional sociolinguistics in the study of schooling. In J. Cook-Gumperz (Ed.), *The social construction of literacy* (pp. 45-68). New York: Cambridge University Press.

Johnston, M. (1997). *Contradictions in collaboration: New thinking on school/university partnerships* (with The Educators for Collaborative Change). New York: Teachers College Press.

Kamii, C., & DeVries, R. (1978). *Physical knowledge in preschool education: Implications of Piaget's theory.* Englewood Cliffs, NJ: Prentice-Hall.

Kantor, R., Elgas, P. M., & Fernie, D. E. (1989). First the look and then the sound: Creating conversations at circle time. *Early Childhood Research Quarterly, 4*(4), 433-448.

Kantor, R., Elgas, P., & Fernie, D. (1993). Cultural knowledge and social competence within a preschool peer culture group. *Early Childhood Research Quarterly, 8*(2), 125-147.

Kantor, R., Miller, S., & Fernie, D. (1992). Diverse paths to literacy in a preschool classroom: A sociocultural perspective. *Reading Research Quarterly, 27*(3), 185-201.

Katz, L. G., & Chard, S. C. (1989). *Engaging children's minds: The project approach.* Norwood, NJ: Ablex.

Kemmis, S., & McTaggart, R. (1988). *The action research planner.* Victoria, Australia: Deakin University Press.

Kessler, S. A. (1991). Alternative perspectives on early childhood education. *Early Childhood Research Quarterly, 6,* 183-197.

Kessler, S., & Swadener, B. B. (1992). *Reconceptualizing the early childhood curriculum: Beginning the dialogue.* New York: Teachers College Press.

Kilpatrick, W. H. (1918). *The project method: The use of the purposeful act in the educative process.* New York: Teachers College, Columbia University.

Kohlberg, L. (1984). *The psychology of moral development.* New York: Harper & Row.

Lubeck, S. (1998). Is developmentally appropriate practice for everyone? *Childhood Education, 74*(5), 283-292, 299-301.

McMurray, P. A. (1992). *The construction, negotiation, and integration of gender, school culture, and peer culture positionings in preschool.* Unpublished doctoral dissertation, The Ohio State University, Columbus.

Miller, S. (1991). *Diverse paths to literacy in a preschool classroom: A sociocultural perspective.* Unpublished doctoral dissertation, The Ohio State University, Columbus.

New, R. (1990). Excellent early education: A city in Italy has it. *Young Children, 45*(6), 4-10.

Noble, N.W. (1990). The infusion of African and African-American content: A question of content and intent. In A. G. Hilliard, III, L. Payton-Stewart, & L.O. Williams (Eds.), *Infusion of African and African-American content in the school curriculum. Proceedings of the first national conference* (pp. 5-24). Morristown, NJ: Aaron Press.

Peterson, R. (1992). *Life in a crowded place: Making a learning community.* Portsmouth, NH: Heinemann.

Piaget, J. (1952). *The origins of intelligence in children.* New York: International Universities Press.

Piaget, J. (1964). *Judgment and reasoning in the child.* Totowa, NJ: Littlefield, Adams.

Scott, J. A. (1992). *The social construction of "outsiders" in a preschool classroom.* Unpublished doctoral dissertation, The Ohio State University, Columbus.

Selman, R. (1980). *The growth of interpersonal understanding.* New York: Academic Press.

Tobin, J. (1997). *Making a place for pleasure in early childhood education.* New Haven, CT: Yale University Press.

Whaley, K. L., & Rubenstein, T. S. (1994). How toddlers "do" friendship: A descriptive analysis of naturally occurring friendships in a group child care setting. *Journal of Social and Personal Relationships, 11,* 383-400.

Williams, D. (1988). *The complexities of small group process for beginning preschoolers.* Unpublished masters thesis, The Ohio State University, Columbus.

Zaharlick, A., & Green, J.L. (1991). Ethnographic research. In J. Flood & D. Lapp (Eds.). *Handbook of research in teaching the English language arts* (pp. 205-225). New York: MacMillan.

Author Index

Subject Index

Printed in the United States
1168600002B/58-167